Changing Nature's Course

The Ethical Challenge of Biotechnology

Changing Nature's Course

The Ethical Challenge of Biotechnology

Edited by
Gerhold K. Becker

in association with
James P. Buchanan

Hong Kong University Press
香港大學出版社

Hong Kong University Press
139 Pokfulam Road, Hong Kong

ISBN 962 209 403 1

Printed in Hong Kong by Condor Production Ltd.

Contents

Contributors

GERHOLD K. BECKER
Chair Professor of Philosophy and Religion; Director, Centre for Applied Ethics, Hong Kong Baptist University, HONG KONG

PHILIP BEREANO
Professor of Engineering, Department of Technical Communication; Director of Biotechnology Working Group, University of Washington, Seattle, USA

JAMES P. BUCHANAN
Caroline Werner Gannett Chair in Humanities, College of Liberal Arts, Rochester Institute of Technology, Rochester, USA

ANTHONY O. DYSON
Samuel Ferguson Professor of Social and Pastoral Theology, Department of Religions and Theology; Senior Fellow, Centre for Social Ethics and Policy, University of Manchester, UNITED KINGDOM

EDWARD S. GOLUB
Professor of Biology; President, Pacific Center for Ethics and Applied Biology, San Diego, USA

KAZUMASA HOSHINO
Professor Emeritus, Kyoto University; Director, International Bioethics Research Center, Kyoto Women's University, Kyoto, JAPAN

RITA KIELSTEIN
Professor of Nephrology, Otto von Guericke University, Magdeburg, GERMANY

REINHARD LÖW (†)
Professor of Philosophy; Co-Director, Research Institute for Philosophy, Hannover, GERMANY

DARRYL MACER
Associate Professor, Institute of Biological Sciences, University of Tsukuba, JAPAN

HANS-MARTIN SASS
Professor of Philosophy; Director, Centre for Medical Ethics, Ruhr University Bochum, GERMANY; Senior Research Fellow, The Kennedy Institute of Ethics, Washington, USA

DA-PU SHI
Professor of Medical Ethics, Xian Medical University; Deputy Director, Education Committee of Shaanxie Provincial Government, Xian, CHINA

PO TIEN
Professor of Biology; Director, Institute of Microbiology, Chinese Academy of Sciences, Beijing, CHINA

RAYMOND WACKS
Professor of Law, The University of Hong Kong, HONG KONG

LIN YU
Editor, Journal of Chinese Medical Ethics, Xian Medical University, Xian, CHINA

JOEL ZIMBELMAN
Fulbright Scholar, Centre for Applied Ethics 1993-94, Hong Kong Baptist University; Associate Professor, Department of Religious Studies, and Director, Centre for Applied & Professional Ethics, California State University, Chico, USA

Foreword

This collection of articles grew out of the symposium 'Biotechnology and Ethics: Scientific Liberty and Moral Responsibility'. The symposium, held in November 1993, was organized and sponsored by the Centre for Applied Ethics at Hong Kong Baptist University in cooperation with the Hong Kong University of Science and Technology and the Goethe Institut. The sponsorship of the symposium through these institutions as well as the financial support provided by the Centre for Applied Ethics towards the publication of the present volume are highly appreciated and gratefully acknowledged.

The symposium and this volume are significant for a number of reasons. First, this was the first conference in Hong Kong which explored the ethical issues arising from the vitally important and increasingly complex area of biotechnology. Second, the participants in the symposium and contributors to this volume represent both multiple cultures (Hong Kong, China, Japan, England, the United States, and Germany) as well as multiple disciplines (biology, chemistry, health sciences, economics, engineering, philosophy, law, and theology).

While this volume does provide a great deal of information about biotechnology, its more appropriate use is as a stimulus for discussion. Towards this end the articles often raise more questions than they answer. The complexity of the ethical dilemmas posed by biotechnology is such that we are still trying to identify what questions should be asked. The volume recognizes that the first step in making the types of ethical decisions which are increasingly demanded of us is searching for the right questions. The articles vary greatly in both length and orientation. This will make it useable by a wide range of groups — from students in the classroom, to professionals such as scientists, medical doctors, business people, lawyers, and ethicists, as well as environmental and other socially active groups. What becomes obvious from the articles collected here is that the issues arising from biotechnology are dramatic and will impact all of us and thus are in need of wide-ranging public debate. It is hoped that this volume will contribute to that debate.

Gerhold K. Becker
James P. Buchanan

1

Biotechnology — The New Ethical Frontier: An Introduction

Gerhold K. Becker

The twentieth century is certainly not short of important scientific discoveries, yet few have had greater impact on our lives than the unravelling of the structure of the atom and the genetic make-up of organisms. Both marked the arrival of a new age of scientific development which has successfully forged the rise of a powerful alliance between pure and applied science, between scientific theory and technological practice (and application). Besides pushing society 'into the era of high technology'[1] it has forced scientists to reconsider their social role and to accept greater responsibility for the consequences their research may hold for the rest of us. This new situation is clearly reflected in Max Born's remark:

> When I was young, it was still possible to be a pure scientist without being much concerned about the applications, the technology. Nowadays this is no longer possible, for natural science is inextricably intertwined with the social and political life (. . .) Today every scientist is a link within the technological and industrial system in which he lives. By that he has on his part also to be responsible for the reasonable use of his results.[2]

While the end of the Cold War somewhat de-dramatized our fear of atomic weapons, the potential threat from nuclear power plants continues to be the source of great anxiety. It is only rivaled by recent advances in biotechnology which have captured our imagination and propelled our expectations of the immense benefits as well as the fears of the equally immense dangers. As a report by the Office of Technology Assessment has pointed out, the arrival of the Age of Biology marks a new 'scientific revolution that could change the lives and futures of its citizens as dramatically as did the Industrial Revolution two centuries ago and the computer revolution today.' [3]

For its proponents, biotechnology holds the promise of generating almost limitless resources to meet the needs of a rapidly growing world population in its fight against hunger, diseases and the devastation of the natural environment through human intervention. From the development of designer foods to the creation of biodegradable pesticides, virus-resistant plants, and bacteria which consume oil spills; from gene therapy to eugenics, the impact of biotechnology can hardly be overestimated. The cover story in *Time* magazine of 17 January 1994 noted: 'The ability to manipulate genes could eventually change everything: what we eat, what we wear, how we live, how we die and how we see ourselves in relation to our fate.'

For its critics, biotechnology is more a nightmare than the answer to our current problems. It has been argued that, instead of creating genuine opportunities for a more humane future, biotechnology will jeopardize even our past achievements and add numerous incalculable risks to our future. The human body will be commodified and objectified, becoming a source of patentable raw materials which can be combined to produce tissues and living organisms that cannot develop naturally.[4] Nature will no longer be 'natural' but be re-created in the image of man. It is an image, some believe, that will have more in common with Dr Frankenstein and his creatures than with Socrates, Confucius, or Mother Teresa.

Outline of a Revolutionary Technology

In spite of the singular, biotechnology is in fact a combination of several technologies which draw on a number of scientific disciplines.[5] Biotechnology as it has developed over the last 15 to 20 years is usually taken to refer to three significant technologies:
- recombinant DNA technology
- *in vitro* manipulation of cells (also called cell culture technology, or bioprocessing)
- monoclonal antibody technology

The European Federation of Biotechnology defined biotechnology accordingly as the 'integrated use of biochemistry, microbiology and engineering sciences in order to achieve technological (industrial) application of the capabilities of micro-organisms, cultured tissue cells, and parts thereof.'[6]

Modern biotechnology is based on the discovery by James Watson and Francis Crick some forty years ago (1953) of the structure of DNA (deoxyribonucleic acid). Its famous double helix is made up of long and complex molecules which form two coiling strands of sugar-phosphate linked together like the steps of a spiralling staircase by four subunits.[7] These molecular components are called nucleotides (or nucleotide bases) and contain, apart from a sugar-phosphate combination, one of four kinds of differently shaped bases: adenine (A), guanine (G), cytosine (C), thymine (T). The genetic information which determines the whole structure and the biochemical functions of the cells of any organism is encoded in the sequence, or order of these four subunits. It has been estimated that there are about three billion base pairs which are the 'steps' of the 'staircase' containing all the genetic information of a human cell.

This principle of coded information resembles that in the sequence of the letters of our alphabet, complete with stop- ('periods') and start-codes (markers for word beginnings), by which we obtain all the words of our language through the combination of just 26 letters. Similarly, the chemical substances of DNA are combined into distinct functional units — the genes — which form individual, consecutive stretches of base pairs encoding sufficient genetic information to produce simple chains of amino acids. Although the term gene preceded modern biotechnology and was first coined in 1909 to refer to Mendel's rather mysterious units of biological inheritance, its full implications emerged only when the high-tech form of biotechnology gained ascendancy. Genes vary considerably in size, and 'a typical gene might include 1,000 base-pair steps in the DNA staircase and about 100 turns in the DNA double helix.' [8] The genes represent the various words in a long text and work like commands to produce (express) all the hereditary traits in any organism. An organism's complete set of genes, comprising the totality of its genetic information, is called the organism's genome. It has been estimated that the three billion base pairs of the human genome include 50,000 to 100,000 genes. 'The rest of the genome — perhaps 95 percent of it — is nongenic sequences with unkown function, sometimes called "junk".' [9]

The chemical components of DNA are the same in all organisms and are found in the most primitive bacterium as well as in human beings. What distinguishes one organism from the other is not the overall structure of the molecules but the different sequences of the subunits within the DNAs. 'Once isolated, any DNA molecule is the same as any other, and all can be treated with the same tools and techniques in the laboratory.' [10]

The most dramatic implication of biotechnology lies in this fact of the sameness of DNA components and the possibility of re-arranging their order and substituting one gene for another. Although the technology for such an unprecedented manipulation of genetic information — recombinant DNA technology — began to become available only in 1973, it has 'undergone the most spectacular development' (Gendel). It quickly evolved into a powerful instrument which is now routinely used to alter the genetic make-up of a broad range of organisms, including microbes, plants and mammals.

The technology seems in principle rather simple although it requires highly sophisticated tools and clever methods to slice out a piece of genetic information of the host organism, manipulate it and transfer it to a cell of another organism. Recombinant DNA technology has developed rapidly and can now be used for a variety of purposes including the breaking down, manipulation and recombination of molecules. 'The power of recombinant DNA technology is that it permits researchers specifically to reprogram an organism to produce any desirable or useful biological product.'[11]

The *in vitro* manipulation of cells is bound to revolutionize agriculture and livestock farming, and will have a strong impact on our natural environment including its fauna and flora. Although applied to the development of a variety of new bio-products both in plants and animals, the most dramatic impact of this technology lies in its capability of breaking down the species barrier by engineering transgenic plants and animals. This is based on a combination of recombinant DNA technology and cell culture technology which allows the introduction of desirable traits from various sources into the genetic make-up of an organism. 'A transgenic organism is one that carries and expresses genetic information not normally found in that species of organism.' Whereas 'traditional methods can only manipulate genetic capabilities already present within the gene pool of an individual species', 'modern biotechnological innovations allow creation of organisms with genetic capabilities not normally found in that particular species.' [12]

Currently, this technique is most commonly used to improve the nutritional qualities in both plants and animals and to develop natural defense mechanisms against diseases. The application in plant production includes further strengthening of their natural properties against cold or heat, and a higher tolerance to pesticides and polluted environments.

Antibodies are extremely sensitive proteins capable of recognizing a foreign molecule from among billions of others and hooking themselves to a very specific location of it. Monoclonal antibody technology then makes use of these exceptionally important properties of antibodies to produce a variety of specific indicators of other substances to which they react. It will allow the development of numerous diagnostic testing procedures of extremely high accuracy.

A New Ethical Landscape

There can be no doubt that biotechnology represents a major breakthrough in scientific research and a triumph of human ingenuity. It will be the most powerful ally in our fight against diseases and disabilities, hunger and poverty on a world scale. It will help us cope better with the devastation of nature brought about by the earlier industrial revolution and over-population in the wake of what has been described as 'the demographic explosion' (Paul Kennedy).

However, the downside of biotechnology has largely to do with this unprecedented power, its use and its control. The implications and social impact of biotechnology have been compared to those of the splitting of the atom and the technological exploitation of nuclear power. As with nuclear technology, biotechnology has put enormous power in our hands. Yet, power is essentially ambiguous, it can be used for good and evil purposes. And there is growing concern that this new technology may redefine our relationship to nature by irreversibly and detrimentally changing nature's course. In altering natural evolution through human tampering with the gene pool, biotechnology would cause incalculable risks for human integrity, well-being and freedom.

This ethical concern is reflected in an increasing number of publications which cover a wide range of issues. There is also the fear that biotechnology might even have begun to change the rules of ethical decision making. In the past, ethics was based on widely (and frequently cross-culturally) shared beliefs about human nature, personhood and social responsibilities. The consequences of individual actions were never as dramatic as they are now; in addition, they were usually confined to one's own life circle. Clearly, this situation has changed, since we are now capable of literally blowing up the whole planet, destroying its ecosystem and changing humanity beyond recognition. Hans Jonas has pointed out that for the first time in history it is up to us to decide whether mankind should be at all; for the first time, the very existence of humanity is put in our hands. In the past, ethics never had to deal with such daunting questions, instead it operated on the assumption that nature was not within the reach of man[13] but ultimately inviolable. Her self-healing powers were thought to always prevail and out-do the damage man could possibly inflict on her. Certainly, this can no longer be taken for granted.

A sober reflection on the ethical implications of biotechnology as such is therefore, above all, confronted with two fundamental questions:

Firstly, does biotechnology represent a qualitatively new step in the history of science which calls for a new ethics, or is it something that can and should be understood along the lines of traditional values and within the well-established framework of moral philosophy. To put it differently: Has biotech just opened a new chapter in the long history of the scientific conquest of nature, or has it effectively closed the old volume and begun to write the first lines of an entirely different story? This text would be as much about the conquest of nature as it would be about its potential devastation, its manipulation and re-creation; in any case, it would be about changing nature's course altogether.[14]

Secondly, what impact should we allow biotechnology to have on the hidden assumptions as to how we view ourselves? Can we utilize its potential and carry on with our familiar worldviews and religious interpretations of the world, or is biotechnology in itself some sort of new ideology which challenges our traditional place in nature? Is it endowing us with the creative powers of God, or rather reducing us and the mystery of life to mere genetic components at the molecular level?

Strachan Donnelley very aptly summed up the ethical problem of biotechnology as follows: 'What should be the ethically self-imposed limits, if any, to our interventions into nature, for what reasons, in service of what moral values?'[15]

Biotechnology's Major Ethical Challenges

Apart from ethical considerations on our general relationship to high technologies, most notably biotechnology, a number of research areas have attracted particular attention. They combine most of the features of complex ethical dilemmas with a relatively well-defined research activity within the larger framework of biotechnology. The more prominent of them are represented in this book through articles on both the latest research developments and in-depth analyses of their ethical implications. These areas of biotechnological research include the following:

- human genetic engineering
- genetic screening and testing
- the engineering of transgenic plants and animals
- the patenting of life forms

The Human Genome Project and Gene Therapy

The ethical issues with regard to the Human Genome Project which will ultimately lead to a full map of the genetic information as it is encoded in the human DNA concern not so much the project itself but the potential use of the information thus acquired. Since it will be possible to produce the genetic profile of any individual, the ethical questions revolve around issues of privacy, confidentiality, ownership and autonomy: 'How should information be protected? Who should have access to the information and under what circumstances? What rights, if any, do employers, insurers, and family members have to an individual's genetic information?'[16]

Yet, the larger question looming in the background is related to human gene therapy. Although there seems widespread agreement that somatic cell gene therapy poses little ethical concern, germ-line gene therapy is highly controversial and generally rejected on ethical grounds. Whereas the former therapy could be understood along the lines of traditional medical intervention such as organ transplantation, the latter is different. It allows that changes could be made in the genetic information which would be passed on to all future generations. It raises also questions about how to understand what is normal and what is abnormal, what is deviant or deficient, and what is genuinely human.

There are mainly two kinds of ethical arguments against the use of germ line gene therapy. The first one is a consequential argument that doubts the moral right of anyone to induce genetic changes whose potentially harmful consequences cannot be anticipated and whose results will affect future generations. The second argument is categorical (deontological) in nature and rules out as a matter of principle any moral right to tamper with the human gene pool and to manipulate the genetic inheritance of the human race.

Ultimately, germ line genetic therapy leads directly back to the extremely difficult questions which have been raised in conjunction with biotechnology and its impact on our fundamental beliefs about ourselves, our species and human nature as such. To what extent will biotechnology change how we view ourselves? On what ideological assumptions will scientists base their research on the human genome? Will they regard human beings as nothing more than the products of interacting genes, or will they allow for some qualitative differences between the genes and their 'product'?

It seems that the answer to questions such as these will depend on whether we will enter a new era of eugenics where we might not only aim at decreasing the number of harmful or less desirable genes (negative eugenics) but tamper with the genetic make-up of our species by introducing new or altered genes thought to 'improve' the quality of the human gene pool (positive eugenics). Unless we have arrived at an universally shared, normative conception of humanity in the comprehensive sense of the term which can ethically guide this kind of intervention, and unless we can claim solid knowledge about the long-term consequences of positive eugenics, experiments of this nature should not be allowed.[17]

Transgenic Organisms

Similar questions have been raised with regard to the development of transgenic organisms. Yet, there are also a number of more specific issues which have become the focus of ethical concern. A research project on the Ethics of Animal Biotechnology sponsored by the Hastings Center has identified three issues of particular significance:

Firstly, the concept of the species and its possible moral implications: The possibility to bridge the species barrier brings to the fore not only the very concept of the species itself but also its significance and function in the natural order of beings. It is noteworthy that in most cultures the crossing of species lines used to be the subject of taboos for humans and was exclusively reserved to superhuman beings. This indicates a strong sense for the inviolability of the natural order and its hierarchy where everything is believed to have been assigned its proper place. The attempt to change this place was tantamount to an attack on the eternal order of creation and a rebellion against its creator. It is not only in Christian iconography that the devil as the embodiment of such a rebellion is usually depicted as some sort of 'transgenic being', which has merged the properties of a number of different species (man, goat, ass, reptile, etc).

It appears then that the question as to whether species are 'real biological entities so inherent in the fabric of nature that we become morally culpable in breaking the barrier between them'[18] requires an interdisciplinary and cross-cultural approach. It would have to draw on the wisdom enshrined in the philosophical and religious traditions of mankind as well as on the discoveries of the biological sciences.[19]

Secondly, the potential pain and suffering caused to genetically engineered animals: This concern is closely related to the more general one of the treatment of animals as subjects of research and experimentation, and raises the question of the moral status and the potential (range of) rights of animals. The commercial benefits of genetically engineered livestock (greater weight, greater feed efficiency, reduction in fat) have frequently been offset by a host of painful side effects such as a high incidence of gastric ulcers, arthritis, cardiomegaly, dermatitis, and renal disease.[28]

It seems that the production of genetically engineered animals on a large scale for exclusively commercial purposes requires a strong justification of the harm done to their well-being and the pain inflicted; at present, such a justification may not be readily available. The extremes of the ethical debate are marked by conservationists and advocates of animal rights who argue against any form of human intervention in the life cycles and the natural habitats of animals, and the defenders of a more anthropocentric approach which would allow for the exploitation of animals if the benefit for mankind clearly out-weighed the harm done to them.

Thirdly, the possible ecological impact: The engineering of transgenic plants has been particularly successful and resulted in a number of new products; their commercialization is about to begin.[21] In the last five years, the UK Ministry of Agriculture, Fisheries and Food has approved the marketing of nine different types of genetically engineered food. In Britain alone, seven genetically altered organisms are scheduled for release in the fields in the second half of 1995.[22]

Researchers usually point out the many benefits this kind of genetic intervention will bring to mankind and tend to minimize the risks the intentional or accidental release of genetically altered plants could have on the environment. Although our understanding of the potential role and impact of transgenic organisms on the environment is still in its infancy and has so far brought only scanty results, this is no reason for complacency. We should, however, equally avoid falling into the opposite trap of painting risks in too gloomy colours, since this will only foster in many of us a sense of helpless despair in the face of what seems to be the inevitable course history will take. The anticipated dangers may involve: health hazards for humans and animals alike; economic losses especially in developing countries caused by a combination of unaffordable prices for patented crop seeds and changed patterns of soil cultivation (monocultures, cattle breeding); species imbalances or depletion which could lead to a host of subsequent perils ranging from soil erosion and deforestation to climatic changes.

Risk Assessment and Regulatory Policies

It is a matter of great urgency to develop adequate methodologies of risk assessment for all areas of high-technology, particularly biotechnology. In pondering the socio-cultural consequences of these advanced technologies and their ethical implications, researchers in biotechnology need to draw on the results of the emerging discipline of risk assessment and utilize its methodology. One major difficulty, however, lies in the fact that ecological and evolutionary risks can only be simulated to a very limited extent in computer models. Their full-scale assessment relies heavily on hypotheses which could be tested only when the events had been realized. This amounts to a rather paradoxical situation: one would have to await the outcome of certain artificially induced evolutionary developments in order to decide whether they should have been prevented from occurring! This perplexing and dilemmatic scenario has led to opposing views as to how one should proceed with regard to the release of transgenic organisms. Whereas some have argued for a moratorium, others have favoured an even accelerated release. They envisage greater overall dangers in the mistaken belief that we could ever be able to design and manage flawless experiments. Unless we decide to give up science altogether, there will always be surprises and unexpected results in the outcome of experiments. Yet, even failed experiments appear to be better than no experiments whatsoever. Since, according to this view, the knowledge thus provided is of greater significance for the well-being of mankind and makes it much more likely that we will be able to cope with undesirable side effects, it is better to promote research than to abstain from it. [23]

Despite these complex problems, the development of assessment strategies and the study of short- and long-term ecological effects of transgenic organisms remains a high priority. Yet, in the case of decisions where the stakes are as high as in biotechnology, one can never rely exclusively on scientific methods to determine how one should act. Unless risk assessment strategies are comprehensive enough to incorporate also the fundamental beliefs on which our society rests, they can at best provide the information which is vitally needed for responsible action but not serve as its substitution. The desirability of biotechnology as such cannot be exclusively determined on the basis of scientific data and knowledge. The evaluation of the implications biotechnology is likely to have for our life, for our society and our culture reaches beyond the expertise of the scientist qua scientist and calls for a comprehensive discourse in which the various moral, social and cultural interests will find the attention they deserve. It is for our society as a whole to decide on the way we want to live.

It is therefore not surprising to see the conviction gaining ground that research in biotechnology in general and in transgenic organisms in particular needs to be carried out with extreme caution and a high degree of (individual and public) responsibility. This has prompted many countries to develop regulatory policies and to legislate against uncontrolled research.[24]

It is obvious that, in spite of its undoubted significance, such legislation must be balanced against another social good which deserves protection: the liberty of science and research. Any regulatory policy has to tread a fine line and aim at safeguarding the overall interests and the well-being of society without stifling science and research.

Finally, the impression must be avoided that any kind of legislation could ever release the indvidual researcher from his moral responsibility for the consequences of his research.[25] This is particularly necessary since there will always remain a certain gap between the stipulations of the law and their practical implementation and enforcement.

Paradigm-shift

This introduction would be incomplete without the attempt to map biotechnology onto the canvass of the philosophical tradition in the West, since this can help to clarify the extent to which biotechnology has begun to redefine our traditional relationship to nature. Although the following remarks can only give a rough outline of this relationship and its ideological implications, they will lend support to the claim expressed above that biotechnology represents a decisive turn away from a tradition which for centuries provided our moral perspective with inspiration and direction. Following a Nietzschean line of thought, it will be argued that biotechnology is the culmination of a larger development and the clearest indication to date of the paradigm-shift it stands for.

Western philosophy derives much of its strength from the intuition that in spite of its various tumultuous events the world is no chaos but a 'cosmos': a beautifully and intelligibly arranged system of order. This order not only permeates everything from the lowest to the highest scale of beings but defines also to each its proper (metaphysical) place. It is this assumption of intelligibility and order which provided the fundament for Plato's philosophy and set the philosophical agenda for centuries to come.

Plato's metaphysics entailed what Lovejoy has called the principle of plenitude. This principle required 'the realization of conceptual possibility in actuality'.[26] The universe then is composed of 'an infinite number of links ranging in hierarchical order from the meagerest kind of existents, which barely escape non-existence, through 'every possible' grade up to the *ens perfectissimum*.'[27] In allusion to Homer's *catena aurea*, this order of nature was called the Great Chain of Being which, on Lovejoy's account, held sway from the Platonic beginnings of Western philosohy up to the nineteenth century. Alexander Pope's *Essay on Man* (1733/34) bears witness to the prominence of this 'vast chain of being' extending from God through the whole range of creatures all the way down to mere 'nothing'.

Man's place in the order of beings was precariously set in the middle. Drawing on both Greek metaphysics and Christian theology, Thomas Aquinas called man the 'horizon and border' which connects as well as separates the material and the spiritual (intellectual) world. This view is still valid in the seventeenth and eighteenth centuries when Pascal sees in man 'a middle point between all and nothing' [28] and when Pope has him 'placed on this isthmus of a middle state'[29].

About a hundred years ago Nietzsche stated that this order no longer existed and that its underlying metaphysical worldview had definitively come to its end. With the chain 'broken', man lost his metaphysical place in the hierarchy of beings. His 'essence' is no longer set from eternity by the divine order of things but malleable as clay in the hands of a potter. Man is emphatically the 'animal which is not yet fixed'.

Consequently, Nietzsche's Zarathustra declared the end of man which derived essence and identity from his preordained place in nature. Man is now 'something that must be overcome', is merely 'a bridge and not a goal',[30] a 'passage' to something greater than what he used to think of himself. 'Man is a rope, fastened between animal and superman'[31] who ultimately will replace him, and whose arrival was already announced.

Nietzsche's philosophy of the superman draws as much on the traditional worldview as he rejects it. Whereas previous ages saw man encouraged to improve on himself within the limits set to him by the divine laws of nature, Nietzsche's philosophy advocates a qualitative step which leads beyond the boundaries of nature, metaphysics and religion.

Nietzsche was convinced that his philosophy marked the turning point in Western intellectual history and that he anticipated things to come on a much larger scale. His intuition is based on two 'events' in the intellectual history of humankind which in his view are deeply intertwined: the 'death of God' and the ascent of modern science.

Nietzsche's 'madman' proclaims that there 'has never been a greater deed' than the death of God from the hands of man since it makes man become part of 'a higher history than all history hitherto'. In Nietzsche's reading, the rejection of theistic metaphysics is a structural condition of modern science which puts it squarely on the basis of what has been called methodological atheism. Yet, with God the whole metaphysical structure has been lost which once defined man's nature and his place in the universe. Since this 'entire horizon' was wiped away with our sponge, we lost orientation and are now 'plunging continually', — 'backward, sideward, forward, in all directions'.[32]

Whereas the 'death of God' implies the demise of the metaphysical frame of reference (worldview) for man's theoretical as well as practical orientation, modern science compensated man for this loss by cutting his imagination loose from past constraints and inviting him to define for himself who he wants to be.

The collapse of the metaphysical basis, however, is quite ambiguous. It opens the door for the existentialist reading of man's freedom which is as much a condemnation as it is a blessing. In the ontological phraseology of Sartre, this means that 'existence comes before its essence'. Consequently, 'there is no human nature' and 'man is nothing else but that which he makes of himself'.[33] Yet, already Nietzsche knew of the anguish which comes with this new and radical freedom. If freedom lacks a grandiose vision of the future of man, the ensuing disorientation is bound to lead to suppression and degradation at the hands of petty and selfish individuals, 'the last men'. These have no qualms to violate nature 'with the aid of machines and the heedless inventiveness of our technicians', and 'to experiment with ourselves in a way we would never permit ourselves to experiment with animals.'[34] The vision which makes the difference is that of superman. It sets out a new, higher goal for humankind and at the same time prevents human scientific endeavours from going astray.

Nietzsche accepted that the time for his bold vision had not come yet. He took comfort in the fact that 'some are being borne posthumously', and that he was merely the prophet of a new age that would arrive anyway.

That age may finally have come. Biotech, so it seems, represents both the pinnacle of modern science and its eclipse, the power and the inability of reason. It vindicates admirably the Baconian formula that knowledge is power while illustrating at the same time the loss of moral orientation. The enormous advances we have made in science and technology are quite obviously not matched by a similar progress in our moral awareness that would enable us to put our scientific knowledge in the service of a shared vision of 'the good life'. It needs the combined efforts of all concerned, including scientists, policy makers, social planners and philosophers to take up the challenge which has begun to change nature's course and to impact our lives more than anything before in the history of mankind. Nietzsche's sketch of the ideological implications of modern science has been etched out with crude tools (he called this proudly 'to philosophize with a hammer'); it can, however, serve as a vivid reminder of what is at stake.

Notes

1. Lawrence Busch, William B. Lacy, Jeffrey Burkhardt, and Laura R. Lacy, *Plants Power and Profit. Social, Economic, and Ethical Consequences of the New Biotechnologies* (Cambridge, Ma and Oxford: Blackwell, 1992) 3. See also W. B. Lacy and L. Busch, 'Changing Division of Labor Between the University and Industry: The Case of Agricultural Biotechnology'. In J. Molnar and H. Kinnucan, eds., *Biotechnology and the New Agricultural Revolution* (Boulder: Westview Press, 1989) 21–50.
2. Max Born, *Physik und Politik* (Göttingen: Vandenhoeck & Ruprecht, 1960) 45 (my translation).
3. Office of Technology Assessment, *New Developments in Biotechnology: Public Perceptions of Biotechnology* (Washington, DC: US Government Printing Office, 1987) 9.
4. Andrew Kimbrell, *The Human Body Shop. The Engineering and Marketing of Life* (San Francisco: Harper San Francisco, 1993) 188f.; 268f.
5. Stephen M. Gendel, 'Foreword'. In William F. Woodman, Mack C. Shelley II, and Brian J. Reichel, *Biotechnology and the Research Enterprise* (Ames: Iowa State University Press, 1989) VII-XII, VIII.
6. M. Chiara Mantegazzini, *The Environmental Risks from Biotechnology* (London: Frances Pinter, 1986) 136. A somewhat biased definition is found in Pat Spallone, *Generation Games. Genetic Engineering and the Future of Our Lives* (Philadelphia: Temple University Press, 1992) 4: 'Biotechnology is the exploitation of living things, and of substances from living thing, to create products and processes for many different purposes.'
7. David Suzuki and Peter Knudtson, *Genethics. The Ethics of Engineering Life* (London: Unwin Paperbacks, 1988) 30–51; here and in the following I refer particularly to pages 32–34 of their acclaimed explanation of a rather complicated matter.
8. Ibid., 34.
9. Sharon J. Durfry and Amy E. Grotevant, 'The Human Genome Project', *Kennedy Institute of Ethics Journal* (December 1991) 1 (Scope Note 17): 347–362, 347.

10. Gendel, loc. cit. IX.

11. *The International Biotechnology Handbook* (London: Euromonitor Publications, 1988) 28–33, 33.

12. Rivers Singleton, et al., 'Transgenic Organisms, Science, and Society', *Hastings Center Report* (1994) 24, 1. *Special Supplement*: S4-S14, S4.

13. Here and in the following, 'man' is always used as a gender-neutral term.

14. Whereas the proponents of biotechnology tend to emphasize its continuity with past technologies and processes of natural selection and cultivation, the skeptics and 'opponents of rapid development stress discontinuities and the harms that can come from bold departures.' Vivian Weil concludes: 'Whether or not there is a radical break with the past, it has to be conceded that living organisms are less predictable than mechanical systems.' Vivian Weil, 'Ethics and Biotechnology — Identifying Issues in the Face of Uncertainties'. In Matthias Kaiser, and Stellan Welin, eds., *Ethical Aspects of Modern Biotechnology* (Goeteborg: Centre for Research Ethics, 1995) 7–24, 8.

15. Strachan Donnelley, 'Exploring Ethical Landscapes', *Hastings Center Report* (1994) 24, 1. *Special Supplement*. S1-S4, S3.

16. Sharon J. Durfry, and Amy E. Grotevant, ibid. 350.

17. For a more positive assessment of germ line therapy see: John Harris, *Wonderwoman and Superman: The Ethics of Human Biotechnology* (Oxford: Oxford University Press, 1992). See also: Matti Häyry, 'Categorical Objections to Genetic Engineering — A Critique'. In Anthony Dyson, and John Harris, eds., *Ethics and Biotechnology* (London/New York: Routledge, 1994) 202–215.

18. Rivers Singleton, et al., loc. cit. S5.

19. The groundwork for this research has already been laid in the work of Ernst Mayr who distinguished between three different conceptualizations: essentialist, nominalist and modern. See Ernst Mayr, *The Growth of Biological Thought* (Cambridge, Mass.: Belknap Press, 1982) esp. chapter 6: 'Microtaxonomy, the Science of Species'. See also: Marc Ereshefsky, *The Units of Evolution. Essays on the Nature of Species* (Cambridge, Mass: MIT Press, 1992).

20. Daniel Koshland, 'The Engineering of Species', *Science* (1989) 244: 1233.

21. The first genetically modified agricultural product was Calgene's Flavr Savr tomato which has now reached the marketplace in the Unites States.

22. *Gen Ethics News* 7(1995): 4, 12.

23. A. Wildavsky, *Searching for Safety* (New Brunswick: Transaction, 1988).

24. As regards Hong Kong, it seems that there are presently no rules governing the growth of any kind of transgenic plants. This lack of regulations could prove very attractive to biotechnology firms interested in potentially dangerous experiments which are prohibited in their own countries of origin.

25. Vivian Weil has argued that since the increased complexity of modern research and the various factors which drive it still leave some latitude to the individual scientist for defining the research even in large, hierarchical organization, researchers have to 'accept responsibility for contributing to foreseeable outcomes beyond the laboratory and the company'. Loc. cit., 19.

26. Arthur O. Lovejoy, *The Great Chain of Being. A Study of the History of an Idea* (Cambridge, Mass.: Harvard University Press, 1978) 52.

27. Ibid., 59.

28. Blaise Pascal, *Pensées* (1670), Léon Brunschvicg, ed. (Paris: Librairie Générale Française, 1972) fr. 199.

29. Alexander Pope, *Essay on Man*, II, 3.

30. See: Friedrich Nietzsche, *Thus Spoke Zarathustra. A Book for Everyone and No One*. Tr. by R. J. Hollingdale (Harmondsworth: Penguin Books, 1972) 215–216.
31. Ibid., Prologue, 4.
32. Friedrich Nietzsche, *The Gay Science*. Tr. by W. Kaufmann (New York: Vintage Books, 1974) 181 (§ 125).
33. Jean-Paul Sartre, *Existentialism and Humanism*. Tr. by Philip Mairet (Brooklyn: Haskell House Publ., 1977) 28.
34. Friedrich Nietzsche, *On the Genealogy of Morals*. Tr. by W. Kaufmann (New York: Vintage Books, 1989) 113 (III, 9).

Part I

Ethical Concerns in the Age of Biotechnology

* * * * * * * * * * * * * *

Part IA

Biotechnology and the Environment

2

Production, Use and Biosafety of Genetically Engineering Resistance to Plant Virus Diseases

Po Tien

One successful application of genetic engineering in crop improvement is in the production of virus-resistant plants. This has been achieved by genetic transformation of plants with novel resistance genes based on nucleotide sequences derived from the viruses themselves or from virus-associated nucleic acid as well as genes from other sources.

The demonstration that the expression of tobacco mosaic virus (TMV) coat protein (CP) in transgenic plants protects the plants against virus infection[1] has led to explorations of using other viral or virus-associated genes in producing genetically engineered resistance against in plant virus. Transgenic plants expressing Sat-RNAs have been obtained in a number of laboratories and have been tested in greenhouses and fields.[2] Recent studies with defective interfering RNA or DNA protection and sense-antisense-ribozyme RNA-mediated protection offer much promise for a broad range virus resistance in plants.[3]

Our laboratory has successfully produced satellite RNA-mediated resistance to cucumber mosaic virus (CMV) in tobacco and tomato, CP-mediated resistance to rice stripe virus in rice and fusion protein (CP and nuclease) mediated high resistance to tobacco mosaic virus in tobacco. One way to confer more effective and durable field resistance to virus disease in transgenic crop is to use a combination of multiple resistance genes. Transgenic commercial tobacco cultivars expressing CP and satellite RNA of CMV are being used in tobacco production in China. Safety, from a public point of view, was ensured by biologically containing the modified plants. Assessing and monitoring the risks of releasing genetically manipulated plants will be discussed.

Satellite RNA in Engineering Resistance to Plant-Virus Diseases

Since 1981, Sat-RNAs have been used as a biological control agent (BCA) of diseases caused by CMV on a large scale in China.[4] The results show that the BCA is effective in controlling diseases caused by virulent CMV strains in many crops and, in addition, induces resistance to certain types of fungal diseases.[5] The protective effects of CMV Sat-RNAs have been demonstrated in a number of greenhouse and field tests. These studies have provided the basis for engineering plant resistance to virus infection by introducing the Sat-RNA as a transgene.

In our laboratory, the cDNA of an attenuating Sat-RNA monomer from CMV strain 1 was synthesized and constructed into the plant expression vector pRok2. The Sat-RNA cDNA was introduced into different plant species including tobacco[6] and tomato.[7] When transgenic tobacco and tomato plants were tested in the greenhouse for resistance against challenge infection by CMV, they showed a significant decrease in disease index compared to non-transformed plants. In an experimental scale field test conducted in the spring of 1990, the transgenic tomato plants inoculated artificially with CMV gave about 50% higher fruit yield than the non-transformed control plants and showed a decrease in disease index (Table 1). However, there was no significant difference in leaf yield between the satellite transgenic and the control tobacco plants, although the disease index of transgenic tobacco was about 10% lower than that of the control. Due to an insufficient level of Sat-RNA in the plants at an early stage of infection, the transgenic tobacco plants showed only a weak resistance to CMV, which directly affected the leaf yield, since it is the early leaves that are harvested in tobacco production.[8]

Although Sat-RNAs confer some extent of resistance to virus infection, field tests carried out in China from 1990–1992 show that the resistance of the transgenic plants is not strong enough to fully protect tobacco and tomato plants from the damage caused by natural virus infections (Table 1).

Table 1
Resistance and yield of transgenic tomato expressing Sat-RNA in field test (1990–1992)

Year	Treated area	Disease index		Fruit yield kg mu⁻¹		
		Transgenic	Control	Transgenic	Control	Increase (%)
1990	121 plants	56.4[†] (DI)[‡]	100[†] (DI)	16.2 (10 plants)	10.6 (10 plants)	43
1991	1 mu[*]	20.0[§]	42.8[§]	4289	4010	6.9
1992	2 mu	8.7[§]	16.1[§]	6100	5439	11.1

[*]mu. Chinese unit for area (= 0.0667 hectares).
[†]Sap inoculation.
[‡]DI. Disease index, see footnote of Table 2.
[§]Natural infection.

Sat-RNA in a Multiple Gene Strategy of Engineering Resistance

One way to obtain more effective and durable resistance to virus diseases in transgenic plants may be to use a combination of multiple resistance genes. In this strategy, different genes that produce blockage or interference at different stages of a virus infection are used to obtain engineered resistance. Transgenic lines of tobacco expressing both CP and Sat-RNA of CMV were obtained through transformation using a chimeric vector containing two expression cassettes of the two genes under the control of the CaMV 35S promoter.[9] When challenged with CMV, the virus concentration of challenging CMV in transformed plants that express only Sat-RNA was about 10–20% of that in non-transformed plants, while in CP + Sat-RNA transformed plants it was only 4–5%. A comparison of disease incidence and disease index of CP + Sat-RNA, CP alone or Sat-RNA alone transformed tobacco plants is shown in Table 2. The resistance of CP + Sat-RNA transformed plants was about twice as strong as that of Sat-RNA alone or CP alone transformed plants. Since the CP level expressed in CP + Sat-RNA transformed plants was similar to that in transformed plants that contained only the CP gene, the two-fold increase in resistance of CP + Sat-RNA transformed plants was not due to higher levels of CP expression. On the other hand, the level of Sat-RNA accumulation in the CP + Sat-RNA transformed plants was lower than that in the Sat-RNA alone transformed plants. This may be due to the effect of the CP gene conferring resistance at an early stage in CMV infection, reducing the replication of CMV as well as Sat-RNA. Preliminary data from a field test of 1992 confirmed the enhanced resistance of the CP + Sat-RNA transformed plants to CMV. The CP + Sat-RNA transformed plants show stronger resistance to natural CMV infections than either the CP alone or Sat-RNA alone transformed plants.

Table 2
Comparison of disease incidence and disease index[*] of CP + Sat, CP alone and Sat-RNA alone transgenic tobacco after CMV inoculation

Transformed genotype	Number of plants analyzed	Days post inoculation with 25 µg/mL CMV					
		30 days		60 days		90 days	
		Disease incidence (%)	Disease index (%)	Disease incidence (%)	Disease index (%)	Disease incidence (%)	Disease index (%)
Sat-RNA	20	80	23.7	95	30.0	100	45.0
CP	20	50	37.5	60	40.0	60	46.25
Sat-CP	20	25	7.5	30	10.0	30	20.0
Inoculated control	20	100	63.7	100	28.0	100	100.0
Control without inoculation	20	0	0	0	0	0	0

$$*\text{Disease index} = \frac{\Sigma \text{ (No. of plants of each grade)} \times \text{(Severity)}}{\text{(Total no. of plants)} \times \text{(The highest severity)}} \times 100$$

Severity of symptoms was rated on a scale of 0–3, where 0 = no symptoms and 3 = severe symptoms.

Fast Homozygosity of Transgenic Tobacco Plants Resistant to Cucumber Mosaic Virus by Expressing Satellite RNA and Coat Protein

Since *Nicotiana tabacuum* is an amphidipoid species, the tetraploid transgenic plants will segregate extensively in their progenies. It needs to be propagated several generations before obtaining a homozygous line. In order to speed up this process, a procedure for a fast production of homozygosity of transgenic plants was devised in our work (Figure 1). Leaf discs of diploid tobacco plant derived from anther cultures of a commercial cultivar NC-89 were transformed with a chimeric vector of CP and Sat-RNA genes of CMV. The kanamycin resistant diploid plants were selected by their expression of CP and Sat-RNA. Then the transgenic plants were tested for their resistance to CMV after inoculation with high concentration of CMV (50–100 µg/mL). Only the plants with high resistance to CMV were tetraploidized with colchicine. The transgenic homozygous tetraploid progeny can therefore be obtained after only one generation. A certain amount of transgenic seeds will be produced within one growing season. After propagation of the transgenic seeds once in Hainan Province a large scale of field test can be achieved in the main tobacco producing area in the second year. Table 3 showed the results of resistance of transgenic tobacco cultivar NC-89 through the procedure of fast homozygosity generation in Hainan Province.

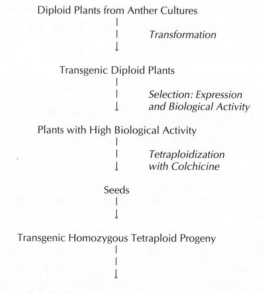

Figure 1 A procedure for fast homozygosity generation in transgenic plants.

Table 3
Field resistance of transgenic commercial tobacco cultivar NC-89 expressing CP and satellite RNA and CP Alone on infection by CMV. A field trial in an area of several hectares has been carried out in Henan Province in 1993.
(1992 in Hainan Province)

Homozygous Progeny of Transformed genotype		Area (Mu)*	Plants with Symptoms (%)	Disease Index
	N3-5	1	26	15
	N3-8	1	28	16
CP + Sat-RNA				
	N26-4	1	37	20
	N26-20	1	13	8
CP alone		1	76	44
Control		2	100	100

*1 hectare = 15 Mu

Resistance to Rice Stripe Virus in Transgenic Indica Rice Plants Expressing Coat Protein

Rice stripe disease occurs in rice growing areas of China, Japan, Korea and the Commonwealth of Independent State, and causes significant reduction in rice yield. The coat protein (CP) gene of a Chinese isolate of rice stripe virus (RSV-C) was synthesized, cloned and sequenced, which is very similar to the Japanese strain.

Cell suspension cultures were initiated from embrogenic calli of rice Annong S-1 (indica rice) by inoculating yellowish, compact and embryogenic calli derived from seeds into a suspension culture medium containing proline and maltose. After being cultured at 26°C in the dark for about half a year, finely-dispersed and embryogenic suspension culture was established. Before bombardment, the suspension culture was evenly applied onto three-layer-filter-paper discs in a petri dish. Cells were bombarded with 1 μm diameter tungsten particles coated with DNA of the expression vector pROK2 containing the CP gene under control of the 35S promoter. The plasmid DNA was absorbed to tungsten particles using a calcium-spermidine precipitation procedure. 2.5 μL of the coated particles was loaded onto macroprojectile and each dish with the suspension culture was bombarded three times under a partial vacuum. Following bombardment, the suspensions were cultured in a modified N_6 medium. Two days later the suspensions were transferred to the same medium containing G418 (40 μg/mL), which were subcultured every week. Being subject to G418 selection for two months, white and fast-growing colonies were emerged from the browny cultures. Green plants could be regenerated when the resistant calli were transferred to a differentiation medium. In one experiment ten plantlets regenerated from G418 resistant calli were tested for their transgenic nature by Southern blot analysis using a-^{32}P-dCTP-labelled CP gene as a probe. The genomic DNA extracted from the selected as well as the control plants were digested with EcoR1 and BamH1 and then hybridized with the probe. Two plants showed two hybridization bands of 0.6 kbp and 0.7 kbp corresponding to the CP gene. Western blot and ELISA further analyses demonstrated that CP (32 kDa) was expressed in the transgenic rice plants.

Sixteen transgenic thus obtained and 100 non-transformed rice plants were inoculated with RSV-carrying leaf hoppers, 24 days post inoculation feeding, most of the untransformed plants developed chlorotic stripes and chlorosis in the young leaves, the disease index (DI) being 53%. After 40 days post inoculation feeding, most of the control plants showed severe symptoms, being stunted and the leaves developing chlorotic and brown necrotic streaks, with the DI being 88%. In contrast, the transgenic rice plants subject to the inoculation feeding developed no or mild symptoms. After 24 and 40 days post inoculation feeding, the disease index of the transgenic plants was 15% and 25% respectively.

Increased Resistance to Tobacco Mosaic Virus Conferred by a Fusion Protein of TMV Coat Protein and Staphylococcal Nuclease in Transgenic Tobacco Plants

Coat protein-mediated resistance (CPMR) has been proved to be successful against several families of plant viruses. Recently CPMR was obtained by expressing a truncated CP of tobacco virus.[10] Our work has indicated that expression of a fusion protein of TMV-CP and Staphylococcal nuclease (SN) in transgenic tobacco plants significantly enhances the CPMR to TMV. TMV-CP or SN gene alone and CP→SN or SN→CP fusion protein genes were obtained by PCR, inserted downstream of 35S promoter of a binary vector pROK2 and transformed into tobacco leaf discs. No SN gene alone transformed tissues could be regenerated, but the tissues containing CP→SN or SN→CP fusion genes grew normally and could be regenerated into plants. The transformed nature of the regenerated tobacco plants were confirmed by Southern blot hybridization and PCR analysis. It was demonstrated that the fusion proteins of CP→SN and SN→CP were expressed in the transgenic plants by Western blot analysis. CP→SN- or SN→CP-transformed plants exhibited higher resistance to TMV than CP alone transformed ones. 50% of CP→SN- and SN→CP-transformed tobacco plants were symptomless for three months after inoculation with 1 μg/mL TMV (Figure 2).

Nuclease activity test of the fusion protein expressed in transgenic plants was carried out *in vitro*. Fusion proteins of SN and CP were extracted from the transgenic plants and were obtained by immunoprecipitation with antiserum of TMV. The precipitated proteins were infiltrated with 2% SDS and then with water containing excess amount of TMV-CP, and reacted at 30°C with the incubation mixture of 25 mM Tris-HCl (pH 8.8), 10 mM $CaCl_2$ and 40 ng ^{32}P-5'-end-labelled oligdeoxynucleotide. The result showed that no nuclease activity was observed (Table 4). No obvious difference in structure and

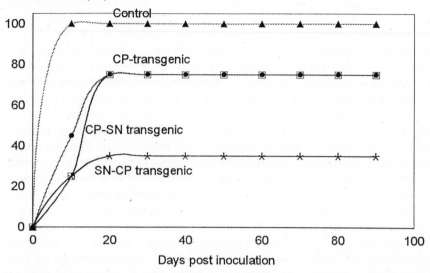

Figure 2 Development of systemic symptoms in CP-SN and SN-CP transformed and nontransformed control tobacco plants after inoculation with 1 µg/mL TMV.

Table 4
DNase activity of fusion protein from transgenic plant expression CP→SN or SN→CP and CP

Sources of protein	0 min	60 min	The observed DNase activity
		cpm	
CP-transgenic plants	12015.29	11983.76	-
CP→SN-transgenic plants	13874.67	13832.19	-
SN→CP-transgenic plants	16352.31	16300.22	-
pROK II-transgenic plants	13988.72	13902.18	-
SN from *S. aureus*	19761.82	1501.01	+
SN infiltrated with 2% SDS and water	18896.74	2437.11	+

infectivity of virion isolated from SN-CP transgenic and non-transgenic plants has been found.

The mechanism of resistance to virus by expression of a fusion CP was unknown. We speculate that the fusion CP is somehow dysfunctional and more effective to disrupt the normal virus-host relationship than CP does alone. The disruption may be at the level of virus movement throughout the plant or the fusion CP is encapsidated into virion to generate defective virus particle.

Risks Assessment of Releasing Genetically Engineered Plants

Some transgenic organisms, such as micro-organisms and animals will be grown under controlled conditions and only released to the environment accidentally. However transgenic plants will be grown on a large scale in the open environment. There is concern that transgenic plants may produce risks.[11]

1. *Spread of transgene by pollen.* Because genetic engineering will often result in the introduction of genes not previously present in a species, there is concern that such genes may spread to other plants and to weeds by cross-pollination. It is important to have information on pollen transfer distances and the range of species that can be pollinated. To obviate this problem trial release of transgenic plants have often required the removal of flowers to prevent pollen spread as for the transgenic tobacco production. However, if such plants are to be used for the seeds or fruits, unlimited spread of pollen will occur.[12]

2. *Releasing of antibiotic resistance genes.* Antibiotic resistance genes are often used as a selective marker in transformation procedure. In the case of antibiotic resistance, it will be a problem only if it is inherited by pathogenic micro-organisms which are being controlled by the antibiotic in question. The risk of a pathogen inheriting and being able to express an antibiotic resistance gene derived from a plant is at least a million-fold lower than such resistance being obtained from other micro-organisms.[13]

3. *Pollution of honey.* A further problem that might be encountered is the presence of cloned gene products in pollen. This could harm the bee larvae which are fed pollen, pollutes honey with minute amounts of the gene products, and makes the pollen more allergenic. Most gene products will not be found in or on pollen in other than minute amounts and thus contamination should not be a problem.

4. *Transgenic plants becoming weedy.* Potentially the greatest risk is that certain types of transgenic plants might become weedy, for example, the acquisition of herbicide resistance genes which will make them less easy to control in subsequent generations. On the one hand herbicide resistance genes are used as selective markers in many laboratories; on the other hand large companies are attempting to encourage growers to use more herbicides, and are using genetic engineering for purely commercial reasons.

5. *Safety of application Sat-RNA for virus diseases control.* Safety concerns about the use of Sat-RNAs remain. Even though virus replication is inhibited in transgenic plant, a small amount of Sat-RNA can still be encapsidated into helper virus particles and transmitted to other plant species, which it may cause more severe diseases. Moreover, because the exacerbating and attenuating Sat-RNAs can differ in only a few nucleotides, there is always a possibility that a symptom attenuating Sat-RNA can mutate into an exacerbating one.

During a decade of using Sat-RNAs as biological control agents in China, a number of facts concerning the safety of using Sat-RNA in agriculture have been realized. In spite of the large scale application of the BCAs on different crops, no necrogenic or other harmful Sat-RNA variant was found in a systematic field survey in which random plant tissue samples were analysed by temperature-gradient gel electrophoresis (TGGE) to detect Sat-RNA sequence variants. Secondly, the efficiency of aphid transmission of CMV in the presence of the Sat-RNA is reduced to about 10% of that in the absence of the Sat-RNA. The reduced transmission efficiency, due to the low concentration of CMV when the Sat-RNA is present, lowers the chance that the Sat-RNA will be released in the field. Finally, it is possible to maintain the benign property of the Sat-RNA by periodic and detailed quality control of the BCA stocks. It is our hope that the use of Sat-RNA as a viral control strategy will become increasingly safe as our knowledge of Sat-RNA structure-function relationship increases. Indeed, it has recently been found that the Sat-RNA of CMV can lose its ability of being encapsidated into CMV CP by changing a few nucleotides; this in turn excludes the possibility of Sat-RNA transmission (D. Baulcombe, personal communication).

6. *Safety of viral coat protein-mediated resistance.* Transencapsidation of viral nucleic acid by transgenically expressed CP may induce heteroencapsidated virion, which might be transmitted by new vectors and to new host plants (Wilson, 1993). The CP of plum pox potyvirus has been shown to confer aphid-transmissibility on a non-transmissible isolate of zucchini yellow mosaic virus. However, recent studies showed that intentionally truncated, antisense or nonexpression (-AUG) CP genes could provide measurable protection or even complete immunity against the appropriate parent virus;[14] this in turn excludes the possibility of heteroencapsidation of viral nucleic acid by transgenically expressed CP.

In conclusion, safety, from a public view, was ensured by biologically containing the transgenic plants so that they would not induce risk. The emphasis on biological containment has meant that for release to be permissible it is necessary to demonstrate beyond reasonable doubt that the transgenic plants are safe. But nothing is completely safe, and safety *per se* is not always desired; for example, plant species without any toxic metabolites would be exquisitely sensitive to pests.

Notes

1. Abel et al., 1986, 738–743.
2. Baulcombe et al., 1986, 263–272; Wu et al., 1988, 948–956.
3. Wilson, 1993.
4. Tien and Wu, 1991; Tien and Zhang, 1983.
5. Qin et al., 1992; Tien, 1992.
6. Wu et al., 1989.
7. Zhao et al., 1990.
8. Yin and Tien, 1993.
9. Yie et al., 1992.
10. Malpica et al., 1993.
11. Beringer et al., 1992, 135–140.
12. Ibid.
13. Ibid.
14. Wilson, 1993.

References

P. P. Abel, R. S. Nelson, B. De, H. Hottmann, S. G. Rogers, R. T. Fraley, and R. N. Beachy, 'Delay of Disease Development in Transgenic Plants that Express Tobacco Mosaic Virus Coat Protein Gene', *Science* 232 (1986): 738–743.

D. Baulcombe, M. Devid, and M. Jaegle, 'The Molecular Biology of Satellite RNA from Cucumber Mosaic Virus'. In R. S. S. Fraser, ed., *Recognition and Response in Plant-Virus Interactions* (Berlin: Springer, 1990).

J. E. Beringer, M. J. Bale, P. K. Hayes, and C. M. Lazarus, 'Assessing and Monitoring the Risks of Releasing Genetically Manipulated Plants'. *Proceedings of the Royal Society of Edinburgh* 99B(3/4) (1992): 135–140.

Y. L. Liu, F. Zhu, Z. Y. Wei, Y. Yie, L. Y. Kang, and P. Tien, 'Increased Resistance to Virus Disease by Expressing a Fusion Protein of Tobacco Mosaic Virus Coat Protein and Staphylococcal Nuclease in Transgenic Tobacco Plant'. Abstract of the 9th International Congress of Virology, 1993.

B. Y. Qin, X. H. Zhang, G. S. Wu and P. Tien, 'Plant Resistance to Fungal Diseases Induced by the Infection of Cucumber Mosaic Virus Attenuated by Satellite RNA', *Annals of Applied Biology* 120 (1992): 361–366.

P. Tien, 'Effects of Cucumber Mosaic Virus Satellite RNA and its Helper Virus on the Resistance of Plants to Different Pathogens'. Symposium on *Satellites and Defective-Interfering RNAs of Plant Virus* (New York, Cornell University, 1992).

P. Tien and G. S. Wu, 'Satellite RNA for the Biocontrol of Plant Disease'. In K. Maramorosch, F. A. Murphy, and A. J. Shatkin, eds., *Advances in Virus Research*, Vol. 39 (London: Academic Press, 1991).

P. Tien and X. H. Zhang, 'Control of Two Plant Viruses by Protection Inoculation', *China Seed Science and Technology* 11 (1983): 969–972.

T. M. A. Wilson, 'Strategies to Protect Crop Plants Against Viruses. Pathogen-derived resistance blossoms', *Proceedings of the National Academy of Science* 90 (1993): 3134–3141.

S. X. Wu, S. Z. Zhao, G. J. Wang, X. C. Yang, C. X. Zhang, X. Wang X, and P. Tien, 'Transgenic Tobacco Plants with Resistance to Cucumber Mosaic Virus by Expressing Satellite cDNA', *Scientia Sinica (B)* 9 (1988): 948–956.

Y. T. Yan, J. F. Wang, B. S. Qiu, X. M. He, S. Z. Zhao, X. F. Wang, and P. Tien, 'Expression of Rice Stripe Virus Coat Protein Gene in Transgenic Rice Plants', *Acta Botanica Sinica* 31 (1992): 899–906.

Y. T. Yan, J. F. Wang, B. S. Qiu, X. M. He, S. Z. Zhao, and P. Tien, 'Resistance to Rice Stripe Virus of Transgenic Indca Rice Regenerated from Bombarded Suspension Culture and Expression Coat Protein' (in preparation).

Y. Yin and P. Tien, 'Plant Virus Satellite RNAs and Their Role in Engineering Resistance to Virus Diseases', *Seminars in Virology* 4 (1993).

Y. Yie, F. Zhao, S. Z. Zhao, Y. Z. Liu, Y. L. Liu, and P. Tien, 'Transgenic Commercial Tobacco Cultivar G-140 with High Resistance to Cucumber Mosaic Virus Conferred by Expressing Satellite RNA and Coat Protein. *Mol Plant-Micriobe Interact* 5(b) (1992): 460–465.

S. Z. Zhao, X. Wang, G. J. Wang, and P. Tien, 'Transgenic Tomato Resistant to Cucumber Mosaic Virus by Expressing its Monomer and Dimer Satellite cDNA', *Scientia Sinica (B)* 7 (1990): 708–713.

3

Some Environmental and Ethical Considerations of Genetically Engineered Plants and Foods

Philip L. Bereano

At a symposium at the University of Washington Law School in October 1993 (on the eve of President Clinton's Asian Pacific Economic Council 'Summit'), when discussing the 'Future of Intellectual Property Protection for Biotechnology in the US, EC, and Japan', Joseph Straus of the Max Planck Institute (Germany) warned the participants against 'ethics and other irrational considerations'. Indeed, except for a very narrow band of 'moral dilemma' situations which are the stock-in-trade of professional biomedical ethicists, the ethical aspects of genetic engineering have been routinely ignored by government policy-makers and corporate technology promoters.

My thesis is that it has been the corporate promoters and their governmental handmaidens who have been 'irrational' in their systematic refusal to acknowledge the environmental and ethical considerations of genetic manipulation.

Technologies, by definition, are neither acts of God nor nature; they are the embodiment of specific human purposes and intentionality. Far from being inevitable, they are researched and developed by those entities with sufficient power to mobilize social institutions to bring the technology into being, according to their own goals and normative considerations. 'Biotechnology is not neutral. It shares the propensity of modern materialistic science to desacralise, dominate and manipulate life. It reduces all living things to a mechanism which it can manipulate according to engineering standards.'[1]

Genetic engineering is a technological process for undertaking activities which do not, and cannot, occur in nature. In this sense it is perfectly legitimate, therefore, to label genetic engineering as 'unnatural'. The European Community has incorporated this concept in its definition of genetically modified organisms, and it has been adopted by the UN Environment Program (in the working of its Fourth Expert Panel set up under the Biodiversity Convention as part of the follow through to the United Nations Conference on the Environment and Development held in Rio de Janeiro in June 1992): 'organisms in which the genetic material has been altered in a way that does not occur naturally by mating and/or natural recombination'. Thus, hybrids and other modified organisms obtained by traditional breeding techniques are excluded from the definition of genetically modified organisms.

It is important to note that the process as well as the products are novel. The promoters of the new technology believe that a concern for the process itself is specious, downplaying its novelty whenever confronted by discussions of regulatory oversight. However, one of the bases of the decision of the US Supreme Court in the *Chakrabarti* case (which, 5 to 4, upheld the patentability of genetically engineered microbes, and which has been unquestionably accepted by foreign governments as disposative of the issue of patentability of genetically engineered life forms) was that the element of 'novelty' required by the patent law was to be found in the process by which the microbe had been created.

One reason why we cannot ignore the powerful novel aspects of the processes of genetic manipulation is because we are not omniscient as to what will, in fact, happen when we alter genomes. Genetic manipulation is not like a child's game of Legos or Tinkertoy, in which parts can be rearranged or linked up with only simple mechanical and relatively predictable consequences.

> [In] calculating any risk from a transgenic organism, one should consider four elements: the host organism, the foreign genes, the interaction between the foreign genes and the rest of the genome, and the environment in which the organisms will be used. . . . [in regard to the last two elements] the literature contains many examples of genetic manipulations where inserted genes did not respond in their new environments the way they did in their old ones or where alterations with one part of the genome caused surprising activity in other parts of the genome.[2]

There is an element of arrogance to scientific assertions which assure us that the process itself poses no risks, since scientists know so little about actual ecosystems; for example, I have been told by agronomists that over 80% of the organisms which can be identified in a soil sample from my garden are completely unknown to the scientific literature. Indeed, the Ecological Society of America itself has specifically warned about the problems presented in our lack of ecological knowledge and the resulting consequences from releasing (intentionally or accidentally) genetically altered organisms into ecological systems.[3]

Foods

In May 1992, the US Food and Drug Administration, responding to corporate pressures to remove the prospect of regulation of genetically altered foods, issued a set of rules which have largely left responsibility for protecting the public health and safety in the hands of the industry, permitting products to be marketed without scrutiny unless the industry indicated to the agency that it believed governmental oversight was justifiable. However, the proposal as published by the FDA in the Federal Register[4] perversely noted several important problem areas: creating allergens, additions of genes from sources which might violate religious and cultural norms (of vegetarians, Jews or Muslims, etc.), and implications for animal welfare and well-being (for example, the incorporation of human growth hormone-producing gene into a pig's genome produced a highly arthritic animal). Indeed, the commissioner of the FDA, David A. Kessler, and his colleagues noted the possibility that genetically engineered food might 'contain high levels of unexpected, acutely toxic substances'.[5]

In order to begin to address ethical issues presented by the genetic modification of foodstuffs, we need to have some ideas of the purposes for which these modifications are performed. (For example, if we wish to approach an analysis on utilitarian cost-benefit grounds.) Despite a great number of general statements, human nutrition and hunger do not appear to be the actual driving forces behind the development of genetically engineered foods. Other than claiming increased shelf life (which can be indirectly related to nutrition in the sense of reducing spoilage or the consumption of foods that have begun to spoil), there is hardly any indication at all that genetic engineering is being directed to create nutritious substances out of non-nutritious ones; similarly, there are few real instances of genetic engineering reducing the cost of foodstuffs, or increasing the quantities of foods actually available to populations that are hungry because of the non-existence of consumables (as opposed to hungry because they lack money to buy sufficient foods, no matter how produced). Indeed, early genetic manipulations seemed perversely designed to minimize the achievement of such goals: the creation of 'herbicide tolerant plants' which do not reduce the applications of dangerous chemicals to agricultural fields (which might occur if genetic manipulations of food crops were designed to make them resistant to insects, fungi, or disease) but instead permit higher levels of chemical application, or the introduction of recombinant bovine growth hormone to produce more milk at a time when developed countries suffer from milk gluts and have instituted programmes to kill cows and physically dump milk (milk as a commodity is price inelastic; quantity increases do not lead to price decreases).

Indeed, as the above examples indicate, the goals of genetically engineering foods seem to be more closely tied to increasing the economic gain and power of the corporations involved in food production (for example, the development of herbicide-tolerant farm crops has been led by corporations which manufacture herbicides), making production easier for corporations, reducing or altering packaging and transportation costs for the corporations, etc.

Environment

Industrial societies around the world are faced by massive pollution legacies from the previous emphases on chemical and nuclear industrial activities. The inability of the US Department of Energy to find a suitable site for a long-term nuclear waste repository illustrates our very poor track record for dealing with the scientific, technical, economic, and socio-political aspects of prior technological 'revolutions'. The environmental problems posed by genetically engineered organisms are likely to be substantially more intractable than those posed by these earlier instances of pollution because genetic wastes multiply, migrate, and mutate. A genetically engineered organism once free in the environment is impossible to recall. (Impacts which are irreversible must be considered with higher scrutiny than those which can be undone.)

Examples of environmental problems which need to be assessed include the risks of transgenic crops themselves becoming weeds; the risk of gene flow to wild relatives which might become weeds or pests;[6] the growth of antibiotic resistance in species (particularly animals), since resistance genes are used as markers for the genetic engineering sites; the problem of exotic or non-native species taking over ecological niches (such as gypsy moth, starling, kudzu, rabbits in Australia, etc.) leading to extraordinary economic losses as well as ecological ones; the restriction (rather than increase) of biodiversity by selective advantageous breeding of transgenic organisms as opposed to natural ones, or the predatory results of expanding exotic species (such as the Dutch Elm micro-organism destroying the American Elm and severely restricting the biodiversity of certain areas in the Northeast United States); health issues (both of plant and animal species, as well as humans — worker health and safety as well as community security); and the occurrence of the completely unexpected, the inability to eliminate uncertainty (for example, the late 1993 floods in the Mississippi valley included the flooding of a field of genetically engineered corn and the dispersal of this plant material to unknown sites within the thousands of square miles of downstream flood plain).[7] Prospective ecological assessment is not being performed, despite the fact that its need has long since been recognized.[8] And economic priorities, particularly those accruing directly to the promoters, as well as the nebulous spur of 'competition' with foreign countries, oftentimes overwhelms any interest in doing environmental impact analysis.

Ethical Concerns

In this section I want to raise a number of practical issues of social ethics. I am not going to pursue the perspective of the individualistic moral dilemma which is so common among professional ethicists. Increasingly, indigenous peoples, Third World activists, and environmentalists in developed countries are raising concerns about the 'desacralisation' of nature and its reification/commoditization.

. . . [The GATT treaty] is not just a trade treaty. It is also an environmental treaty. Accepting it in its present form amounts to accepting the ethical framework that all species are only for human use and exploitation and their value is defined by how much some human groups can profit from that exploitation. It also condemns all people and all societies to the abhorrent position of accepting that the living diversity of this planet can be reduced to patented private property. These implications go against all notions of the environmental ethic. . . .[9]

In its more extreme forms, we are now witnessing what is called 'bio-prospecting', not just of plants and animals[10] but also of human beings. The Human Genome Diversity Project is an effort to collect samples from several hundred isolated and 'endangered' or 'vanishing' human communities in order to detect and preserve (and presumably commercially exploit) minute differences in the human genome which might have some major implications in terms of factors such as disease resistance (for example, the inhabitants of the Italian village of Limone in the Dolomite mountains have an unusually low incidence of coronary problems despite the similarity of their diet and life experiences to other Italian mountain communities).

In September 1993 the chief of the Global Environment Division of the World Bank, Kenneth Newcombe, addressed a group of environmental foundations urging them to put up some money for 'investment opportunities in the natural world.' According to the notes of one of the participants:

The three examples that Newcombe gave of investment opportunities through the Global Environmental Fund [of the United Nations] were:
- eco-tourism
- genetic material screening
- commercialization of traditional medicines

Under eco-tourism, he spoke of auctioning the rights to 'charismatic ecosystems' to multi-national corporations, partly for the PR benefial. Under genetic material screening, he talked vaguely about 'under-used crop varieties'. When pressed for a more specific example he talked about Papua New Guinea forests where the GEF could supervise the 'bidding of tracts for genetic prospecting'.

His example in commercializing of traditional medicines concerned the traditional plant knowledge thought to be in the Ethiopian Coptic Church. He said, 'let's screen that knowledge stock', and suggested that we 'explore how it might be commercialized'. The speakers indicated in response to another question that intellectual property rights questions were not a big problem and could be 'dealt with'.

One foundation person asked why they were coming to foundations first, instead of going to people in the South who might be directly affected by this project. The response was that there was no point in going to people in the South because they don't have money to invest.[11]

Although many people see these activities as the latest form of neo-colonialism, the ultimate attempt of communities in the North to own, control, and exploit the resources of less powerful communities, they are often presented as helpfulness by well-intentioned liberals. Western scientists and some environmentalists, in their rush to help local shamans patent centuries-old medicinal knowledge so that indigenous tribes are not stripped bare by marauding corporations, seem to ignore the ethical quandary of how such peoples can participate at all in a foreign intellectual legal regime (the patent system) and still maintain their indigenous culture (which, of course, contains no such concepts). Nor do they seem to find it ethically troubling that we are always insisting that such people need to harmonize cultural differences by adopting our way of doing things, rather than the reverse.[12] Perhaps we should follow indigenous norms, forbidding the private ownership of this medicinal knowledge and treating it as the common property of all.

The fascination with genetic engineering, with its endless repetition of the mantra that it is to be the defining characteristic of the forthcoming civilization (just as we had 'the industrial age' or 'the nuclear age'), represents an expansion of technocratic consciousness crowding out other elements of the collective human persona. Thus, biotechnology reinforces an ideological spirit of conquest, arrogance, and hubris in which a technocratic-commercial stratum seeks to maintain and extend domination over nature and a related domination over other humans. This ideology is well-encapsulated in the statement of James Watson when he became the original head of the Human Genome Project that 'at last we will know what it truly means to be human' (as if Shakespeare, for example, had no inkling).[13]

An additional ethical issue is raised by the severe socio-economic dislocations which biotechnology can cause, particularly where they are not mitigated or compensated for. The report of UNEP's Fourth Expert Panel referred to above noted that 'the conservation and sustainable use of biological diversity, especially in the case of domesticated plants and animals, is dependent on the socio-economic conditions of the people who have been maintaining it. It is, therefore, essential that the socio-economic risks posed by the use of GMOs be evaluated and that any probable adverse effects be mitigated.'[14] Yet the highly publicized contract between Merck Pharmaceutical and INBio (a Costa Rican foundation) providing the latter with approximately $1 million for exploration rights to the Costa Rican rain forest means, since Costa Rica is estimated to contain approximately 5% of total global rain forest biodiversity, that the companies of the North are putting an economic value of only $20 million on all of tropical biodiversity, irrespective of the fact that those regions have provided sustenance to their own inhabitants for millennia and also commercial plant species (coffee, cocoa, etc.) clearly worth far in excess of such an amount. By way of comparison, pharmaceutical firms such as Merck spend an average of $125 million to develop a single drug for the market.

At the same time, corporations in the First World are seeking to develop means to synthesize, through genetic engineering, equivalents for products which may be commercial mainstays of developing countries. A US company is developing a way to produce vanilla extract which, if successful, will be able, through the productive facilities of a single vat located here, to undercut the economic livelihood of approximately 100,000 Third World farming families in Madagascar and South Asia.[15] Institutions in developed countries are not hesitant, either, to export biohazards, by doing testing in Third World countries where information and/or regulatory procedures may be lacking. Sometimes outright deception is used, as in the situation when the Wistar Institute tested a rabies vaccine in cattle in Argentina without providing any information to the Argentine government or the local cow herders.[16]

Many of the issues above are becoming embedded in the tremendous push in the past decade to expand the reach of the patent system. Not only have new intellectual constructs been advanced (such as the patentability of micro-organisms, plants, and animals), but the actual legal reach of these intellectual regimes has been extended (as in the GATT negotiations). Indeed, there have even been instances of attempts to patent portions of the human genome of Third World peoples and human genetic body parts.[17]

As in many other ethical considerations it is difficult to ascertain where it might be appropriate to draw the line between socially permissible and unsavory activities. This slippery slope is best understood by looking at the applications of genetic engineering to issues of human 'disease'. The commonplace announcement that genes are being discovered 'for' a particular disease ignores the fact that very few human physical characteristics are directly dependent upon a single gene or that the genes usually represent, in fact, merely contingent possibilities whose manifestation depends on very complex intragenomic and environmental interactions. Such announcements become an application of the ideology that genes are the 'blueprints' or determinants of human destiny and behavior, leading inevitably to situations of genetic discrimination. The increasing mania for genetic screening (an outgrowth of pressures for testing of all sorts — for drug use, diseases, and the like) has forced people to confront situations where they are unable to obtain insurance (life, medical and — in at least one instance we know of — automobile liability coverage).[18]

Despite the fact that the discovery of many so-called genes 'for' diseases has very little implication regarding treatment modalities (we have known for 25 years which gene causes sickle-cell anaemia, but are nowhere nearer today than we were then to a cure), adventuresome scientists pushed for somatic cell 'therapy' and this inevitably led to calls for germ-line interventions. There are arguments to be made, both technical and ethical, against germline therapy[19] but the main troubling reality is that the acceptance of such procedures leads inevitably to calls for human 'enhancement' or outright eugenics. Astonishing as it may seem, Daniel Koshland, the editor of *Science* magazine, has actually talked about finding the genetic 'cause' for homelessness, and improving our children's mathematical and computer abilities through genetic manipulation so that they are better able to compete with the Germans and Japanese.[20] Finally, the implications of genetic engineering for rapidly proliferating reproductive technologies opens up truly astonishing issues which humans have never before had to contemplate; for example, the announcement in late 1993 that it was possible to clone human embryos let to the passage of a resolution in the European Parliament against human embryo 'farming'.

In all of this we can see the potential (or actual) diminution of the democratic ethos. People are seen as passive consumers rather than citizens living the *vita activa*.[21] The development of decision-making elites is encouraged, persons whose professional and social lives are characterized by an abundance of experiences which are systematically denied to the great mass of human beings.[22] The technology of genetic engineering is not developing democratically and, indeed, is leading to the exacerbation of power differentials within our societies. This is perhaps its most substantial ethical affront.

Notes

1. Nicanor Perlas, Center for Alternative Development Initiatives, Philippines, *Third World Resurgence,* Issue No. 38, 1993, Third World Network, Penang, Malaysia.
2. Philip L. Bereano and Nachama L. Wilker, Council for Responsible Genetics, Letter, *Science*, Vol. 258, 4 December 1992: 1561–1562.
3. M. Tiedje, *et al*, 'The Planned Introduction of Genetically Engineered Organisms: Ecological Considerations and Recommendations,' *Ecology*, Vol. 70, 1989: 298–315.
4. Vol. 59, pp. 22984–23005 (29 May 1992).
5. *Science*, Policy Forum, 26 June 1992: 1747.
6. These two problems are analysed extensively in Jane Rissler and Margaret Mellon, *Perils Amidst the Promise: Ecological Risks of Transgenic Crops in a Global Market*, Union of Concerned Scientists, Washington DC, December 1993.
7. 'Flood Uproots Transgenic Crop,' *Science*, 'Random Samples' (ed. Christopher Anderson), Vol. 261, 3 September 1993: 127.
8. See Note 3 above.
9. Vandana Shiva, *Third World Resurgence*, No 38, Third World Network, Penang, Malaysia, 1993.
10. *Science*, 'NIH Biodiversity Grants Could Benefit Shamans,' 10 December 1993, Vol. 262: 1635.
11. Personal communication.
12. See Note 10 above.
13. For a fuller exploration of this ideology and a countervailing point of view see Ruth Hubbard and Elijah Wald, *Exploding the Gene Myth*, Boston: Beacon Press, 1993.
14. Martin Khor, *Third World Resurgence*, No. 38, Penang, Malaysia, 1993.
15. Rural Advancement Foundation International, 'Communique: Vanilla and Biotechnology,' January 1987; see update, July 1991.

16. *New York Times*, 11 November 1986: B20.
17. Edmund L. Andrews, 'US Seeks Patent on Genetic Codes, Setting Off Furor, *New York Times*, 21 October 1991: A1; G. Kolata, 'Biologist's Speedy Gene Method Scares Peers but Gains Backer,' *New York Times*, 25 July 1992: B5,8; US Patent Application No. WO 92/08784 A1 (on a part of the genome of a woman of the Guaymi people, Panama; withdrawn, Autumn 1993); US Patent Application No. WO 93/03759 (on the Hagahai of Papua New Guinea); US Patent Application No. WO 92/15325-A (on the genome of a Solomon Islander); Marcia Barinaga, 'A Muted Victory for the Biotech Industry,' *Science*, 20 July 1990: 239 (the Moore case — researchers held to own cell line derived from patient to exclusion of patient).
18. Paul R. Billings, et al, 'Discrimination as a Consequence of Genetic Testing,' *American Journal of Human Genetics*, (1992) Vol. 50: 476–482. Philip L. Bereano, testimony on DNA Identification Systems and Civil Liberties, Hearings before Subcommittee on Civil and Constitutional Rights, Committee on the Judiciary, House of Representatives, 22 March 1989, 101 Cong., First Session, Serial No. 48; Council for Responsible Genetics, 'Position Paper on Genetic Discrimination,' Cambridge, Mass., 1990; Institute of Medicine, National Academy of Science, *Assessing Genetic Risks: Implications for Health and Social Policy*, 1993.
19. See *Council for Responsible Genetics*, 'Position Paper on Human Germline Manipulation', Cambridge, Mass., Fall 1992.
20. See Koshland, 'The Future of Biological Research: What is Possible and What Is Ethical?', *MBL Science*, winter 1988–1989, for an early version of his views.
21. Hannah Arendt, *The Human Condition*, (Chicago: University of Chicago Press, 1958).
22. John McDermott, 'Technology: the Opiate of the Masses,' in Bereano ed. *Technology as a Social and Political Phenomenon* (John Wiley & Sons, 1976).

4

Sacrificed for Science:
Are Animal Experiments Morally Defensible?

Raymond Wacks

> There is no impersonal reason for regarding the interests of human
> beings as more important than those of animals. We can destroy
> animals more easily than they can destroy us; that is the only solid
> basis of our claim to superiority. We value art and science and
> literature because these are things in which we excel. But whales
> might value spouting, and donkeys might maintain that a good bray
> is more exquisite than the music of Bach. We cannot prove them
> wrong except by the exercise of arbitrary power. All ethical systems,
> in the last analysis, depend upon weapons of war.
>
> Bertrand Russell[1]

Some 140 million animal experiments are performed annually.[2] Protests against
these and other practices involving animals (including the fur trade, battery
farming, hunting, trapping, circuses, zoos, and rodeos) have, in recent years,
increased significantly.[3] Though many experiments inflict pain and distress
on animals, it is worth noting that some do not. Nor will all be 'sacrificed',
the researcher's euphemism for killing.[4] Moreover, it is hard to deny the fact
that eating animals 'is responsible for a vastly greater quantity of death and
suffering than experimentation'.[5]

While what follows is confined to the use of animals in scientific research,
any analysis of this difficult question entails a consideration of our attitude
to, and relationship with, non-human animals.[6] I shall, however, make four
assumptions, none of which is uncontentious, in order to facilitate a clearer
statement of what seem to me to be the principal issues.

1.   That human and non-human animals occupy a continuum.[7]
2.   That a line can be drawn between 'higher' and 'lower' animals; the difference between vertebrates and invertebrates does not appear to be a wholly unreasonable one.[8]
3.   That animal experiments have produced some practical benefits to both human and nonhuman animals.[9]
4.   That 'higher' animals have the capacity to suffer pain and distress.[10]

The justification for these assumptions should become a little clearer in the course of this paper, but I have neither the space nor the expertise to explore any of them at length. My purpose is rather to sketch the nature of the (inevitable?) conflict between those who advocate the continued use of animals in research, on the one hand, and those who believe that such activities are unacceptable, on the other. Unless animals are regarded simply as replaceable commodities (a position which few would adopt) the argument is ultimately a moral one. The use of animals in scientific experiments therefore requires a moral foundation.[11] And I shall attempt to examine the case, from an ethical standpoint, both for and against such use.

Animals in the Laboratory

Accounts, often vivid,[12] of the experiments to which animals are subjected, seriously challenge the spirit of objectivity and detachment which is generally regarded as the hallmark of academic enquiry. Many of these reports (which I do not propose to repeat here) cause profound distress and anger in many who read or learn of them. I cannot pretend that they do not have similar effects on me. Chomsky may be right:

> By entering the arena of argument and counter-argument, of technical feasability and tactics, of footnotes and citation, by accepting the legitimacy of debate on certain issues, one has already lost one's humanity.[13]

I hope he is wrong, and that it is possible for moral sensibility and logical argument to co-exist. It seems important to me that they can.

Animals, especially rats, are widely used to test the efficacy and toxicity of new drugs.[14] Thus the so-called LD50 test (LD = lethal dose) seeks to establish the single dose required to kill 50% of test animals.[15] Rabbits have been routinely used to test for skin irritancy of cosmetics and shampoo.[16] The Draize test is used to determine eye irritancy.[17] Animals, principally primates, are also used in cancer research (the image of smoking beagles provoked strong, and occasionally violent, protest from organizations such as the Animal Liberation Front), behavioural research, surgery, artificial insemination, agricultural research, and in weapons and safety testing. It is often suggested that significant differences between humans and animals render a good deal of these experiments of dubious value and possibly even dangerous.[18] One scientist concludes:

. . . since animal-based research is unable to combat our major health problems and, more dangerously, often diverts attention from the study of humans, the real choice is not between animals and people, rather it is between good science and bad science. In medical research animal experiments are generally bad science because they tell us about animals, usually under artificial conditions, when we really need to know about people.[19]

Whatever the benefits of vivisection, unless one is to adopt a strict utilitarian position (which I consider below), the pain and distress it causes to its victims call for some justification.

Justifying Animal Suffering

Subjectivism and Intuitionism

Why is any justification required? The simplest (and least successful) response is to claim that to inflict suffering on animals is unacceptable 'because it is wrong'. And it is wrong, according to this subjectivist view, because it is obviously the case. Or, it might more plausibly be argued, it is wrong on the ground that our intuition or our common sense tells us so. A serious difficulty with this form of moral intuitionism is generally thought to be that it suggests that there are certain objective standards 'out there' which ought to guide our behaviour. But the source and content of these standards is, to say the least, debatable, unless it could be shown that, as Chomsky suggests in respect of language, we are genetically endowed with a system of non-deductive norms.[20] Subjectivism and moral intuitionism seem fragile foundations upon which to build a defence against animal suffering,[21] though the strongest and most coherent argument in support of animal rights (considered below) appears to be founded on intuitionist claims.

Utilitarianism

A firmer basis may be found in utilitarianism. Utilitarians take as their premise the proposition that the fundamental basis of morality and justice is that happiness should be maximized. Though there are a number of classical utilitarian theories (including those of John Stuart Mill and Henry Sidgwick) it is Jeremy Bentham's classic formulation that is well captured in the following passage from *An Introduction to the Principles of Morals and Legislation*:

Nature has placed mankind under the governance of two sovereign masters, pain and pleasure. It is for them alone to point out what we ought to do, as well as to determine what we shall do. On the one hand the standard of right and wrong, on the other the chain of causes and effects, are fastened to their throne. . . The principle of utility recognises this subjection, and assumes it for the foundation of that system, the object of which is to rear the fabric of felicity by the hands of reason and of law. Systems which attempt to question it, deal in sounds instead of sense, in caprice instead of reason, in darkness instead of light.

A fundamental assault on utilitarianism consists in the view[22] that it fails to recognize the 'separateness of persons'. It suggests that utilitarianism, at least in its pure form, treats human and non-human beings as means rather than ends in themselves. This important attack consists, in H.L.A. Hart's view,[23] of four principal criticisms which may be summarized as follows:[24]

1.   Separate individuals are important only in so far as they are 'the channels or locations where what is of value is to be found'.
2.   Utilitarianism treats individual persons equally, but only by effectively treating them as having *no* worth, for their value is not *as persons*, but as 'experiencers' of pleasure or happiness.
3.   Why should we regard as a valuable moral goal the mere increase in totals of pleasure or happiness abstracted from all questions of *distribution* of happiness, welfare etc.?
4.   The analogy used by utilitarians of a rational single individual prudently sacrificing present happiness for later satisfaction, is false for it treats my pleasure as replaceable by the greater pleasure of others.

These arguments seriously undermine the utilitarian project in the present as well as other contexts.[25] The pain of a few may in principle be justified by the pleasure of (or at least the benefits to) the many. The utilitarian objection to killing a conscious being rests on the destruction of the prospect of future pleasures. Killing an animal is therefore wrong, not because it harms the animal killed, but because its death diminishes the sum of the utilitarian calculus.

The leading text on animal welfare, Peter Singer's *Animal Liberation*[26] proceeds from an act-utilitarian standpoint. His central argument is that in calculating the consequences of our actions, the pain suffered or pleasure enjoyed by animals counts no less than our own. To regard their experience is in some way inferior to ours is 'speciesism'. Animals have moral worth; their lives are not simply expendable or to be exploited for our own ends. Singer does not claim that the lives of humans and animals have equal worth or that they call for identical treatment — except in respect of the capacity to experience pleasure and pain. Animals need not be *treated* equally, but they are entitled to equal *consideration*.

Thus, animal experiments are justifiable, provided pain is restricted to a minimum and the research is highly likely to produce aggregate benefits outweighing individual pain. His test is whether it would be morally acceptable to perform such experiments on mentally retarded human orphans.[27] If it would not, it would be 'speciesist' to inflict pain on animals of similar intelligence.

The strength of the utilitarian argument lies in its focus upon actual suffering, a concern that seems to accord with our intuitive view of animals, captured two centuries in Bentham's oft-quoted observation that the question to ask about animals '. . . is not Can they *reason*? nor Can they *talk*? but, Can they *suffer*?' Its weakness lies in its neglect of *individual* animals and its willingness to accept the use of animals where expected benefits outweigh the costs of suffering.[28]

Animal Rights?

A deontologist is an animal's best friend. The utilitarian, in order to prove his case for treating animals humanely, must show that the consequences of such humanity outweigh the consequences of any of a number of alternatives, and this may stretch his empirical evidence to breaking-point. The proponent of a right-based argument, on the other hand, needs to overcome not only the objection that animals cannot really be said to possess rights, but that talk of moral rights is, in Bentham's words 'nonsense on stilts'. To invoke the categorical imperative that cruelty to animals is simply *wrong*, the deontologist is more likely to enable a dog to have his day.[29]

In view of the importance the argument for animal rights has recently assumed, a brief foray into the concept of rights is necessary. Right-based theories are understandably fashionable. They have a strong political and rhetorical appeal. A modern trilogy (first introduced by Ronald Dworkin) of legal and moral theories which are right-based, duty-based and goal-based has emerged. J. Waldron[30] provides an example which illuminates this (sometimes elusive) distinction. We are opposed to torture. If our opposition is based on the suffering of the victim, our approach is right-based. If we believe that torture debases the torturer, our concern is duty-based. If we regard torture as unacceptable only when it affects the interests of those other than the parties involved, our approach is utilitarian goal-based.

To reply that since animals cannot be the subject of duties, they cannot be 'moral agents' and are thus incapable of being objects of rights is to beg the question about what it takes to be a right-holder. In particular, it presumes a choice-based rather than an interest-based theory of rights.[31] (See below.)

Rights talk immediately raises the distinction between what a right is, on the one hand, and what rights people actually have or should have, on the other — in other words, the distinction between moral rights and legal rights. The two are often confused, and it is by no means certain that even the most influential (and perhaps the most satisfying) analysis of rights (that undertaken by Wesley Hohfeld)[32] is applicable to moral rights. It probably is not.[33] Hohfeld seeks to clarify the proposition 'X has a right to do R' which may, in his view, mean one of four things:

1. That Y (or anyone else) is under a duty to allow X to do R; this means, in effect, that X has a claim against Y. He calls this claim right simply a 'right'.
2. That X is free to do or refrain from doing something; Y owes no duty to X. He calls this a 'privilege' (though it is often described as a 'liberty').

3. That X has a power to do R; X is simply free to do an act which alters
    legal rights and duties or legal relations in general (e.g., sell his property)
    whether or not he has a claim right or privilege to do so. Hohfeld calls
    this a 'power'.
4. That X is not subject to Y's (or anyone's) power to change X's legal
    position. He calls this an 'immunity'.

It is important to note that, for Hohfeld, claim rights (i.e., rights in the
normal sense) are strictly correlative to duties. To say that X has a claim right
of some kind is to say that Y (or someone else) owes a certain duty to X. But
to say that X has a certain liberty is not to say that anyone owes him a duty.
Thus if X has a privilege (or liberty) to wear a hat, Y does not have a duty to
X, but a no-right that X should not wear a hat. In other words, the correlative
of a liberty is a no-right. Similarly, the correlative of a power is a liability
(i.e., being liable to have one's legal relations changed by another), the
correlative of an immunity is a disability (i.e., the inability to change another's
legal relations).

But is Hohfeld correct? Is it true that whenever I am under some duty
someone else has a corresponding right? Or vice versa? In the first case,
surely it is possible for me to have a duty without you (or anyone else) having
a right that I should perform it. In the criminal law certain duties are imposed
upon me, but no one has a correlative right to my performing these duties.
This is because it is possible for there to be a duty to do something which is
not a duty to *someone*; for instance, the duty imposed on a policeman to
report offenders — he owes this duty to no one in particular, and, hence, it
gives rise to no right in anyone. And even where someone owes a duty to
someone to do something, the person to whom he owes such a duty does not
necessarily have any corresponding right. Thus, my moral duty to give charity
to X implies no right vesting in X. Similarly, I have certain duties toward my
students, but this does not necessarily confer any rights upon them (though
perhaps it should!) Or the duty to observe road signs contains no reference to
any duty to others and therefore implies no rights vested in anyone.

On the other hand, it is, of course, common for me to have a right to do
something, without you (or anyone else) having a corresponding duty. Lawyers,
however, often mistakenly assume that right and duty are correlatives. But
this Hohfeldian notion does help to clarify the concept of a right, as J.W.
Harris[34] demonstrates. It is true that, in order to make sense of legal relations
between persons, correlativity is part of the law's lowest common denominator,
because every judicial issue involves at least two persons. In practice, therefore,
litigation gives rise to opposing parties — even where, strictly speaking, the
defendant does not owe a duty to the plaintiff. Thus, my duty to pay tax on
my income does not necessarily give rise to a right held by another; but the
taxman will pursue me in the courts in order to recover tax owing. Hence,
the court has to answer the question: does the defendant owe a duty to the
plaintiff. Similarly, in those recent decisions in which the courts have had to
consider whether private individuals have *locus standi* to enforce the duties

imposed by the criminal law, or the duty of public authorities to provide various facilities such as health care and housing, the question is whether the defendant's conduct was in some way privileged in relation to the plaintiff.

What of moral rights? A moral right is an entitlement which confers moral liberties on those who have them to do certain things, and the moral constraint on others to abstain from interference.[35] A legal right is one recognized by the law. Statutes imposing a duty on persons not to inflict cruelty on animals (with their normal sanctions for violation)[36] could be said to confer on animals a legal right to humane treatment.[37] Does the same follow in respect of *moral* rights? I shall briefly consider this difficult question and then address the problem of whether (notwithstanding my confidence in respect of legal rights) animals, or, to enable me to put the strongest case, 'higher' animals, can be bearers of rights.

McCloskey argues that '(t)o show that animals possess moral rights, moral rights against persons, it is not sufficient to establish that persons have duties in respect of animals.'[38] His argument rests on the view that there is no strict correlativity of rights, a position accepted above in respect of legal rights. He then proceeds along the following lines:

1. Central to the concept of moral rights is the notion of *exercising* such rights. The paradigm possessor of a right is an actor or potential actor who can act by doing what he is entitled to do, or act by demanding, claiming, requiring what he is entitled to demand claim, require. In the absence of the possibility of such action in the being towards whom duties are owed, and where the being is not a member of a kind which is normally capable of action, we withhold talk of rights and confine ourselves to talk of duties. Moral rights are ascribed to beings who are capable of moral autonomy, moral self-direction and self-determination.

2. We can therefore deny the capacity for rights to 'ex-persons' (the brain damaged, or extremely senile) and 'non-persons' (those born with damaged or under-developed brains), but not to 'potential persons' (infants who will become persons). We also deny this capacity to inanimate objects and plants, even though they (like ex-persons and non-persons) may be the object of duties. This is because they cannot exercise rights or have them exercised for them.

3. The capacity to have interests is insufficient to establish a capacity to bear rights. This is because, though non-humans (including corporate bodies, churches, states, clubs etc), may be said to have interests, the idea that non-human animals have interests relies on an equation of interests with desires, aims and beliefs, and it would therefore still need to be shown that the possession of *these* capacities is a ground for the attribution of rights. Moreover, 'rights and interests are completely different things.'[39] There will be circumstances where a right-bearer may wish to exercise his rights *against* his own interests. Equally it may be in his interests to deprive him of his freedom to exercise rights. And where a putative right-bearer is incapable of expressing his wishes (if he has any) his mind would have to be read. Where he has no mind or will to be read, he

cannot be a representation of his rights or the exercising or waiving of moral rights.

4. Since most animals lack the relevant moral capacity, they do not have moral rights. Some animals (whales and dolphins) may be found to have such capacity: it may therefore be 'morally appropriate for us meanwhile to act towards (whales and dolphins) *as if* they are possessors of rights'.[40]

This is an important and careful argument, but it does not seem to me to be a particularly convincing one. Indeed, some of its claims do not appear to advance its own case. Thus, it is difficult to see how a right-bearer's inability to express his wishes leads ineluctably to the conclusion (in point 3) that he has no rights that can be represented. To argue (as McCloskey does)[41] that the paternalism it involves would offend liberal values may call for an examination of those values. Nor is the speculative empirical move (in point 4) a particularly solid foundation for the benevolence towards a limited range of creatures.

Non-human animals have interests and needs. In particular, they have a clear interest in avoiding pain and an untimely death. But this does not dispose of the matter. It enables one to reject one of the two main theories of rights (the 'choice' theory) which is plainly less congenial to animals than the 'interest' theory. The main virtue of an interest-based theory is that it enables us more easily to ground *duties* toward animals,[42] but, as I shall try to show, it has a considerably wider application.

The 'choice' theory (advanced, most notably, by Hart[43]) holds that when I have a right to do something, what is essentially protected is my choice whether or not to do it. It stresses the freedom and individual self-fulfilment that are regarded as essential values which the law ought to guarantee. The 'interest' theory, on the other hand (most effectively espoused by D.N. MacCormick)[44] claims that the purpose of rights is to protect, not individual choice, but certain interests of the right-holder. It should be noted that the advocates of both theories (though not Professor MacCormick) normally accept the correlativity of rights and duties; indeed, this is often central to their arguments.

In attacking the choice theory, proponents of the interest theory raise two main arguments. First, they reject the view that the essence of a right is the power to waive someone else's duty. Sometimes, they argue, the law limits my power of waiver without destroying my substantive right (e.g., I cannot consent to murder or contract out of certain rights). Secondly, there is a distinction between the substantive right and the right to enforce it. MacCormick gives the example of children: their rights are exercised by their parents or guardians; how can it be said, therefore, that the right-holder (i.e., the child) has any *choice* whether or not to waive such rights? It must, he argues, be concluded that children have no rights — which is absurd. And a similar point could, of course, be made in relation to animals.

While the choice theory, by arguing that the enforcement of Y's duty requires the exercise of will by X (or someone else), rests on the assumption of the correlativity of rights and duties, it is possible to postulate the interest theory (as MacCormick does) independently. Thus, it may be argued that conferring a right on someone (e.g., to housing) constitutes an acceptance that the interest represented by that right ought to be recognized and protected. There are two main versions of this theory. One asserts that X has a right whenever he is in a position to benefit from the performance of a duty. The other claims that X has a right whenever the protection of his interest is recognized as a reason for imposing duties — whether or not they are actually imposed.

Tom Regan's sentimental anthropomorphicism argues for the similarities between a human and an animal life. In particular, animals, like us, are 'subjects-of-a-life'. They have inherent, not merely instrumental, value or worth. This entitles them to the absolute right to live their lives with respect and autonomy:

> The most reasonable criterion of right-possession . . . is not that of sentience or having interests, since neither of these by themselves can account for why it is wrong to treat humans who are not irreversibly comatose merely as means; rather the criterion that most adequately accounts for this is the criterion of inherent value: All those beings (and only those beings) which have inherent value have rights.

Hence, no amount of benefit to humans (from, say, vivisection) can justify the violation of this absolute right:

> The laudatory achievements of science, including the many genuine benefits obtained for both humans and animals, do not justify the unjust means used to secure them . . . (T)he rights view does not call for the cessation of scientific research. Such research should go on — but not at the expense of laboratory animals.[45]

While the idea of rights lends support to the animal case (as it does to many causes) it is often rejected by many who might otherwise be enlisted to the animal cause. Hence communitarians stigmatize rights as individualist. They are seen to operate formally not necessarily to assist those (the poor, oppressed, alienated) who most need them. They are disparaged as 'excess baggage' superfluous in the condemnation of cruelty or exploitation.[46] All we need, it is argued, is a fully developed theory of right and wrong. Moreover, as I shall suggest below, Regan's argument that animals have an inherent value does not lead ineluctably to a rights-based conclusion. A second attack conceives of rights as weapons of last resort: 'the really desperate word'.[47] And the source of Regan's notion of inherent value is often questioned; is his theory no more than a form of sophisticated intuitionism?[48] Though Regan seeks to distinguish his case from that held by classic intuitionists like G.E. Moore, there is always the danger that your intuition might lead in the opposite direction to mine. How are we to determine who is right? Some rights-sceptics therefore prefer to prescribe duties without recourse to the precarious problems generated by animal rights through the mechanism of a social contract which I shall now briefly examine.

Animals and Social Contractarianism

In essence, contractarianism seeks to establish a moral system on the basis of what rational agents would agree under ideal circumstances. In its most modern, sophisticated version, as postulated by John Rawls,[49] these 'people in the original position' are shrouded in a 'veil of ignorance' which prevents them from knowing to which sex, class, religion or social position they belong. Each person represents a social class, but they do not know whether they are clever or stupid, strong or weak. Nor do they know in which country or in what period they are living. They possess only certain elementary knowledge about the laws of science and psychology. In this state of blissful ignorance they must unanimously decide upon the general principles that will define the terms under which they will live as a society. And, in doing so, they are moved by rational self-interest: each seeks those principles which will give him or her the best chance of attaining his or her chosen conception of the good life once the veil of ignorance is lifted. Objective standards are thus guaranteed.

I cannot discuss here the conclusions reached by Rawls as to what principles of justice these agents would select (he explicitly excludes animals as rational agents). But it is not altogether implausible that, in pursuit of objectivity, (even though we do not ask them to imagine themselves members of another species) they would choose a moral system which included respect for animals. At most the social contract may require *indirect* duties to animals because of the (contingent) characteristics of the social contract struck in any particular society, or out of respect for the feelings of humans. But this seems too delicate a foundation upon which to construct a protective framework for non-humans.

Intrinsic Worth

Resting the welfare of animals on any of the arguments canvassed briefly above is unlikely to supply a convincing case. Perhaps, in the same way as the heated debate about abortion has missed the central issue, this controversy has lost its way. Ronald Dworkin distinguishes between two positions that are taken by those who oppose abortion.[50] The first he calls a derivative objection for it derives from the rights and interests that it assumes all human beings, including *foetuses*, have. A second objection rests on the claim that human life has an intrinsic value, that it is sacred or inviolable; abortion is therefore wrong because it infringes this value even in the case of an unborn human being. This he calls the detached objection.

Dworkin contends that the critical question in the abortion debate is the violation, not of the rights or interests of the *foetus* (an impossibly difficult metaphysical problem anyway) but of the importance of life itself:

Abortion wastes the intrinsic value — the sanctity, the inviolability — of a human life and is therefore a grave moral wrong unless the intrinsic value of other human lives would be wasted in a decision *against* abortion.[51]

The sterility of the disagreement concerning whether an animal may be said to be a 'person'[52] or (if or it is) whether it can or should have rights, gives rise to similar difficulties. And to a similar solution. The determination of the circumstances under which it is morally defensible to subject a living creature to pain or death seems to require coherent detached arguments that seek to show why the inherent worth of other lives (human and animal) are more valuable. The arguments sketched above appear, as in the case of the dispute concerning abortion, to generate a good deal of vitriol and rhetoric, and little in the way of constructive results. An essential element in the search for a happy ending is, of course, to find alternatives to the use of live animals in the laboratory.

Alternatives to Experiments

Many experiments on animals are unnecessary.[53] Alternatives often exist. The use of tissue culture, *in vitro* methods, mathematical and chemical modelling, computer simulation, and human volunteers is not uncommon, but is far from being generally accepted, even though the 'number of major contributions that replacement techniques have made to Nobel Prize-winning research is astonishing'.[54]

Inadequate funding for alternative methods and researchers' hostility have, at least in the past, conspired against what is misleadingly and unfairly described as the 'anti-science' posture of advocates of animal welfare. Cruelty aside, in today's world of advanced technolgy, the whole process of vivisection seems slightly anachronistic. Perhaps the Nobel Laureate in medicine and physiology, Sir Peter Medawar, was correct when he declared in 1972: 'the use of experimental animals on the present scale is a temporary episode in biological and medical history'.[55]

Regulating Experiments

Legislation to control and regulate the use of animals for experiments exists in a number of European jurisdictions.[56] Though they differ in scope they share five principal objectives:[57]

1. to define the legitimate purposes for which animals may be used,
2. to exert control over permissible levels of pain and distress,
3. to provide for inspection of facilities and procedures,
4. to ensure humane standards of animal husbandry and care,
5. to provide for public accountability.

The British statute is the most far-reaching. Enacted in 1986 the Animals (Scientific Procedures) Act establishes an elaborate system of licensing and inspection operated by a government department. In particular, it requires researchers to demonstrate that the potential results of their experiments are sufficiently significant to justify the use of animals, that their proposed research could not be done without live animals, and that the minimum number of animals will be used.[58] Other forms of non-legislative regulation are in place in the USA,[59] Canada, Australia, and New Zealand.

In 1986 a European Convention for the Protection of Vertebrate Animals Used for Experimental and Other Scientific Purposes was formulated. It requires each of the members of the Council of Europe, should they decide to ratify it, to give effect to its (fairly weak) provisions by legislation. In 1987 the European Commission itself became a signatory to the Convention. The EC Directive[60] provides for the limitation of severe pain and distress and for control by the Competent Authority in each member state of experiments likely to cause severe pain, including a requirement to weigh the likely benefit against the pain suffered. It does not, however, impose a duty upon member states to reduce experiments involving animals or to use available alternatives. Nor is a system of inspection to monitor state practices established. The requirements to limit pain are not strong.

Legislation plainly cannot stand on its own. Even if enforced, it needs to be buttressed by a programme of education and a consciousness of and support for its moral purpose. Without the endorsement and commitment of government and researchers, it is likely to have only limited effect. There is evidence to suggest that the British Act, at any rate, is beginning to improve the lot of laboratory animals.

Conclusion

Those who oppose animal experiments tend to adopt the single-minded pursuit of arguments in support of the proposition that animals have *rights*. This is hardly surprising.

In moral discourse the power of rights is formidable. Moral claims are routinely translated into moral rights: individuals assert their rights to life, work, health, education, housing and so on. Communities and putative nations demand a right to self-determination, sovereignty, free trade. In the legal context rights have assumed a prominence so great that they are sometimes regarded as synonymous with law itself;[61] declarations of political rights are often conceived to be the hallmark of the modern democratic state. And the inevitable contest between competing rights is one of the self-justifying characteristics of a liberal society. Whether the choice or the interest model of rights is adopted, 'it is quite inconceivable that that the extension of any right should coincide exactly with the boundaries of our species'.[62]

But the language rights does not seem to present a promising basis for the protection of animals against avoidable suffering. Rights need not feature in the case for a naturalist strategy to secure and protect the material, social and psychological well-being of all animals, and perhaps even plants.

The harm that scientific and economic 'progress' can inflict on our environment and all who share it is plain. The attraction of rights as a weapon by which both to safeguard the interests of living things against harm, and to promote the circumstances under which they are able to flourish is understandable. Yet the traditional concept of rights is problematic and, in any event, may be unable to deliver these goods. The case for a fundamental shift in our social and economic systems and structures may be the only way in which to secure a sustainable future for our planet and its inhabitants. The importance of the sanctity of all life and its flourishing offers a powerful means to this end.

Whatever conceptual strategy is deployed, there are a number of fundamental practical changes that need to take place in the approach to animal experiments. First, ethical committees (whose members are not confined to scientists) need to be established (along Australian and New Zealand lines)[63] to allow the moral issues to be properly considered. In particular, since the central criterion of acceptability is (or ought to be) the 'benefits' of the proposed experiment, those who will allegedly enjoy the principal benefits, ought to be involved in fixing the meaning of what often looks like a dangerous weasel-word.[64] Secondly, it is essential that the public (whose taxes tend to support such scientific ends) have access to information on experiments. Participation in ethical committees would assist, but there is plainly a requirement for comprehensible accounts of the nature, purpose, and controls exercised over experiments. Thirdly, a good deal of repetition, pain, and pointless experiments could be avoided if experimenters included in their published papers details of alternatives to the use of animals in the particular experiment, the adverse effects associated with certain procedures, special signs of suffering, results of early failures (to prevent other scientists from repeating them), and painkillers used.[65]

The argument is sometimes heard that concern for animals is misplaced. Human beings, it is contended, are manifestly more important than non-humans. Energy spent on animal causes is better directed against human suffering. Indeed one writer asserts that the popular movement in support of animal rights is a 'reflection of moral decadence'.[66] This argument seems to be driven by the idea that those who are engaged in animal rights or welfare activities either subordinate human interests to animal interests, or that they have a pathological indifference towards human beings.[67] In my experience, at least, the opposite tends to be true. Individuals involved in the animal welfare movement are frequently dedicated as well to the alleviation of suffering of oppressed or disadvantaged humans.[68] And even if this were not so, our concern for animals is inseparable from our anxiety about the ravages we continue to inflict on our environment, and the consequences of this damage on all living things.

The (highly questionable) notion that science is somehow value-neutral appears sometimes to blind scientists to the suffering of animals and deny them subjective awareness and moral status.[69]

Cruelty to animals and indifference to the extinction of endangered species, is, especially in this region, sometimes defended in the name of cultural or ethical relativism. This is a neglected issue that warrants close attention. It is true that, as in the case of human rights, 'since people are more likely to observe normative propositions if they believe them to be sanctioned by their own cultural standards, observance of human rights standards can be improved through the enhancement of the cultural legitimacy of those standards.'[70] Yet, all too often, these arguments merely camouflage injustice. Where suffering is caused (and especially where international norms are infringed) we should resist such claims.

If the argument about our use of animals in research is best considered as an aspect of our attitude towards the planet we inhabit, it requires an understanding of the circumstances that give rise to animal experimentation in the first place. Are experiments (if that is what they are) performed by large pharmaceutical companies[71] a kind of insurance policy against potential claims for negligence? Do the criteria for academic career advancement place undue emphasis on research conducted on animals? Is the practice of animal experimentation so ingrained into the methodology and reward-system of the scientific community that it inevitably generates more experiments?[72] These questions warrant the closest examination.

Was Bentham too sanguine when he declared:

Why should the law refuse its protection to any sensitive being? The time will come when humanity will extend its mantle over everything which breathes. We have begun by attending to the condition of slaves; we shall finish by softening that of all the animals which assist our labours or supply our wants.[73]

Who could hope that he was?

Notes

1. 'If Animals Could Talk' [1932] in H. Ruja (ed) *Mortals and Others: Bertrand Russell's American Essays 1931–1935* (London: Allen & Unwin, 1975) vol.1, 120–121, quoted in P.A.B. Clarke and A. Linzey (eds) *Political Theory and Animal Rights* (London: Pluto Press, 1990) 92.
2. This figure (which happily declines each year) can only be an estimate and does not include all countries; it is based on the following estimates: US: 90 m, Japan: 13 m, Austria: 8 m, Australia: 8 m, UK: 5 m, France: 4.4 m, Netherlands: 3 m, South Africa: 2 m, Canada: 2 m, Finland: 1.6 m, India: 1 m, Sweden: 0.9 m, Israel: 0.5 m, Norway: 0.09 m. The statistics are from G. Mitchell, 'Guarding the Middle Ground: The Ethics of Experiments on Animals' (1989) 85 *S.Afr.J.Sci.*285.
3. See P. Singer, *Animal Liberation* (New York: Avon, 1975), T. Regan, *The Struggle for Animal Rights* (Clarks Summit,Penn.: International Society for Animal Rights, 1987), J.M. Jasper and D. Nelkin, *The Animal Rights Crusade: The Growth of a Moral Protest* (New York: The Free Press, 1992)

4. Other euphemisms used by experimenters describe animals as being 'dispatched', 'terminated', 'cervically dislocated', 'exsanguinated', 'decapitated', or 'put down'. Whole rooms are 'depopulated' or simply 'cleaned'. In this survey of 15 laboratories, the animals themselves were routinely reified as 'controls', 'recipients', 'donors', 'carriers', 'bleeders' and so on, A. Arluke, 'Trapped in a Guilt Cage' (1992) *New Scientist*, 4 April, 33, 35.

5. R. Rodd, *Biology, Ethics, and Animals* (Oxford: Clarendon Press, 1990) 145. But it is hard to accept that in extreme cases certain 'experiments' do not cause significantly greater suffering to individual animals than is caused by meat-eating.

6. This enquiry invites in turn a deeper question about our attitude to nature in general. For a account of some of the central issues see J. Passmore, *Man's Responsibility for Nature* (London: Duckworth, 1974). But his analysis of our attitude to non-humans is not always especially perspicuous or convincing. For more sympathetic accounts see, for example, R. Attfield, *The Ethics of Environmental Concern* (Oxford: Basil Blackwell, 1983), P.S. Wenz, *Environmental Justice*, (Albany: State University of New York Press, 1988), H. Rolston, *Environmental Ethics* (Philadelphia: Temple University Press, 1988), T. Benton, *Natural Relations: Ecology, Animal Rights and Social Justice* (London: Verso, 1993). See too M. Midgley, *Animals and Why They Matter* (Harmondsworth: Penguin, 1983).

7. This is an especially controversial assertion. It is based on the idea of ontological naturalism advanced by Ted Benton, *Natural Relations*, see Note 6 above, which informs and reflects many of my own views on the subject of the moral status of animals. Most writers reject this continuism; the criteria upon which their differentiation is drawn are numerous, and none is without logical flaws or traces of speciesism. Thus Finnis contends that human consciousness, unlike that experienced by animals is 'expressive of decision, choice, reflectiveness, commitment, as fruition of purpose, or of self-discipline or self-abandonment, and as the action of a responsible personality,' *Natural Law and Natural Rights* (Oxford: Clarendon Press, 1980), 194. But I see no reason why this naturalistic argument for 'human flourishing' (though anthropocentrically rooted) should not be extended to all life forms. Finnis's assertion that '(t)hose who propose that animals have rights have a deficient appreciation of the basic forms of human good' strikes me as tautologous.

8. I would prefer not to draw such a distinction, but I shall allow this assumption to save my having to explain how we are to justify what may otherwise be classified as cruelty to a carrot or a virus.

9. It is difficult, as a layman, to assess the claims and counterclaims on this critical issue. Professor Paton seeks to demonstrate that animal experiments have been essential not only to our understanding of our bodies, but in the treatment of numerous diseases (including pneumonia, rheumatic fever, diptheria, polio, measles, whooping cough, smallpox, childhood leukaemia, and cancer) as well as the development of surgery, hygiene and preventive medicine. Many of the drugs and procedures which have been discovered have, he argues, been available to veterinary surgeons to treat sick animals, W. Paton, *Man and Mouse: Animals in Medical Research* (Oxford: Oxford University Press, 1984), 40–79. Patrick Wall, Professor of Anatomy at University College, London, refers to the 'revolution' over the last 25 years in our understanding of pain mechanisms which, he says, was 'generated by experimantal work on animals' (which does not mean, of course, that it might not have been 'generated' *without* the use of animal experiments). He adds that

'by great good fortune' these tests have resulted in a series of new therapies including transcutaneous electrical nerve stimulation, dorsal column stimulation, and epidural narcotics. See P. Wall, 'Neglected Benefits of Animal Research' (1992) *New Scientist* 18 April, 30, 31. The House of Lords in *National Anti-Vivisection Society v Inland Revenue Commissioners* [1947] 2 All ER 217 refers to 'the immense and incalculable benefits which have resulted from vivisection. . . The scientist who inflicts pain in the course of vivisection is fulfilling a moral duty to mankind which is higher in degree than the moralist or sentimentalist who thinks only of the animals,' (*per* Lord Wright at 223). It is doubtful whether today even the most ardent defender of vivisection would express his support in such unqualified rhetorical terms. A powerful argument against such claims is made by Robert Sharpe who tries to demonstrate that animal experiments 'are generally bad science because they tell us about animals, usually under artificial conditions, when we really need to know about people,' R. Sharpe, 'Animal Experiments: A Failed Technology' in G. Langley (ed) *Animal Experimentation: The Consensus Changes* (Basingstoke: Macmillan, 1989) 111. He quotes (at 88) Professor Sir George Pickering, former Professor of Medicine at Oxford who in 1964 wrote: 'The idea, as I understand it, is that fundamental truths are revealed in laboratory experiments on lower animals and are then applied to the problems of the sick patient. Having been myself trained as a physiologist I feel in a way competent to assess such a claim. It is plain nonsense,' 'Physician and Scientist (1964) 2 *Br.Med.J.* 1615. As will become evident below, the utilitarian calculus implicit in the way in which I have formulated the assumption is by no means the only way of evaluating the 'benefits' of animal experiments.

10. That this should be in doubt is, at least to a pet-owning layman, extraordinary. The evidence appears to be irresistible, see B.E. Rollin, *The Unheeded Cry: Animal Consciousness, Animal Pain and Science* (Oxford: Oxford University Press, 1989), M. Dawkins, *Animal Pain: The Science of Animal Welfare* (London: Chapman & Hall, 1980). But see M.P.T. Leahy, *Against Liberation: Putting Animals in Perspective* (London: Routledge, 1991) 124–131, 222–228.

11. Though, according to Arluke's study, see Note 4 above, most experimenters 'did not have elaborate moral justifications for their use of animals. Instead, many of them appeared ethically inarticulate'. (35).

12. See, for instance, P. Singer, *Animal Liberation*, Note 3 above, and R. Ryder, *Victims of Science* (London: Davis-Poynter, 1975) for numerous unsettling descriptions.

13. N. Chomsky, *American Power and the New Mandarins* (Harmondsworth: Penguin, 1969) 11, quoted in S. Clark, *The Moral Status of Animals* (Oxford: Clarendon Press, 1977) 1.

14. For a comprehensive list of scientific references, see R. Sharpe, Note 9 above, 111–117.

15. For a sceptical analysis of the reliability of this test, see G. Zbinden and M. Flury-Roversi, 'Significance of the LD50 test for the toxicological evaluation of chemical substances' (1981) 47 *Arch. Toxicol.* 77.

16. According to a distinguished human toxicologist, Roy Goulding, 'the subject and practice of toxicology has become exalted to the eminence of a religion . . . (and) like a religion it relies rather more on faith than reason,' quoted in M. Balls, 'Time to Reform Toxic Tests' (1992) *New Scientist*, 2 May 1992, 31, 33. See C. Hollands, 'Trivial and Questionable Research on Animals' in Langley (ed) see Note 9 above, 118. But one ought to acknowledge, as Paton points out, that

cosmetics sometimes perform more than a trivial role when used, for example, to conceal unsightly birthmarks, Paton, see Note 9 above, 140. *In vitro* tests, developed by ICI in the early 1980s, offer a promising alternative to animals. This is formally recognized by the OECD which, in its 1992 revision of its guidelines on skin irritation/corrosion states that 'it may not be necessary to test *in vivo* materials for which corrosive properties are predicted on the basis of results from *in vitro* tests'. It does, however, add that it is highly unlikely that in vitro tests would replace the rabbit test completely for at least another ten years. See P. Botham and I. Purchase, 'Why Laboratory Rats Are Here to Stay' (1992) *New Scientist*, 2 May, 29, 30.

17. See B. Ballantyne and D.W. Swanson 'The scope and limitations of acute eye irritation tests' in B. Ballantyne (ed) *Current Approaches in Toxicology* (Bristol: John Wright) 139.

18. It is frequently suggested that even if thalidomide had been tested on pregnant rats, no malformations would have occurred, for the drug does not cause birth defects in rats or in several other species, see P. Lewis, 'Animal tests for teratogenicity, their relevance to clinical practice' in D.F. Hawkins (ed), *Drugs and Pregnancy: Human Teratogenesis and Related Problems* (Edinburgh: Churchill Livingstone, 1983) 17.

19. R. Sharpe, see Note 9 above, 111.

20. For an argument along these lines see D.L. Perrott, 'Has Law a Deep Structure: The Origins of Fundamental Duties' in D. Lasok, A.J.E. Jaffey, D.L. Perrott and C. Sachs, *Fundamental Duties* (Oxford: Pergamon Press, 1980) 1.

21. Though they often provide the most strongly held and persuasive reasons for action. For a lucid introduction to these issues, albeit from a morally sceptical point of view, see J. L. Mackie, *Ethics: Inventing Right and Wrong* (Harmondsworth: Penguin, 1977, reprinted 1990).

22. It is made most forcefully by Bernard Williams. See J.J.C. Smart and B. Williams, *Utilitarianism: For and Against* (London: Cambridge University Press, 1973).

23. H.L.A. Hart, 'Between Utility and Rights' in his *Essays in Jurisprudence and Philosophy* (Oxford: Clarendon Press, 1983) 198, 200-202.

24. These four criticisms contain most of the issues that lie at the heart of many of the other attacks, of which the following may be mentioned. Why *should* we seek to satisfy people's desires? Certain desires are unworthy of satisfaction (e.g. the sadist who wants to torture cats). A third attack is one made by Johns Rawls, *A Theory of Justice* (Oxford: Oxford University Press, 1973) who argues that utilitarianism defines what is right in terms of what is 'good'; but this means, he says, that it begins with a conception of what is 'good' (e.g. happiness) and then concludes that an action is *right* in so far as it maximizes that 'good'. Fourthly, utilitarianism is concerned only with maximizing welfare; many regard the more important question as the just *distribution* of welfare. Fifthly, many critics point to the impracticability of *calculating* the consequences of one's actions: how can we know in advance what results will follow from what we propose to do. Sixthly, are our wants and desires not manipulated by persuasion, advertising and the like? Can we, in other words, separate our *'real'* preferences from our *'conditioned'* ones? Seventhly, is it possible (and, if it is, is it anyway desirable) to balance my pleasure against another's pain? Eighthly, how far into the future do (or can) we extend the consequences of our actions? Or to put it slighly differently, as Bernard Williams does (op. cit. 82): 'No one can hold that everything, of whatever category, that has value, has it in virtue of its consequences. If that were

so, one would just go on for ever, and there would be an obviously hopeless regress.'

25. But see R.G. Frey, *Interests and Rights: The Case Against Animals* (Oxford: Clarendon Press, 1980) for a rejection of the argument, from a utilitarian position, that animals can be said to have either rights or interests.

26. See Note 3 above. See also Singer's *Practical Ethics* (Cambridge: Cambridge University Press, 1979). For a similar argument from pain and suffering see S. Clarke, *The Moral Status of Animals*, Note 13 above.

27. See *Practical Ethics*, 59. Orphans in order to exclude the possibility of vicarious suffering to relatives.

28. Another feature of utilitarianism is sometimes viewed as helpful in developing a sound moral approach towards animals is Mill's view [advanced in a more sophisticated form by R.M. Hare (see *Moral Thinking* (Oxford: Clarendon Press, 1983)] that our primary duty is to develop certain qualitites of character which would promote the greatest overall utility. But this may impose unreasonable demands on moral actors. It is not impossible to reconcile consequentialism with rights, see, for example, L.W. Sumner, *The Moral Foundation of Rights* (Oxford: Clarendon Press, 1987).

29. The strongest argument in support of animals as right-bearers is made by Tom Regan, *The Case for Animal Rights* (London: Routledge, 1984). For assaults on this view, see R.G. Frey, *Rights, Killing and Suffering: Moral Vegetarianism and Applied Ethics* (Oxford: Basil Blackwell, 1983) which I reviewed in (1986) 49 *Modern Law Review* 403, and P. Carruthers, *The Animals Issue: Moral Theory in Practice* (Cambridge: Cambridge University Press, 1992).

30. J. Waldron (ed), *Theories of Rights* (Oxford: Oxford University Press, 1984) 13.

31. In any event, is it wholly implausible that animals may indeed be subjects of certain duties (eg a watchdog)?

32. W.N. Hohfeld, *Fundamental Legal Conceptions as Applied in Judicial Reasoning*, W.W. Cook (ed) (New Haven, Conn; London: Yale University Press, 1964).

33. See J. Raz, 'Legal Rights' (1984) 4 *Oxford Journal of Legal Studies* 1.

34. J.W. Harris, *Legal Philosophies* (London: Butterworths, 1980) 81-83.

35. See the useful essay by H.J. McCloskey, 'Moral Rights and Animals' (1978) 22 *Inquiry* 23. 27–28.

36. The most comprehensive statute is the British Protection of Animals Act of 1911. The use of animals for experimentation is now regulated by the Animals (Scientific Procedures) Act 1986 which establishes a licensing regime controlled by the Home Office. By the admission of a number of scientists (let alone animal welfare groups) the Act, though a major advance, is not providing the expected benefits for laboratory animals.

37. See J. Feinberg, 'Human Duties and Human Rights', 188–9, and 'The Rights of Animals and Unborn Generations', 159, both reproduced in his *Rights, Justice and the Bounds of Liberty: Essays in Social Philosophy* (Princeton: Princeton University Press, 1980).

38. McCloskey, see Note 35 above, 27–28.

39. McCloskey, see Note 35 above, 39. Here McCloskey departs from his earlier view expressed in 'Rights' (1965) 15 *Philosophical Quarterly*. See also T. Regan, 'McCloskey on Why Animals Cannot have Rights' (1976) 26 *Philosophical Quarterly*. Joseph Raz argues (as part of a larger and sophisticated defence of freedom) that '(A)ll rights are based on interests', J. Raz, *The Morality of Freedom* 191.

40. McClosky, 42–43. McCloskey proposes, instead of a rights-based argument, a

justice-based argument in support of animals. A full account would require an analysis of how considerations such as desert, merit, well-being, needs, wishes etc figure in the structure of a theory of justice towards animals.

41. McCloskey, 39.

42. This is not, of course, to say either that all duties derive from rights or that morality is right-based. See J. Raz, *The Morality of Freedom* (Oxford: Clarendon Press, 1986) chap 7.

43. See H.L.A. Hart, *Essays on Bentham* (Oxford: Clarendon Press, 1982) chap. 7.

44. D.N. MacCormick, *Legal Rights and Social Democracy* (Oxford: Clarendon Press, 1982) esp. chap. 8, and 'Rights in Legislation' in P.M.S. Hacker and J.Raz (eds.), *Law, Morality and Society* (Oxford: Clarendon Press, 1977).

45. Regan, Note 29 above, 397.

46. See in particular the works by R.G. Frey referred to above.

47. M. Midgley, *Animals And Why They Matter*, Note 6 above, 61–64.

48. See Carruthers, Note 29 above, 21–24.

49. J. Rawls, *A Theory Of Justice* (Oxford: Oxford University Press, 1972).

50. R. Dworkin, *Life's Dominion: An Argument about Abortion and Euthanasia* (London: Harper Collins, 1993, paperback ed, 1995) 11 and *passim*.

51. *Ibid*, 60.

52. The question whether animals can be 'persons' is often connected to the issue of whether they can have legal rights, particularly to inheritance. In English law an animal is a chattel which cannot inherit. The German Civil Code was recently amended to give animals the status of 'beings' rather than 'things'. The Privy Council has accepted that a bronze Hindu idol has legal personality and *locus standi: Union Bank of India v Bumper Development Corporation Ltd* (1988) QBD (17 February, unreported) cited in L.V. Prott and P.J. O'Keefe, *Law and the Cultural Heritage* Vol 3 (London: Butterworths, 1989) 546–7. See also A. D'Amato and S.K. Chopra, 'Whales: Their Emerging Right to Life' (1991) 85 *American Journal of International Law* 21. I am indebted to my colleagues David Murphy and Roda Mushkat for drawing my attention to these sources. Some African legal systems recognize the juristic personality of trees, rocks and even spirits. For a powerful argument (adopted by three Supreme Court judges) in support of legal rights for natural objects, see C.D. Stone, 'Should Trees Have Standing? — Towards Legal Rights for Natural Objects' (1972) 45 *S.Cal.L.Rev* 450.

53. Animals are also widely used in medical education. This raises questions about the right of students to object to such practices, and the academic consequences of such conscientious objection. In a recent survey, 93% of physicians questioned by the American Medical Association (AMA) supported the continued use of animals in medical education. Almost 90% said they had used animals for educational purposes. See J. Foreman, 'Physicians Support Use of Animals in Medical Education' (1992) 110 *Arch Opthalmol* 324. The AMA has recommended guidelines for the use of animals in medical school curricula and continuing medical education.

54. M. Stephens, 'Replacing Animal Experiments' in G. Langley (ed) *Animal Experimentation: The Consensus Changes*, Note 9 above.

55. Quoted by Stephens, Note 54 above, 165.

56. Notably Britain, France, Germany, Holland, Belgium, Switzerland, Denmark, Ireland, Greece, Italy.

57. See J. Hampson, 'Legislation and the Changing Consensus' in G. Langley (ed), *Animal Experimentation: The Consensus Changes*, Note 9 above, 219, 220.

58. Researchers often raise what seems to me a genuine point about the difficulty of predicting (and hence specifying, as required by section 5 of the Act) the value of many proposed research projects. The evidence is fairly strong that a high percentage of experiments, (41% in one survey) bears 'no relation whatever to the disease that it later helped to prevent, diagnose, treat or alleviate,' Comroe and Dripps, quoted by M.A. Fox, *The Case for Animal Experimentation* (London: University of California Press, 1986) 140.

59. The US Animal Welfare Act of 1966 (amended in 1970, 1976, and 1985) is not intended to control research, but the amendment in 1985 require the establishment of Animal Care and Use Committees at institutions where experiments are conducted. For a useful summary of the controls, see J. Hampson, quoted in Langley (ed), see Note 9 above, 229–240.

60. *On The Approximation of Laws, Regulations and Administrative Provisions of the Member States Regarding the Protection of Animals Used for Experimental and Other Scientific Purposes*, November 1986. It was intended that the directive would be incorporated into the domestic laws of member states by 1988. But only Britain, Germany, the Netherlands, France and Italy appear to be in the process of adopting it. Opposition to the directive has been expressed by Spain, Portugal, and Greece.

61. See R. Dworkin, *Taking Rights Seriously* (Cambridge MA: Harvard University Press, 1977).

62. L.W. Sumner, *The Moral Foundation of Rights*, Note 28 above, 206.

63. See J. Hampson, 'The Secret World of Animal Experiments' (1992) *New Scientist* 11 April, 24. Such committees (with lay representation) exist also in Sweden and Denmark. Useful accounts of developments in Australia and New Zealand are provided by reports published by the Australian and New Zealand Council for the Care of Animals in Research and Teaching (ANZCCART) an 'independent' body established in 1987 sponsored by the Commonwealth Scientific and Industrial Research Organization, the National Health and Medical Research Council, the Australian Vice-Chancellors' Committee and the Australian Research Council.

64. The 1986 British statute creates an Animal Procedures Committee, but this deals with only a fraction of cases referred to it by the Home Office, and is not the appropriate forum for genuine moral debate.

65. See D. Morton, 'A Fair Press for Animals' (1992) *New Scientist* 11 April, 28.

66. P. Carruthers, *The Animals Issue*, Note 29 above, xi.

67. For one writer 'there is no real difference in the basic grounds on which we should condemn man's inhumanity to animals and man's inhumanity to man,' T.L.S. Sprigge, 'Metaphysics, Physicalism, and Animal Rights' (1979) 22 *Inquiry* 101, 103.

68. There is a strong connection between the feminist and the anti-vivisection campaigns of the nineteenth century in Britain. See O. Banks, *Faces of Feminism* (Oxford: Blackwell, 1986) 81–2 quoted in L. Birke, *Women, Feminism and Biology: The Feminist Challenge* (Brighton: Harvester, 1986) 120.

69. '(A)nimals have been allowed to suffer in research not through cruelty, but rather, because consideration of suffering is forgotten in the thrill of the pursuit, by nature ultimately ruthless, complementedby an ideology which discounts the cogency of moral reflection in scientific activity and denies the meaningfulness of attributing feelings to animals, and is coupled with practical pressures,' B.E. Rollin, *The Unheeded Cry*, Note 10 above.

70. A.A. An-Na Im, 'Problems of Universal Cultural Legitimacy for Human Rights'

in An-Na Im and F. Deng (eds), *Human Rights in Africa: Cross-Cultural Perspectives* (Washington DC: Brookings Institution, 1990) p. 331. See R. Wacks, 'The End of Human Rights?' (1994) 24 *Hong Kong Law Journal* 372, 392. See too R. Wacks, 'Human Rights: Confronting Bangkok and Beijing' (1994) 24 *Hong Kong Law Journal* 313.

71. It is I think fair to say that industry (especially the pharmaceutical companies) are responsible for most of the experiments conducted on animals. Indeed, Michael Balls, Professor of Medical Cell Biology at the University of Nottingham, laments the fact that under the 1986 Act 'while individual academics must struggle hard to to convince their Home Office inspectors that their use of small numbers of animals in fundamental biomedical research should be permitted, a single industrial project licence may permit the whole range of regulatory tests, involving tens or hundreds of personal licencees and the annual use of thousands, or even tens of thousands of animals,' M. Balls, see Note 16 above, 31.

72. 'It is in the name of science, and with the specious bribe of release from all our ills, that we have been cajoled and threatened and insulted into permitting the continued torture of our kindred and the continued blunting of the sensibilities of those who come to work in our laboratories. Let no-one rely on common decency in such a situation: the pressure of one's professional peer-group, the atmosphere of dismissive tolerance of all outside the clan, the calm assumption that this is what we do, are all far too strong for most of us to resist,' S. Clark, *The Moral Status of Animals*, see Note 13 above, 141–142.

73. J. Bentham, quoted in A. Brown, *Who Cares for Animals?* (London: Heinemann, 1974).

Part I

Ethical Concerns in the Age
of Biotechnology

* * * * * * * * * * * * * *

Part IB

Biotechnology and Genetics

5

Clinical and Ethical Challenges of Genetic Markers for Severe Human Hereditary Disorders

Rita Kielstein

The Winter Family History

I met Mrs Winter, 55, in 1981, when she became a dialysis patient in our dialysis unit. As a carrier of autosomal dominant polycystic kidney disease (ADPKD), she had developed chronic renal insuffiency and had to have dialysis treatment three times a week. In 1977 large cysts in both kidneys and in the liver were confirmed by ultrasound diagnosis. After Mrs Winter became a dialysis patient, her four sons underwent ultrasound screening which showed that all sons were presymptomatic carriers of ADPKD living healthy lives. These were the reactions of the sons after they learned about their carrier status: First of all the sons accused their mother for having as many as four children, even though she knew, that this severe disease was running in the family. Mrs Winter's father and his two brothers had also died in renal insuffiency caused by ADPKD. Albert, 32, married, and father of a six-year old son, committed suicide when he developed first symptoms of pain and renal dysfunction three years later. Otto, 30, married, sold a house, which was half completed, when he learned about the diagnosis. He did not want to make long-term plans for his life and burden his family with a mortgage. Karl, 25, and his fiancé dissolved their engagement because Karl did not want to have children, nor burden his fiancé with his own genetic prediction. Paul, 21, the youngest, a student did not complete his studies and took a job in order to make money and enjoy life while it lasted.

The Winter family story demonstrates very clearly different ways of translating DNA prediction into real life situations. This is in short the clinical and ethical challenge of DNA testing for severe human hereditary disorders.

While I will not discuss these stories, I want to keep them in mind during my discussion to emphasize that severe inherited diseases have a technical, medical, and genetic side as well as a human, real-life side. We are not just talking about genes and DNA, we are talking about fellow humans, brothers and sisters, mothers, families with their hopes, fears, pain, satisfaction and enjoyment for life and suffering in life, discrimination and denial.

DNA-Based Prediction of Severe Genetic Disorders

To date, molecular genetics has identified about 400 factors for hereditary diseases, and every day new factors are described and identified. Two percent of newborns have genetic disorders of the highest severity, which are life threatening, or negatively impact the quality of life or span of life.[1]

Table 1
Severe genetic disorders occurring among four groups of disorders

1. HEMOGLOBINOPATHY: sickle cell anemia, beta-thalassemia

2. ENZYMOPATHY:
   (a)   carbohydrate metabolism: galactosemia
   (b)   amino acid metabolism: phenylketonuria
   (c)   lipid metabolism: Gaucher's disease, Tay-Sachs disease
   (d)   mucopolysaccharid metabolism: Hunter syndrom, Hurler syndrom

3. OTHER DISEASES IN METABOLISM: lack of alpha-trypsin, Lesch-Nyhan disease, xeroderma pigmentosum, Duchenne's disease, cystic fibrosis

4. ONCOLOGICAL and OTHER DISEASES: retinoblastoma, leukemia, lymphoma, Huntington's chorea, Alzheimer's disease, hemophilia A and B, neurofibromatosis Recklinghausen, Friedreichsche Ataxie, ADPKD

Not all hereditary diseases are of the severest form. Among the most severe is cystic fibrosis (autosomal recessive). This is a multisystem disorder which is characterized by an abnormality in exocrine gland function. Nearly all patients develop chronic progressive disease of the respiratory system. Pulmonary disease is the most common cause of death and morbidity. Multiple clinical features include disturbences of the gastrointestinal tract, the reproductive system and the skeletal system. Currently the median survival is about 20 years. The majority of cystic fibrosis patients are diagnosed in infancy or childhood.

One of the most brutal disorders is Huntington's chorea (autosomal dominant), characterised by a combination of involuntary choreoathetotic movements and progressive dementia, usually beginning in mid-adult life. Younger patients, with onset of symptoms in the age group of 15–40 years, suffer a more severe form of disorder than older patients with onset usually between the age of 50 and 60.

Lesch-Nyhan disease is an X-chromosomal-linked disorder of purin-metabolism. Affected patients have hyperuricemia and overproduction of uric acid with uric azid stones. In addition, they have bizarre neurologic disorders, characterized by self-mutilation, hyperreflexia, choreoathetotis, spasticity and retardation of growth and mental function. The onset of symptoms begins at a young age between 15 and 30 years.

Thus, we can see that DNA factors give information about predictibility of disorders, not about severity, time of onset, severity of symptoms, span of life, quality of life and preventive options. Therefore, genetic knowledge has to be translated into real life situations and predictions of families and individuals. Genetic risk factors alone do not predetermine the individual quality and the personal fate of human life.

Risk and Responsibility of Patients With ADPKD

I will dicuss these issues further by presenting the case of ADPKD. This is a systemic disorder producing numerous cysts of varying sizes in both kidneys, in the liver, and the pancreas. There are also structural abnormalities in the gastrointestinal tract, and in the cardiovascular system. About 5 to 10% of all patients on dialysis treatment suffer from cystic kidney disease. The countries of the EEC spend roughly the equivelent of 4 billion ECU each year on renal replacement therapy, dialysis and transplantation. The per capita frequency of ADPKD is 1:1000, which is more frequent than either cystic fibrosis or Huntington's chorea. An estimated half million people have the disease in the United States. There is equal occurance in both sexes. It is inherited as a autosomal-dominant trait with 100% penetrance. Thus, each child of a carrier has a 50% risk to become a carrier.

Genetics

Careful studies of patterns of DNA fragments have revealed consistent differences in the structure of DNA in the short arm of human chromosome 16 in association with ADPKD.[2] Recent observations[3] indicate that at least two different defects can be responsible for a very similiar clinical picture, which cannot be distinguished in a single patient. These PKD-2-carriers live into their 7th to 9th decades and often die of nonrenal causes. PKD-1 carriers have symptoms and signs of the disease in their 4th and 5th decade. It is the usual experience that knowledge about the nature of ADPKD even in affected families, is poor.

Clinical Manifestations and Diagnosis

Cysts are present in the kidneys from the 12th week of gestation. Very slowly these cysts grow in size and number, thereby destroying the functional tissue of the kidneys. End-stage renal failure usually occurs between the age 40 and 60, but in fact varies considerably between patients, even between members of the same family. Autosomal dominant disorders are in general characterized by variability in age of onset and in phenotypic expression. Clinical age of onset is defined by the age at which symptoms appear or cysts can be found. The ages differ, depending upon the circumstances of inquiry.[4] Age of onset is also influenced by the technique used for screening.

The diagnosis of late stage ADPKD is easy: hypertension, abdominal pain, bilateral flank masses, hematuria or azotemia contribute to the typical clinical picture. Ultrasonography, computed-tomography, or magnetic resonance imaging are among procedures known to yield a positive diagnosis among ultimately proven cases. Since only about 60% of the patients will report a family history of this disease,[5] presymptomatic even prenatal and preimplantation diagnosis can be done by methods of molecular genetics.

Symptoms and Signs

Pain, caused by expanding and enlarging kidneys, is the most common clinical symptom of ADPKD in adults. Usually the pain is dull and constant, localized in the flank or lateral abdomen. Acute pain may arise from hemorrhage into a cyst or passage of a blood clot or stone. Sometimes inflammations, spreading to the renal bed from an infected cyst cause discomfort, usually in association with fever. Pain gradually increases over a patient's lifetime, ultimately affecting more than 50% of the individuals. Fifty percent of adult subjects with ADPKD experience hematuria at some time prior to diagnosis. Rupture of the cyst wall is blamed for the episodic hematuria in some patients. Episodes of gross hematuria can occur with strenous physical activity and may last from days to weeks. Gastrointestinal complaints of nausea, vomiting, and diarrhea are less common than renal symptoms, but can pose significant problems for occasional patients. Headaches, often severe and recurrent, are a common occurrence unrelated to hypertension. Headaches may be caused by berry aneurysms of the brain vessels. They occur in 10 to 40% of affected persons and can rupture and cause sudden death. Palpable hepatomegaly can be found in approximately one-half of individuals with ADPKD. They rarely cause symptoms or hepatic dysfunction or pain. Hypertension is a common finding in otherwise healthy patients and occurs in approximately 60% of non-azotemic patients. There are no typical changes in blood chemistry (anemia, serum-creatinin and urea levels) until the onset of renal insuffiency.[6]

ADPKD is considered to be a systemic disorder in which the phenotypic manifestation of the abnormal gene span an array of organ systems. Not every affected individual manifests all the possible aspects. Both interfamilial and intrafamilial variability occur in the extrarenal manifestation of ADPKD. Intrafamily variability is illustrated by differing manifestations and severities of structural defects despite similiar ages. Such intrafamilial variability may reflect the influence of the non-ADPKD allele, of other genes, or enviromental factors.

Risks and Responsibilities of ADPKD-Patients

As we have seen with the Winter brothers and their mother, clinical manifestation as well as presymptomatic knowledge about the ADPKD disorder translates into very different individual life stories. To be informed about one's own carrier status is important for good hypertension prevention and for avoidance of work-related or sports-related rupture of cysts.

Presymptomatic knowledge also seems to be important for making life-plan decisions which take the specifics of the probability of dialysis treatment or kidney transplantation into account. Decisions include carrier planning, occupational, professional, and recreational activities, family planning, social and cultural interactions. Each individual will translate his or her carrier status and symptoms into different parameters of individual life, its qualities, goals, and limitations. Knowledge is equally important for preventive life style for example: first of all, knowledge is the key to effective hypertension control. Second, some recreational activities such as jogging, horseback riding, wrestling, soccer or heavy physical work are not recommended as they might cause haematuria. Third, it is also important to know about one's carrier status when making reproductive choices. The issue of self-determination for each carrier is dependent upon the carrier having adaequate information, knowledge, and counselling in carrier planning, life-style and family planning.

My own clinical experience suggests that there is a duty to inform the carrier concerning his or her status as a carrier of ADPKD. It is the responsibility of the clinicians, geneticists, and families to consult with the carrier on medical and non-medical risks and decisions. A very special responsibility is associated with family planning decisions for carriers. This is because the best 'prevention' of ADPKD might be the 'prevention' of future carriers, which can be done by (a) not having procreative sex or using contraceptives; (b) selective abortion following early prenatal diagnosis; or (c) selective non-implantation following preimplantation diagnosis.

Risks and Responsibilities With Regard to Parenthood

The Case of Anita M.

I will discuss the ethical parameters of responsible parenthood of carriers of severe genetic diseases using the case of Anita M. as an example. Anita M. was diagnosed as a carrier of ADPKD at the age of 16 when she was a subject in a research project studying the family history of patients with this disease. Five years later when she was 21 years old, she became pregnant. Her mother, divorced, was a RDT-patient and her grandmother had just died due to liver complications after being in dialysis treatment for 14 years. Anita requested prenatal testing which now can be done by genetic screening. She was aware that the presence of ADPKD would require dialysis dependency in later years and have a negative impact upon the quality of life, such as renal complications, pain, and hypertension, allowing only for limited quality of life and the type of suffering and dying she had witnessed in her grandmother's final years. She therefore expressed that she felt an obligation not to give birth to a baby with definite diagnosis and prognosis of ADPKD. The test subsequently identified the foetus positively as a carrier. Anita scheduled counselling prior to setting a date for selective abortion, but she missed this appointment, never called back, and probably moved somewhere else and gave birth to her child.

Values at Conflict

Anita's case brings to light at least four different values in conflict: first, respect for life; second, the value of self-determination; third, the issues and values of responsible parenthood; and fourth, family planning. As in most cases of reproductive ethics, Anita faces a special challenge in balancing the respect for unborn life and responsible parenthood. This is a different situation than normal conflicts between right to choose (self-determination of the mother) and right to live (respecting potential interest of the foetus). Anita's foetus carries a severe genetic disorder which, if nothing else, forecasts an uncomfortable quality of life, including such things as dialysis treatment or the possibility of transplantation. In addition, there are the other associated burdens and symptoms of ADPKD already mentioned.[7]

Aborting the foetus might be an ethical option of responsible parenthood and indeed, it was the predetermined choice of Anita. The fact that she did not have the abortion might have been attributable to any of the following reasons: (a) emotional stress; (b) situational ethical uncertainty; (c) the desire to become a mother, regardless of the child's status as a carrier; (d) avoidance of making any decisions; or (f) by faith in the progress of science and the hope of the development of a treatment for ADPKD in the next 30 years, which is roughly the time frame of the onset of her child's symptoms.[8]

Medical Moral Scenario for Responsible Parenthood

I see at least eight scenarios of decision making in reproductive ethics for severe genetic disorder in cases similiar to Anita's:

1. *Giving birth.*   Giving birth and establishing a family by having children is a very normal individual and cultural goal in a woman's life. An ADPKD carrier most likely will be 'healthy' and happy for a long period of time and might even die of other causes a long time before the onset of severe symptoms. The offspring might have a family of his or her own and over the next few decades progress in medicine might develop new methods of prevention and/ or treatment of kidney cysts. On the other hand, should a mother give birth to a carrier of a very severe genetic disorder knowing the many future risks and uncertainties, including expensive and uncomfortable dialysis treatment or transplantation? Giving birth might be viewed as irresponsible from the perspective of the offspring, the spouse, the family at large, the society and the insurance companies.

2. *Abortion.*   Anita could have chosen abortion as her preferred means of contraception because she did not want to give birth to a child having the same disease as her mother, grandmother and herself. But other family planning

methods such as sterilization, the use of contraceptives, or selective abortion after prenatal diagnosis are also available.

3. *Abortion after prenatal diagnosis.* This would place the principle of responsible parenthood above the principle of respect for life or giving birth in general. If parents have responsibilities for the children, then there is a prime parental duty to not harm the unborn by the parent engaging in an unhealthy life-style, such as smoking cigarettes or excessive consumption of alcohol. Might there also be a parallel duty not to give birth to a child 'harmed' by one's own severe genetic disorder.

4. *Preimplantation diagnosis.* Carriers of severe hereditary diseases might, for medical, ethical, and emotional reasons, prefer preimplantation diagnosis over elective abortion. Preimplantation diagnosis has been reported to be successfull in cystic fibrosis[9] and might become the ethical instrument of first choice in responsible parenthood decisions.

5. *Not having children.* This might be a choice for those who, for religious or ethical reasons, do not accept diagnosis or selection of unborn human life.

6. *Not getting married.* Remaining single or having no heterosexual partners most likely will not be based on reproductive decisions but will have the side effect that carriers will not implant their own severe disorder into another generation. In the modern world, the carrier status also could be used as an excuse for a responsibility-free singles life-style.

7. *Adoption.* Adopting a non-carrier would allow one to have a child of one's own who would not be a carrier. Such family planning by adoption would come within the well-known parameters of ethical and emotional 'pros and cons' of adoption.

8. To give birth to a carrier and let the carrier be adopted by others would be a worst case scenario for responsible parenthood.

What must be realized is that each case must be assessed individually. Each case will be different medically and ethically, so will the family situation and the cultural background. I recommend flexible legal and medical standards for handling the complicated issues of reproductive choice with regards to ADPKD carriers or any other carriers of severe genetic disorders. I feel that non-directive counselling would be the best ethical approach by clinicians and geneticists. In my opinion, severe genetic disorders are part of the family history heritage and should be dealt with within the family and not by governmental or medical authorities. In order to assist the patient in making responsible decisions and for reproductive choices, a four-step approach in medical and ethical counselling can be used. This four-step method (Table 2) helps the carrier, presymptomatic or symptomatic, to make decisions for himself or herself or in family planning.

Identifying the Moral Agents

The moral agents for making decisions, exclusively or jointly, could be governed by law, insurance companies or health care systems, religious or societal groups, consulting professionals (clinician and/or geneticists, ethicist, or team),

Table 2
Action guide in patient-centred predictive medicine

---

1 Identify the problem
   (a)   collect genetic data
   (b)   collect human data
   (c)   identify value elements

2. Develop alternative scenarios for action
   (a)   establish medical/genetic prognosis for each scenario
   (b)   identify ethical principles in each scenario
   (c)   discuss ethical issues in each scenario

3. Discuss risks and uncertainties of prediction
   (a)   discuss medical and moral uncertainty and risk
   (b)   identify moral agents
   (c)   assist patient to identify 'best solution'

4. Challenge the patient's medical-moral decision
   (a)   ask patient to clearly specify his or her reasoning
   (b)   help patient to understand risks and uncertainties
   (c)   ask patient to defend his or her decision

---

families, spouses, and women. In this and the following scenarios, my personal choice would be to make the woman the prime moral agent for reproductive choice and responsible parenthood. She is the nucleus, as she carries the future person in her, it is a part of her body, and no one has the same degree of access to it. The wider circle of responsible agents includes spouse, family, physician (primarily clinicians rather than geneticists) and ethicists. All of the latter should play consultative roles but should not be the deciding authority (non-directive counselling!). I see some reasons for moral input on behalf of the payment system (however that is organized), but very minimal rights of the state to intervene in very private family matters. In addition to this, the cultural context must be taken into account. There might be a difference between post-enlightment European individualism and traditional Confucian and Asian thinking with regards to the framework of family network and solidarity which will affect the decision and ethical process.

Final Questions

Let me conclude with questions rather than answers. Answers are not easy in modern pluralistic societies which value individual self-determination; they are even more complicated in the global multicultural world. Predictive medicine presents new scenarios for the physician-patient interaction and will change priorities among traditional principles, maxims, and models of medical ethics. Progress in DNA testing and in predictive medicine is more a challenge to legal ethics than to the medical profession. Acute crisis-style intervention, step-by-step, will have to be replaced by non-acute predictive or preventive discourse. New methods of assessing technical and ethical risks and probabilities will have to be developed in order to translate the 'certainty' hereditary facts into the 'uncertainty' of prognosis and health risks, quality of life parameters, health literacy and self determination of the citizen/patient, and the design of prevention and therapy.

There are five questions which might be helpful in discussion of these issues:

1. Who is the prime moral agent ?
2. Is there a duty to know or a right not to know ?
3. How will predictive medicine influence future medicine ?
4. How will predictive medicine influence future medical ethics ?
5. How will the 'global village' deal with the challenge of these new moral issues ?

Notes

1. Blum, 1993.
2. Breuning, 1990.
3. Kimberling, 1988.
4. Gabow, 1993.
5. Gardner, 1989.
6. Grantham, 1984.
7. Kielstein, 1993.
8. Kielstein and Sass, 1992.
9. Handyside, 1992.

References

H. E. Blum, F. v Weizsäcker, and F. Walter, 'Gentechnologie und Medizinische Bedeutung', *Deutsche Medizinische Wochenschrift* 118 (1993): 629–633.

M. H. Breuning, F. G. M. Snijdewint, H. Brunner, A. Verwest, J. W. Lido, J. J. Saris, J. G. Sauwerse, L. Blonden, T. Keith, D. F. Callen, V. J. Hyland, G. H. Xiao, G. Scherer, D. R. Higgs, P. Harris, L. Bachner, S. T. Reeders, G. Germino, P. L. Pearson, and G. J. B. van Ommen, 'Map of 16 Polymorphic Loci on the Short Arm of Chromosome 16 Close to the Polycystic Kidney Disease Gene (PKD 1), *Journal of Medicine and Genetics* 27 (1990): 603–613.

P. A. Gabow, 'Autosomal Dominant Polycystic Kidney Disease'. In K. D. Gardner Jr. and J. Berstein, eds., *The Cystic Kidney* (Dordrecht: Kluwer Academic Publishers, 1990).

P. A. Gabow, 'Autosomal Dominant Polycystic Kidney Disease', *New England Journal of Medicine* 29 (1993): 332–342.

K. D. Gardner Jr., 'Hereditary and Congenital Renal Disease'. In S. G. Massry and R. J. Glassock, eds., *Textbook of Nephrology Vol. 1*, 2nd Ed. (Baltimore: Williams & Wilkins, 1989).

J. J. Grantham and S. L. Slusher, 'Management of Renal Cystic Disorders'. In W. N. Suki and S. G. Massry, eds., *Therapy of Renal Diseases and Related Disorders* (Boston: Martinus Nijhoff, 1984).

A. H. Handyside, J. G. Lesko, J. J. Taris, M. L. Robert ML, and M. R. Winnton-

Hughes, 'Birth of a Normal Girl After In Vitro Fertilisation and Preimplantation Diagnostic Resting for Cystic Fibrosis', *New England Journal of Medicine* 327(13) (1992): 905–909.

R. Kielstein, 'Klinik, Genetik und Ethik der Autosomal Dominant Polyzystischen Nierenerkrankung'. In *Medizinethische Materialien. Heft* 82 (Bochum: Zentrum für Medizinische Ethik, Ruhr Universität, 1993).

R. Kielstein and H. M. Sass, 'Right Not to Know or Duty to Know?', *Journal of Medical Ethics and Philosophy* 17(4) (1992): 395–405.

W. J. Kimberling, P. R. Fain, J. B. Kenyon, D. Goldgar, E. Sujansky, and P. A. Gabow, 'Linkage Heterogeneity of Autosomal Dominant Polycystic Kidney Disease', *New England Journal of Medicine* 319 (1988): 913–918.

6

Ethical Considerations Arising From Economic Aspects of Human Genetics

Edward S. Golub

Biotechnology can be defined as the creation of the tools that biologists use to study the genes of animals and plants, both to understand life processes, and to use this knowledge for commercial applications.[1] The Scientific Revolution in seventeenth-century Europe brought together of *scientia* and *techne*, knowing and doing so that at this crucial point in western intellectual history the confluence of understanding the world and using that understanding to change it came together to give us the basis of much of our science-based, industrialized world.[2] It is clear that biotechnology is the very visible marriage of *scientia* and *techne*, and because of this we cannot really consider the ethical aspects biotechnology without considering how it is to be used in commerce.

In this paper, I will not discuss biotechnology in terms of the study of the genes of plants, but only in terms of the study of the genes of one small, but extremely interesting group of animals — humans. And I will limit the discussion only to questions of medicine. I use this limited scope to accentuate ethical questions that are of concern not only to professional philosophers and ethicists, but also to scientists and physicians, and to ordinary citizens in society. Because of my background I approach the topic with a completely Eurocentric vision, but I am aware that the topic requires a more ecumenical approach to be really meaningful.

Science, Technology and the Framing of Disease

At the foundation of the association of biotechnology and medicine is the all but universal assumption that the maintenance and improvement of human health is amenable to technological intervention driven by scientific understanding. Science as we know it came late to medicine, and it has had a profound effect not only on how we attempt to maintain health and treat disease, but also on how we frame disease and conceive of health. After the late nineteenth century, when disease was framed in terms of specific causes and for the first time we could think about specific cures, there has been little questioning of the limits of technology in the maintenance and improvement of health. And because of this, until very recently there has been little critical examination of the goals of scientific-medicine.[3] I will argue that this combination of uncritical reliance on technology and lack of questioning of the goals of medicine has led us to potential ethical questions that can no longer be ignored.

In this paper I will address some of the ethical problems in terms of the technology that is coming out of genetics and the Human Genome Project because the great advances in the science of genetics epitomises some potential technological problems we face, and because the Genome Project is the first 'big' science project of modern biology.

Most people would agree with the following dictionary definition of disease: The condition of being (more or less) out of health; illness, sickness.[4] People in all societies and in all periods of history, as far as we can tell, have worried about 'being out of health', and we know that all cultures have variants of their own traditions of maintaining and restoring it. Yet consider these two statement by well-known historians of medicine:

> I assert, to begin with, that 'disease' does not exist.[5]

or a bit less shockingly, that

> [I]n some ways, disease does not exist until we have agreed that it does, by perceiving, naming and responding to it.[6]

These scholars are telling us that the condition of being 'in or out of health' is not absolute; societies define health and disease, and the definition changes with time, even within the same society. And of course, all societies have selected members who are specialists in how the society deals with health and disease. The European tradition of these specialists comes from the Greeks through Hippocrates and Galen, and is one that for over two millennia had as its foundation the idea that health was the proper balance of humours. Over that very long time, collections of symptoms that were regularly seen were given names and identified as unique diseases, and a hierarchy of healers developed who were adept at bringing the humours into balance by various means. But there was little consensus through time and among different factions of healers about what had put the humours out of balance in the first place, and what would be necessary to restore their proper balance. While there were specific collections of symptoms that defined a named disease, diseases themselves were not seen as specific entities with specific causes. Any number of things could put the humours out of balance, many of which we had no control over (climate, miasmas, mephitic vapours, etc.) and so any number of things could put them back into their proper alignment. We know that through most of human history, the diseases that people were most preoccupied with — because they were responsible for the 'constant presence of death' — were infectious diseases.

In my book, *The Limits of Medicine: How Science Shapes Our Hope for the Cure*, I make the point that the major contribution of science to medicine was not the elimination of infectious diseases — because that was brought about by better sanitation and living standards before medicine became scientific — but rather it was the re-framing of disease in terms of specific causes. This had a profound effect because now for the first time, around the middle of the nineteenth century, we could think that if there are specific causes of diseases we should look for specific cures. Modern scientific-medicine is medicine based on this assumption; that all disease has a specific cause and that through science we can find specific cures. Disease became the realm of the scientific-physician; it was to be defined by *scientia* and treated by *techne*.

But this relationship which seems so straightforward opens new ambiguities, and takes us to the very heart of the question of what we call disease, how we treat it, and what we expect from medicine. For example, the prevalence in the United States of clinically apparent prostate cancer in men between the ages of 60 and 70 has for many years been considered to be about 1%. But over 40% of men who have no symptoms and are deemed normal according to the standard physical examination of the prostate have been shown to have microscopic changes in their prostate glands that pathologists associate with very early stages of cancer. And with the increased use of new sophisticated imaging technology, tumours too small to be identified by this kind of physical exam can now be seen in even greater numbers. These are men who exhibit no symptoms of prostate malfunction, or abnormalities during a physical examination; are we to define all of them as having cancer? We had defined the disease by the appearance of clinical symptoms, or the ability of the physician to sense abnormality during the course of a physical examination; are we now to define it as the presence of an image seen by ultrasonography? Should clinicians recommend surgery on the basis of the new tests? If we institute a new definition of the disease the incidence will have gone from 1 to 40% of the population at risk in a few years, does this mean we have an epidemic of prostate cancer?[7]

Remember, the intellectual and emotional impetus for the revolution in framing of disease began when we became convinced that infectious diseases are caused by specific bacteria. We have continued to use this mode of thinking about disease even though we now must deal with diseases that are fundamentally different from infectious diseases. Words like 'epidemic' have entered the language to talk about such diverse topics as the prevalence of breast cancer and urban violence because the idea of a specific cause for being 'out of health' has permeated our thinking. As we enter the twenty-first century we have come to frame as disease, conditions that are the result of our genes. These are not diseases that we 'catch', but diseases that we inherit, and because of our tendency to 'scientificize' and 'medicalize' an increasing number of conditions, we look to the ultimate in specificity, our genes, as causes.

There have been lingering attempts by eugenicists to 'scientifically' categorize behaviour and control the freedom and reproduction of people considered abnormal for many years.[8] Early in 1992 a United States government official suggested that the very serious problem of youth violence, especially in our inner cities, might be addressed by the Public Health Service, the arm of the government responsible for medical research and public health. He suggested that the National Institute of Health examine the genetic component of aggression and violence, and try to find biological markers, especially through brain imaging and genetic testing that would identify those individuals prone to violence. Why even consider a genetic component to youth violence? Because, as the official noted, 78% of violent crimes are committed by 7% of the population, and that population, as every American is repeatedly told, is poor. In the United States the urban poor are preponderantly Black and Hispanic. So on the basis of this social correlation, an apparent genetic association was deduced and a 'violence initiative', similar to the 'genome initiative' that resulted in the Human Genome Project was called for.[9]

Civil rights groups and social scientists immediately claimed that this was a misuse of science; that the social conditions in which those 7% live are the very conditions one would expect to spawn despair and violence among the young. It was pointed out that incarceration rates for black youths was three times that of white youths in 1933, but had risen steadily so that the ratio in 1950 was approximately 4 to 1; in 1960 it was 5 to 1; in 1970 it was 6 to 1; and in 1980 it was 7 to 1.[10] Paradoxically, well into this century one of the traits American whites used as a stereotype of blacks was docility; their acquiescence to the indignities of segregation and other legally sanctioned impediments to full citizenship, and the violence that was perpetrated against them. It has been suggested that if the 'violence initiative' had been initiated in the first decade of this century rather than the last, the genetic correlation would not have been with violence, but rather with meekness.[11] So unless one wanted to argue that evolution was occurring before our very eyes, it seemed only prudent to turn to social factors as the seeds of the problem.[12]

These are just two examples of the kinds of ethical dilemmas we will be creating for ourselves when we to apply twenty-first-century technology to problems we have framed from a nineteenth-century mentality.

Given our growing propensity to look to the authority and technology of science to explain and solve our social problems, and to justify our actions, it is rather predictable that the incredible technical advances that have allowed us to clone and sequence genes has now become the vehicle through which we now want to find specific causes and specific cures. And here is exactly where the danger lies. Technology is only a set of tools, and like all tools, we must suffer the consequences as well as reap the benefits from how we use them. Let me be absolutely clear and explicit; I am not advocating that we do away with scientific-medicine or that technology has no role to play in how we frame and treat disease. My aim is exactly the opposite; I fervently believe that science is one of the great inventions of the human mind and that it is essential for the ordered development of technology as we enter the twenty-first century. I only urge that we examine the possible ethical ramifications of our actions before we do ourselves great harm. If the unexamined life was not worth living for Plato, the unexamined reliance on technology might make our lives quite different from the ones we hope to live.

And how, you ask, is any of this relevant to the commercial aspects of the Genome Project in particular, and genetics in general? The answer lies in the process by which knowing (science) becomes converted into doing (technology). We will focus on the pharmaceutical industry, because that is where biotechnology will be converted into products meant to maintain health and cure disease; an industry firmly built on twentieth-century framing of disease, but producing solutions to twenty-first-century problems.

The Visible Hand of the Market

The modern pharmaceutical industry began in Germany at the turn of the century with the discovery of the antibacterial properties of the sulfonamides, and reached its present form during World War II when it was called on to produce large quantities of penicillin. In fact, penicillin, along with insulin and cortisone, formed the industry as we know it today both in terms of the way it operates and perhaps even more important, in the way the public perceives the importance and efficacy of its products. We have come to have very high expectations of the drugs the industry has produced, and the pharmaceutical companies have, until only last year, been the consistently most profitable corporations in the world. Since throughout most of our history the human population has been concerned almost exclusively with infectious diseases, it is understandable that the lay population saw antibiotics as 'miracle drugs' and then transferred this idea to pharmaceuticals in general. Since the late 1940s infectious diseases have, for the most part, been brought under control in the industrialized nations, and the primary focus of biomedical research has been on non-infectious, chronic diseases, and the primary occupation of the pharmaceutical industry has been in developing drugs to treat these diseases. But as I said, we continue to have an infectious disease mentality in a time when we suffer from chronic diseases.

We have of course come to rely on therapeutic drugs, and the pharmaceutical industry is one of the best examples of society turning over the control and production of an important need to the free market economy. We function on the assumption that factors that affect our health form an industry, and that the forces of the market will ensure that the industry will meet the needs of society. This idea has been a basic tenet of the market economy (Adam Smith's 'invisible hand of the market'), and the pharmaceutical industry worldwide had been assumed to be dramatic proof that the forces of the free market are sufficient to serve the needs of the society.

The recent revelations that the industry spends more money on promoting than developing drugs, and that over half of those drugs developed in the last decade are 'me too' drugs that do not add any therapeutic advantage, has raised questions about just how 'invisible' the hand of the market really is. The assumption that consumers will pay for what they need and want, and that any product that is either un-needed or un-wanted will fail the test of the market has been called into question by this great expenditure of funds on promoting drugs. In one issue of the *New York Times*, the news section reported the fact that more money is spent on advertising (i.e. creating a market) than on research, the financial section stated that the fall in price of the stock of a well regarded biotech company was due to the fact that the market for one of their life-saving drugs (designed of course to treat a specific condition) was not as large as had been predicted and was an indication that the company would have to begin to advertise to create a greater market for their drug (i.e. to treat other conditions).[13]

So in a free market economy in which it is almost an article of faith that the choice of products by the pharmaceutical industry will be determined by the *invisible* hand of the market, it is important to understand how priorities are set and decisions are made about which drugs to develop, test, and market. We must realize that the hand of the market is in fact, very *visible* and look to how it will treat the explosion in genetic information science is giving us.

Established pharmaceutical firms and new start-up biotech companies each face variants of the same fundamental question; will there be a sufficient *return on investment* to justify the development of a product? A start-up biotech firm must attract investors with the promise that there is a large enough market for the potential products to provide an attractive return on their investment, and when the time comes to sell their stock to the public, these companies must also be in a position to assure the larger investing community that there will be sufficient profit to justify investment. Large, established firms also allocate their internal funds based on the potential return on investment; when they decide which of many potential products to develop to keep a flow of products in their 'pipe-line', those with the greatest potential return have a better chance of being developed. The size of the market is therefore crucial in determining if start-ups and established firms will enter into a market. It is always a surprise to those who are not in the industry to realize that market sizes are almost always given in terms of dollar values, not cost of manufacturing and development, incidence of the disease, social needs, etc. (although any of these may be factors in determining the dollar value).

If the dollar value of the market is not large enough to assure a market that will give the desired return on investment, the companies have three options. They can decline to enter into the market, they can raise the unit price of the drug, or they can create an increased need for the drug. But if they choose the third option, there must be enough financial resources in the market they are entering to pay for the product to give the return on investment. Payment is increasingly assured by governments and by private insurers, and governments and insurers are increasingly under pressure from single-disease oriented pressure groups. In the United States, private foundations devoted to calling attention to a particular condition like diabetes, arthritis, or cystic fibrosis have played an increasing role in exerting pressure on insurers and government (a topic that deserves much fuller exploration).[14]

Let me give one example, that of end stage renal disease (ESRD), once known as kidney failure, and before that as Bright's disease. Payment for ESRD treatment by dialysis has for two decades been mandated by federal law, so the diagnosis of ESRD has ceased to be only a medical classification of interest to patients and their doctors, but has become a guarantee of financed treatment. Manufacturers of dialysis machines and reagents, surgeons and hospitals involved in kidney transplantation, and a whole economic apparatus has grown up around this legislative decision.[15] Partly as a result of this example, a great deal of influence is exerted on the choice of disease-areas funded by federal monies, on drugs that are developed by pharmaceutical companies, and on decisions of insurance companies to reimburse. So needs (i.e. markets) can be created in a variety of ways, all of which make the idea of the 'invisible hand' of the market unrealistic. Assuming that there are not inordinate costs projected in the development and testing of a new drug, and that patent protection is adequate for a period of time that will ensure the desired return on investment, what is mythologized as the 'invisible hand' of the market is really aided by the perceptible hand of the manufacturers and special interest groups. The question that we must then ask is, what is there to commercialize from the Genome Project that is relevant to all of this? How can sequencing the entire human genome lead to any products that even those most adept at creating markets can work with? The answer is genetic testing.

Genetic Testing and the Visible Hand of the Market

In the practice of modern scientific-medicine, the decision to treat a patient with a drug is made by the physician, almost always based on one or more laboratory tests. While genetic testing has some place in the differential diagnosis of disease, in general its value is in its ability to predict the probability of the future disease condition of individuals or their offspring. Because of this, the therapeutic interventions resulting directly from the study of our genes are the decision not to have a child, abortion, or gene-transfer (a therapy that is still unproven and one that will not be generally available for many years). Thus, the 'informational medicine' that comes from genetic testing will have as its major emphasis the *diagnosis* of diseases to which the subjects or their children may be susceptible or predisposed.

In fifteen years, we will probably be able to apply a single multiplex test to fetuses in utero, babies at birth, or in many cases, parental carriers, a test that will detect somewhere between 100 and 1,000 of the most common genetic diseases, disease predispositions, and genetic risk factors for environmental insults, drug dose responsiveness, and the like. We will be able to do this extensive fingerprint for any individual, but we will, at least initially, be unable to offer any help based on this information.[16] (Cantor)

So according to this molecular geneticist who is close to the Project, by the early years of the twenty-first century we will have simple tests that will detect the most common genetic diseases, predisposition to those diseases, and the genetic risk factors for environmental insults and drug dose responsiveness. If the twentieth century saw the flowering of biological research, surely the fruits are to be harvested in the twenty-first. What more could science promise than the ability to predict both disease *and* predisposition? But remember, these are promises of solutions for problems that have been framed with an infectious disease viewpoint.

To fully understand the implications of this promise, we must understand two things about our current understanding of genetic diseases. The first is that the diseases for which the tests described above will have predictive value and are caused by a *single* gene defect. There are genetic associations of a great many diseases, but in most of these cases there are *multiple* genes involved, and we have virtually no idea which of them are important and predictive. The second point is that most diseases due to a single gene defect are relatively uncommon; the most common having incidences of around one in 2,000 births. But the most striking thing about them is not so much the number of cases per 1,000 births for any particular trait, but the sheer number of different genetic diseases. The probability of a particular individual being affected by any one of them may be small, but the large number of known, single-gene genetic diseases strikes fear into the heart of any prospective parent. The promise of a test to determine if the parents are carriers of a recessive gene or if the fetus has a rare disease is the fulfillment of the promise of the predictive power of medicine to prevent disease. Some of the single-gene diseases that are currently available for test include:[17]

fragile X syndrome
sickle-cell anemia
Duchenne muscular dystrophy
cystic fibrosis
Huntington's disease
hemophilia
Gaucher and Tay-Sachs

There are less than 1 million people in the United States who suffer from any one of these diseases. This is roughly 2 or 3 per 1,000 of the population.

Now what about the promise that we will be able, with a single test, to determine *predispositions* to disease and genetic risk factors of environmental insults? One reputable source of such potential future tests lists the following susceptibilities to which we can look forward to being screened:

hypertension
dyslexia
atherosclerosis
cancer
manic-depressive disease
schizophrenia
type 1 diabetes
familial Alzheimer's

There are 90 million people in the United States who suffer from one of these eight diseases.[18] This is roughly 500 people per 1,000 population, or one person in every two.

To understand the ethical significance of these numbers, it is necessary to know that in these diseases for which there are 'potential future tests', there is a suspected genetic element (or predisposition) but none of these conditions are caused by a single gene. In other words, if the tests were to be applied to these conditions before it is known which of the genes involved have predictive value for the condition, the predictive value of the tests themselves would be questionable at best.

Now it does not take a knowledge of Aristotle's *Ethics* to realize that to use a test for the genetic 'predisposition' to a disease that has little predictive value because the genetic basis of the predisposition involves many genes, most of which are as yet unknown, is fraught with problems. What is a law firm to make of test results that show that a fifty-year old attorney at the peak of her powers has a 'genetic predisposition' to Alzheimer's disease? Or an airline of the fact that a young pilot in otherwise perfect health has a 'genetic predisposition' to schizophrenia? But if the tests have such low predictive value, why would anyone worry that they will be developed? Will not the forces of the market guarantee that a product with questionable value will not survive? To approach that question, we must return to the factors that will affect the people who will do the developing, manufacturing, marketing, selling, and will be making the profits to return to their investors. I will not insult this audience by suggesting that the free market is an evil cabal that will foist anything on an infinitely malleable public; industry and society often act in concert to create the need for a product. My point is that we must be aware of the factors in society that would act as the 'visible hand' because to a large extent we will be helping to create our own ethical problems.

The Role of the Law in Creating a Market

There are many ways to market the need for massive genetic screening, but one of the most probable is through changes in the law.

> In the UK under the Congenital Disabilities (Civil Liability) Act of 1976 legal action can be brought against a person whose breach of duty to parents results in a child being born disabled, abnormal, or unhealthy. In both the UK and the USA there has been an escalation of litigation concerning genetic disease. Most cases concern physician errors of omission, and it behooves all doctors who provide genetic advice to ensure the validity and up-to-datedness of that information. Thus failure (whether from ignorance or religious objections) to give correct advice, or to refer the consultand to someone who will advise, on the risk of fetal abnormality in a future pregnancy and the possibility of prenatal diagnosis, may constitute medical negligence...*Further, in the USA a physician may now be considered negligent for failing to take a history which includes relevant ethnic and family information.*[19] (emphasis added)

If one aspect of the practice of 'defensive medicine' is to make sure that all patients have undergone a full screen for possible genetic defects, including multifactorial disorders, one need not be a trained economist to see that the market is enormous, and that the economic pressures on corporations to create the atmosphere in which their products can prevent legal actions will be great.

Prospects for the Future

The number of diseases due to mutations at a single gene are not enough to create a market of sufficient size to give the kind of return on investment for gene testing the free market demands. In the US, the total annual market would be around $100 million (at $100/test), the minimum dollar amount for a single blockbuster pharmaceutical. The close to 100 million tests available for conditions in which more than one gene is involved is what the market industry is interested in ($10 billion at $100/test). But for most of the conditions in that list it is not clear that we are close to identifying which of the multiple genes (if any) are predictive, and recent research does not hold out much hope that they soon will be.[20]

The results from 'gene knock out' experiments in mice are showing us that when tested *in vivo*, even the genes whose functions we think are well understood, almost invariably give surprising results causing me to have reservations about the rate at which we will understand the function of multigenic phenomena.[21] If my pessimism is justified, then we must put our faith in the fact that the forces of the market will be able to resist the temptation to wait until science clearly demonstrates that a particular set of genes is unequivocally associated with a conditions before marketing a test.

The problem can be summarized as follows: *large scale* genetic testing of the population is the only way investors can get their return on their money, and society must guard against genes being tested that do not actually predict a tendency or propensity for the condition. The rate of converting science into machines is rapid, that of converting it into drugs is slow; the technology for large scale screening exists and short of legislation, I see no barrier to the visible hand of the market coming into play rapidly. I also see no reason for optimism that advances in genetics will in the near term be able to *reliably* predict alcoholism, schizophrenia or multiple sclerosis by gene testing. I have great fears that whatever genes are available will be screened and large numbers of people will be placed in financial and emotional jeopardy as a result.

Conclusion

The rate of research aimed at understanding the genetic and molecular basis of normal and abnormal metabolic functions is proceeding at a rapid rate and is providing scientists with new insights and surprises. It is already clear that the vast majority of genes that contribute to our development and affect our responses to environmental agents or influence our behaviour act in complex and integrated manners. This research is already revealing redundancies in gene function and properties of emergent systems that will take decades for scientists to fully understand. The Human Genome Project as a major contributor to the interest of the public in gene therapy is aware of its responsibility in educating the public against premature expectations of as yet unproven therapies that have already come from this research, and ethical dangers in the testing for genetic traits that will follow, and has set aside a significant amount of money to explore the ethical and social questions raised by the project.

Historically, commercial forces have created the markets for new technology and we see that the same is true for the commercial uses of the Genome Project and all genetic research. In the present case, however, the commercial forces have been combined with the unbridled enthusiasm of scientists, patient groups lobbying for therapies for individual disease, and a generally uncritical press. Unfortunately, there is no mechanism for the public to make informed decisions if this is the direction it wishes the expenditures in health care to follow. Legislation may be needed for the short term, but society must begin to re-frame disease in light of modern scientific discoveries so that it can have more realistic goals from medicine and the technology that will flow from science.

Notes

1. This definition is loosely taken from a lecture by Lee Hood at the Jackson Laboratory, Bar Harbor, Maine in 1992.
2. Lindberg, 1990; Olson, 1982.
3. I develop these points more fully in my book, *The Limits of Medicine: How Science Shapes Our Hope for the Cure.*
4. Oxford English Dictionary.
5. Francois, 1986, 6.
6. Rosenberg, 1989, supplement 1.
7. Black and Welch, 1993, 1237; Mann, 1993, 102.
8. For extensive discussion, see Chorover, 1979; Kevles, 1985; Duster, 1990; Hubbard and Wald, 1993; Müller-Hill, 1993.
9. Walters, in press.
10. Duster, 1992, 129.
11. Prof. Troy Duster, personal communication.
12. This problem has not gone away however. See Brunner et al., 1993, 578.
13. *New York Times*, 26 February 1993.
14. Marks, 297.
15. Peitzman, 1992.
16. Kelves and Hood, 1992, 105.
17. *Medical World News*, April 11, 1988, 58.
18. Ibid.
19. Connor and Ferguson-Smith, 1984, 121.
20. Gene for Mental Illness Proves Elusive, *New York Times*, 13 Jan 1993.
21. Harlow, 1992, 270.

References

W. Black and G. H. Welch, 'Advances in Diagnostic Imaging and Overestimations of Disease Prevalence and the Benefits of Therapy', *New England Journal of Medicine* 328 (1993): 1237.

H. G. Brunner et al., Abnormal Behaviour Associated with a Point Mutation in the Structural Gene for Monoamine Oxidase A', *Science* 262 (1993): 578.

S. Chorover, *From Genesis to Genocide. The Meaning of Human Nature and the Power of Behavioural Control* (MIT Press, 1979).

J. M. Connor and M. A. Ferguson-Smith, *Essential Medical Genetics* (Oxford: Blackwell Scientific Publications, 1984).

T. Duster, *Backdoor to Eugenics* (London: Routledge, 1990).

T. Duster, 'Genetics, Race, and Crime: Recurring Seduction to a False Precision'. In *DNA on Trial: Genetic Identification and Criminal Justice* (Cold Spring: Cold Spring Harbour Press, 1992).

D. Francois, *Disease and Civilisation. The Cholera in Paris, 1832* (MIT Press, 1986).

'Gene for Mental Illness Proves Elusive', *New York Times*, 13 January 1993.

E. S. Golub, *The Limits of Medicine: How Science Shapes Our Hope for the Cure.* (New York: Times Books/Random House, 1994).

R. Hubbard and E. Wald, *Exploding the Gene Myth* (Boston: Beacon Press, 1993).

E. Harlow, *Nature* 359 (1992): 270.

D. Kevles, *In the Name of Eugenics: Genetics and the Uses of Human Heredity* (California: University of California Press, 1985).

D. J. Kevles and L. Hood, eds., *The Code of Codes: Scientific and Social Issues in the Human Genome Project* (Cambridge, MA: Harvard University Press, 1992).

D. C. Lindberg, 'Conceptions of the Scientific Revolution from Bacon to Butterfield: A Preliminary Sketch'. In D. C. Lindberg and R. S. Westman, *Reappraisals of the Scientific Revolution* (Cambridge: Cambridge University Press, 1990).

C. C. Mann, 'The Prostate-Cancer Dilemma', *Atlantic Monthly* (November 1993): 102.

H. Marks, 'Notes from the Underground: The Social Organization of Therapeutic Research'. In R. Maulitz and D. E. Long, eds., *Grand Rounds: One Hundred Years of Internal Medicine* (Pennysylvania: University of Pennsylvania Press).

B. Müller-Hill, 'The Shadow of Genetic Injustice', *Nature* 362 (1993): 491.

R. Olson, *Science Deified & Science Defied. The Historical Significance of Science in Western Culture*, Vol. 1 (Berkeley: University of California Press, 1982).

S. J. Peitzman, From Bright's Disease to End-Stage Renal Disease. In C. Rosenberg and J. Golden, eds., *Framing Disease: Studies in Cultural History* (Rutgers University Press, 1992).

C. Rosenberg, 'Disease in History: Frames and Framers', *Milbank Quarterly* 1 (1989): supplement 1.

R. Walters, *The Politics of the Federal Violence Initiative* (in press).

7

Technology Assessment, Ethics and Public Policy in Biotechnology: The Case of the Human Genome Project

Joel Zimbelman

The Technological Imperative

Richard Tarnass suggests that Western culture is in large part defined by its inquisitiveness and its search for knowledge through the use of human cognitive faculties.[1] But the Western mind is also motivated by a humanistic impulse: the desire to 'sustain an ethos in which the purposive control of the natural environment for the attainment of . . . [human betterment] and productive knowledge has been considered an appropriate human activity'.[2] Numerous philosophical and religious writers have reflected on the relationship that holds between human beings and their use of tools.[3] *Homo sapiens* (mind maker) has always been *homo faber* (tool maker). But this ability at technological innovation at times has unreflectively expressed itself. In the recent history of the West, one important manifestation of this uncritical attitude has been the acceptance and ultimate dominance of the technological imperative in guiding much social activity: 'If something is technologically feasible, it is desirable'. In the technological imperative, the possibility of technological progress establishes or implies a self-authenticating moral mandate to undertake that task. A society that embodies the technological imperative possesses a surprisingly upbeat assessment of technology in general and its ability to provide the specific means by which human beings, their history, and their cultures can be transformed for the better. The technological imperative is essentially the product of a progressivist philosophy. From this perspective, technological advances are ontological advances that empower human beings to become what they are supposed to be. The technological imperative assumes that the ability and wisdom exists in individuals, but also in the culture or society, to control nature and its processes; and to limit the negative consequences of such developments.[4]

The technological imperative is not without its opponents. One can discern three types of criticisms.

First, there is the empirical critique. French philosopher and Protestant theologian Jacques Ellul argues that technology — through a 'bluff' or false promise — has created as many if not more problems for human beings and their communities than it has solved.[5] In its increasingly sophisticated form, the empirical critique builds on some form of cost- and risk-benefit analysis that quantitatively analyses and weighs the burdens of definable technological development against corresponding improvements in well-being for identifiable persons or the larger, statistically significant society (including, in some calculations, future generations or the biosphere). The empirical critique is often employed to argue against the introduction or expansion of specific technologies.

Second, there exists a psychological critique of the technological imperative. Again, Ellul argues that modern technologies have established — in the form of an impersonal, hegemonic, and alienating 'technological consciousness' — social arrangements that reinforce the survival and dominance of technologies at the expense of human well-being. Even when specific technological advances makes life easier and better in narrow, immediate ways for some people, there may be consequences of a negative and undesirable sort (environmental damage, the concentration of economic power, dependence on elites, and an accompanying loss of any sense of personal power) that decrease human happiness and well-being; that result in psychological burdens and/or illnesses; and that cement in place technocratic and materialistic views of human existence.[6] As a result, the very presence of the technological consciousness impoverishes and overwhelms individuals, societies, and cultures.

Third, there exist a series of philosophical/metaphysical and religious critiques of the technological imperative. The 'anthropological critique,' for example, argues that the technological imperative possesses a view of human nature and a vision of the place of human beings in history and the world that reads the facts of human existence wrong. It makes false assumptions concerning some human capabilities. The anthropological critique, at times dominated by a stark realism and at times uncharitable view of human nature, questions whether human beings are ultimately wise or good enough to manage their power.[7]

In a related vein, the 'desacralization critique' argues that the setting of specific human goals, tendencies, and programmes of action in the context of technological innovation is misguided and wrong by dint of the fact that such innovation undercuts the given order of things. The myths of Adam and Eve and the tragic flight of Icarus are used to define and criticize the hubris of humans who, in their search for self-authentication, cross thresholds best left inviolate and collapse important distinctions best maintained. Liberal society's belief in the possibility of human moral and ontological progress in the context of its use of technological advances comes under particularly strong attack.[8]

Many of these criticisms are compelling, if not toward our society's philosophy of technology in general, then at least toward the forces that animate some technological developments and their applications. Even if one fails to concede fully the points argued above, it is clear that the technological imperative fails to embody the critical reflection (including analysis, evaluation, suspicion, and caution) on technological innovation that is called for in our present circumstances. One can still affirm technological innovation as a noble, moral, and essential human undertaking and yet concede that neither the dominance of the technological imperative nor the development of any specific technology *per se* is necessary. We can reject the 'monster mythology' that surrounds much technology in the late twentieth century and still affirm that some technologies are not worthy of development or appropriation.[9] But to justify such a judgement, we need to develop functional, discriminating, and critical perspectives and tools to assess technologies.

The Art of Technology Assessment

Technology assessment can be defined as 'a comprehensive approach to the analysis of the efficacy of a technology that considers all possible and probable, present and future, intended and unintended effects of a technology on a society'.[10] Technology assessment is more an art than a science.[11] Construing technology assessment as a science suggests that there is a well-established experimental framework at the foundation of such an undertaking that will provide a high level of empirical certitude in our assessment of a given technology. Such a task, this perspective claims, is predominantly an act of deduction and critical reason grounded in an objective and value-free assessment of a situation; an application of known universal and empirically verifiable principles to the challenge at hand. Appropriating the metaphor of technology assessment as science mitigates against making decisions about affirming or rejecting a given technology based on intuition; or political, aesthetic, religious, moral, or spiritual reasons. From a strictly 'scientific' perspective, choices are not legitimately justified on the basis of non-scientific values; or as a function of concerns about what will be 'in the best interests' of persons; or what will add to the enjoyment of the community; or what will allow the culture to flourish.

In contrast to the language of 'science,' the language of 'art' encourages the development of a framework for assessment that embraces — indeed, requires — 'thick description'; a concern with a myriad of issues in addition to strictly 'scientific' facts and data. As an art, technology assessment reflects several characteristics and affirms numerous methodological presuppositions borrowed from philosophy, cultural anthropology, and ethnographic and linguistic analysis. Affirming this intellectual genealogy allows us to establish technology assessment as a task of cultural reflection, creation, and aspiration.[12] Such analysis includes scientific and phenomenological readings of facts, data and contexts; but moral, visionary, imaginative, and humanistic concerns as well. It requires that we take account of the cosmological, anthropological, philosophical, and religious commitments, values, and loyalties of a society and of those who champion and develop technology. Technology assessment construed in terms of the metaphor of art is at times less definitive or precise in its methodology and in the locus of its analysis than it might be if understood as a science. In part this is so because of the difficulty of observing, evaluating, and understanding human action and motivation; in part because of the centrality of human interpretation to the arena of technology assessment. What 'thick description' sacrifices in terms of precision, clarity, simplicity, and strict logical coherence, it makes up for in terms of its comprehensiveness, its appreciation of the complexity of lived experience and the way that historical and cultural development inform the 'structures of signification' in the contemporary setting.[13]

In light of these observations, an adequate framework of technology assessment will need to address four broad concerns.

1. Technology assessment will need to address the scientific, technical, quantifiable, and verifiable dimensions associated with the development and implementation of a given technology. Is the project based on good science? Is its development possible given the general laws of physics? Is the goal toward which we are aiming technically feasible given the present limits on our knowledge and abilities?

2. Technology assessment will need to clarify the extent and types of risks, costs, and benefits associated with a new technology. Such assessment must address the probability and estimated magnitude of both present and future costs, risks, harms, and benefits. It must account for the political costs of a given choice (society's support or lack of support for a specific undertaking); the 'opportunity costs' of pursuing a technological option (what is given up or sacrificed by making a specific choice); and the moral costs (in terms of values, goals, or ideals compromised or sacrificed) implicit in one's choice. Such risk-benefit assessment cannot be value free because, as Childress notes, 'values determine what will count as harms and benefits and how much various harms and benefits will count'. And since 'a cultural theory of risk perception account[s] for the selection of some risks, rather than others', risk benefit analysis must take account of actual and perceived risks in a situation.[14]

Risk and cost/benefit assessment must avoid the problem of engaging in a technology assessment that considers only the interests of some segments of society; some limited time frames; or only very crude and reductionistic or easily quantifiable measures of costs, risks, and benefits.[15] There is significant political pressure to make such assessments quickly and cleanly so that vexing issues can be set aside. But adequate technological assessment will have to avoid the temptation of not throwing its net far enough — of not including in its assessment considerations and issues that are very difficult to quantify. If a chosen framework of technology assessment affirms a mode of analysis that is narrowly quantifiable, it will fail to accomplish an assessment that truly considers the broad interests and needs of human beings and their cultures.

3. Technology assessment must come to terms with the reality of human

beings as creators and users of technology. Certainly this involves some background reflection on philosophical (and perhaps religious) anthropology. But in a more practical and tangible vein it requires that we seek a better understanding of human motivations, capabilities, and proclivities; and an analysis of past technological undertakings for signs of how we think human beings might deal with present technological challenges. What are human beings capable of both intellectually and morally? Do they possess good judgement? Are they able to choose their goals and values clearly, judiciously, and intelligently? Have they exhibited past responsibility in reshaping their history and cultures? Have past technologies been well conceived, and have human beings put those technologies to good, life-enhancing uses? Or are human beings more fundamentally self-serving and self-deceiving; capable of at best glimmers of beneficent action, but possessing a propensity toward egoism and unauthentic consciousness? There has been a tendency during the past century, in spite of what we know about how human beings function and thrive in settings such as politics and science, business and the academy, to assume that right motives and intentions guarantee desired and virtuous outcomes. But our experience in the past with technological development and the delivery of those technologies to society should raise flags of caution in assuming that nobility of goals means nobility of practice.[16] If such an assessment is an accurate description of human beings in the face of technological power, we may have to admit the possibility that there might exist technologies that we ought to forego. Alternately, affirming such an anthropology might require greater effort and energy in establishing limits, procedural constraints, and regulatory mechanisms around the technologies that we do employ.

4. An adequate framework for technology assessment needs to address the broad issue of whether or not the development of a particular technology is socially acceptable; whether its appropriation is consistent with the beliefs, values, and aspirations held by society. Establishing such consensus may appear nearly impossible. Modern pluralistic societies define themselves by the fact that their members share neither specific material conceptions of the good nor unitary definitions of what counts as 'socially acceptable'. Still, respecting this individual and cultural diversity might still allow for limited agreement about what we as a society would desire concerning some proximate social goods (for example, safe streets, clean drinking water, the elimination of smallpox and scarlet fever, and a system of limited taxation).

Determining the social acceptability of some technologies and policies might be nearly impossible because of people's lack of familiarity with or knowledge of the science behind a technology; the reasons for embarking on technological development; the risks associated with a technology; or social conditioning of the society (which might be skeptical or unsupportive of certain types of technological development). But instead of seeking to determine social acceptability directly (through a kind of subjective technology assessment by direct vote) we might instead ask whether or not a given technology is consistent with, and can be justified by recourse to, the dominant moral values or principles that are affirmed by our society. There are several moral values around which many members of our society structure their lives and employ both for guidance and as a means of justifying and defending their actions.[17] These include a general respect for persons as beings whose interests are worthy of consideration; a commitment to due care; and a desire to embody the moral principles of non-maleficence (avoiding harm) and beneficence (removing harm and doing good) on behalf of persons. In addition, most members of our society recognise the importance of respecting the rights to self-determination and some degree of autonomy that persons in our society possess by dint of their humanity and membership in community. At the same time, all societies to some degree are committed to the integrity of community and culture, and recognise that social and biological sustainability are important considerations in policy choices. In crude form, this commitment to the maximizing of the good for all members of society is captured in the broad moral imperative of utility, which seeks the greatest good for the greatest number of people. In its more sophisticated form, the moral imperatives of procedural and distributive justice establish an obligation to seek the fair distribution of the benefits and burdens of social life and policy choices.

Reflecting on the implications of these principles and their use in moral reason-giving and justification as part of a larger process of technology assessment is not easy. Construals of important moral values differ among members of our society; the stringency with which we affirm these values is not identical; and the weight and priority that we assign to specific values is not uniform. Still, in order to pass the social responsibility test, a programme of technology assessment needs to justify itself in terms of such moral and social values.

In the larger context of assessment just outlined, accepting the challenge of developing an identifiable technology is justified only if that technology can pass the tests established by all four criteria. Significant failure on any one of these criteria is grounds for abandoning the development or use of a given technology. But such technology assessment is never an unambiguous process. Incomplete analysis; disagreement about the relevant facts; interpretive incoherence; and conflicts of interest between interest groups and the larger society muddy the analytic waters.

An Introduction to the Human Genome Project

The Human Genome Project (HGP) is a multi-agency international effort to 'map' the human genome — the series of discrete genes in the chromosomal material of human DNA that serve as the code for the expression or production of individual proteins that are the building blocks of life.[18] 'Gene mapping' constitutes several discreet tasks. It seeks to provide researchers and clinicians with a comprehensive map that will reveal the relative location of specific genes on specific chromosomes. It attempts to establish the linkage between specific genes (the way in which certain genes predispose the expression of other genes or are expressed in tandem with other genes). The project will attempt to sequence the base pairs or chemical building blocks of specific genes of interest selected from the 50–100,000 genes in the human genome. Finally, the HGP will attempt to elucidate relevant non-human genome and base sequences where such research is of interest to our understanding of the human genome. In short, the HGP seeks to construct a human genetic 'dictionary' by providing a 'list' of all human genes; by establishing the proper 'spelling' of each gene; by seeking to attach an unambiguous 'definition' to each gene; and by providing us with an appreciation of a functional genetic 'syntax' that govern the complex relations between genes.

A commitment to beneficence and a desire to overcome the debilitating effects of disease and suffering lie at the centre of scientific and policy justifications for support of the Project.[19] The aspiration of those involved with the Project is to facilitate genetic knowledge of all kinds and provide researchers with a powerful tool for future explorations in human biology and medicine. The discovery of specific techniques that result from this new knowledge should increase our ability to diagnose disease; identify weaknesses or pathologies in specific genes; treat disease (through repair, replacement, or some other forms of therapy); prevent the manifestations of certain diseases; and allow for the enhancement of certain desirable traits.

Discussions of biotechnology in general and the HGP in particular are carried out against a background of historical and contemporary cultural realities which explain in part why the Project generates so much controversy among scientists and the public. The past abuse of genetic research and the improper uses of genetic information on individuals and populations is a partial explanation.[20] The mixed record of success concerning scientific prediction in research; the often reductionistic and selective way in which assessments of new technologies are carried out; and the willingness of specific groups within society (scientists, engineers, the medical community) to support technological innovations for economic and political gain rather than social efficacy are other reasons.[21] These observations notwithstanding, I do not believe that the HGP introduces any new ethical dilemmas for society. All of the concerns associated either directly or indirectly with the HGP have already surfaced and have been discussed in other contexts. Still, the ethical challenge created by the HGP is distinctive in several respects. First, the speed with which the Project was established and the rate of making available the fruits of this research to the public outstrip all other significant technological advances in the life sciences. Second, the complexity of quandaries and moral dilemmas gives the appearance of new problems. Third, the heightened awareness of a large number of persons in the society concerning the power of the knowledge provided by the HGP means that potential problems and dangers are quickly and openly communicated to the society. Fourth, the expense of the Project is significant, and debates about the control of such funding by scientific, political, and policy elites is increasingly troublesome to growing numbers of people. Fifth, the paucity of policy analysis and established procedural protection addressed either before or during the early stages of the research programme raises questions about the appropriateness of the project from a public interest perspective.

Ethical, Legal and Policy Concerns Raised by the Human Genome Project

Many of the ethical, legal, social, and policy concerns that surface in an adequate process of technology assessment relate to the way in which HGP research is carried out. Other concerns are a function of the particular knowledge established by the Project; the regulation of such knowledge; the application of that knowledge; and the development of public policy governing biotechnology.[22] Technology assessment of the HGP uncovers four significant and substantive concerns that involve critical issues of ethics, law, and public policy.

1. *Liberty rights.* One ethical concern surrounding research into the HGP is that of liberty rights. This encompasses a debate over how best to define and respect the rights of researchers, institutions, commercial interests, and the public to pursue their own goals. Included here are debates involving the ownership and patentability of different types of knowledge, information, processes, and applications.[23]

A commitment to liberty rights also shapes discussions of how best to respect the freedoms of individuals in the face of the explosive growth and demand for genetic knowledge. Here, concerns revolve around issues of privacy, confidentiality, and proprietary access to and the sharing of information.[24] As Annas and Elias note, '[t]hese issues include what information can be collected, how, by whom, on whose authority, for what purpose, [and] how and to whom the information is disclosed'.[25] One concern of some feminists and supporters of 'family values' focuses on how knowledge from the HGP might inform and shape law and policy with respect to procreative liberty and reproductive choice. Arguments made in this context are closely tied to philosophical and religious debates over definitions of the human and of human authenticity; and issues of power, oppression, and control.[26] Knowledge of the prognosis of or future prospects for certain foetuses established by genetic testing (itself facilitated by the HGP) will certainly influence foetal testing and abortion policy. It should shape debates about who should have the power to decide on testing and abortion; and who will pay for such diagnosis and surgery.[27]

The application of the fruits of the HGP will also have a profound effect on the degree and type of information available through genetic testing to insurance companies assessing the risk of prospective clients (and rewriting actuarial tables and premium calculations based on such information); and to employers who wish to know the genetic profiles (and perhaps related behavioural proclivities) and biological predispositions of their employees.[28] The testing of students in schools for intellectual capabilities has been a fixture of developed societies for decades. However, several social scientists fear that the fruits of the HGP might be applied to behavioural testing with more significant and pernicious effects on the tracking and educating of children, perhaps even resulting in the limiting of certain educational choices for some children because of their genetic constitution.[29] Similar developments in the forensic sciences and even in the testing of young children to be adopted raise important questions about the right to refuse genetic testing and the use of such information once acquired.[30]

2. *Social goods.* As society deals with the fruits of the HGP, it will need to address social and moral issues that go beyond the concerns of liberty, autonomy, and privacy. How can we best respect the integrity of individual choices and freedoms in situations where there exist competing community goods and interests? Such debates will need to address the relevance of other moral values to the debate about genetic knowledge and its uses, including how to avoid harms to persons (non-maleficence); how to seek their good, including physical, psychological, and spiritual integrity (beneficence); and the most acceptable way to employ and weigh risk-benefit analysis and utility in shaping public policy. Here, related concerns are raised about personal and environmental safety, including concerns surrounding the release of genetically engineered organisms into the environment and the implications of germ-line gene therapy on the environment and future generations.[31] Crucial questions about the development of regulatory and tort law will need to be addressed, including questions about evolving standards of evidence and determinations of proximate cause as the basis for tort claims.[32]

Of increasing interest to ethicists and clinicians are two issues related to how public access to practical genetic applications ought to be determined and enhanced. The first focuses on the ethical propriety of testing or screening for genetic defects or predispositions; or for traits that are present but might be genetically enhanced in specific individuals through genetic manipulation.[33] This is a particularly troubling issue when confronting the 'diagnostic/ therapeutic gap'; testing for defective genes whose physical manifestations may not appear for years, and/or for which no successful treatments or funding for treatment exist.[34]

The second concern seeks to determine how best to educate people about the nature and uses of the information gained from genetic testing and counselling; and how best to integrate the availability of such knowledge into medical practice and the delivery of health care.[35]

3. *Distributive and social justice.* The HGP imposes costs, but promises benefits as well. The moral imperative of justice requires that we seek a fair distribution of these benefits — and the burdens — across society.[36] The challenge of justice in this debate can be recognized at several junctures in our process of thinking about allocating resources.

First, justice requires that we address the question of how to allocate scarce resources for support of the many goods (e.g. housing, health care, scientific research projects, education, defense) which are in demand in our society. It also requires that we consider what scheme of distribution for these resources we will employ. This process will involve assessing the relative merits of such goods from a societal point of view; ranking those goods; and then supporting the establishment of such goods according to this ranking. The goods of scientific research, medicine, and health care are all highly valued in our society. But they are not the only goods which we embrace.

Second, within the confines of its life science research and medical care budget, society will need to decide how to allocate resources to fund the HGP and other projects.[37] Some critics argue that the HGP is not good value for the money and argue for less support for the Project. Others suggest that supporting a project of this kind, whose social benefits will most clearly be realized through screening programmes and gene therapy interventions, will simply exacerbate existing inequities in the expensive and high-tech health care industry.[38] Supporters contend that the HGP will increase the likelihood that basic preventive health care services will be inexpensive and available to all.

Third, even if the decision is made to fund (or continue funding) the HGP, society will be forced to decide how to allocate resources among specific aspects of the Project (mapping, base sequencing, related animal studies); specific institutions and individual researchers; and specific lines of research, genes, or disease constituencies.

Fourth, the society will be forced to decide about how to fairly allocate the burden of financial support for and the benefits of clinical services that will be an outgrowth of the HGP. Will such services be available to a broad segment of the society? Or will the increasing expense of such services and products in an era of diminishing health care budgets mean that they will be available only to the relatively well-to-do as a function of their ability to pay? Critics question whether certain racial and cultural groups will ever receive the clinical benefits of this technology — in part because they fall outside the established health care system; in part because of racial and cultural discrimination; and because there exist tendencies in some cultures to eschew genetic screening programs for various reasons.[39]

Indeed, the concern with — and commitment to — social justice will force us to examine other issues, including the way in which we interpret — and apportion — technical, political, and social power in the context of the genetic revolution; and the way in which social relations will be reordered as a result of the introduction of this technology.[40]

4. *Issues of social ethos, culture, philosophy, and religion.* The debate about how a given technology alters the ethos (general values and cultural climate) of a society is of particular interest to anthropologists, social critics, philosophers, scholars in religious studies, and theologians. Several writers have observed that the HGP might easily alter our powers over and perception of human biology and the accompanying ability to reinvent the concepts of human history, society, and biological existence.[41] Here, discussions focus on issues surrounding changing conceptions of human freedom, human limits, and the spectre of reductionism and biological determinism.[42]

Other writers focus on the practical effects of genetic advances on our concrete views of health and the concept of disease (including new definitions of 'normal' and 'abnormal'); and on the effects of genetic manipulation on the concrete ordering of society.[43] The practical result of such an altered ethos might be the establishment of a drive toward human perfectibility through eugenics. Such a programme might too quickly blur the practices of positive and negative eugenics and then fail to distinguish between the correcting of diseases and enhancing certain human traits.[44]

Establishing Policy in Biotechnology After the HGP: Some Issues to Consider

Asking for absolute certainty with respect to the safe and ethical development and implementation of any technology is perhaps futile. One cannot ask for greater prescience and certainty than is compatible with human nature. But as we back into the future, we can at least make sure that our heads are turned.

The opportunity of fully informed and leisurely debate over whether or not to embark on the HGP is past. The initial phase of crude relative gene mapping that is one basic goal of the HGP has been completed. Sequencing of disease-linked genes and other genes of interest in both humans and animals is proceeding vigorously. Some critics argue that society's opportunity for limiting in any significant way the scope and trajectory of the HGP has evaporated. It would be disingenuous, they argue, to act as if technological assessments and ethical or policy discussions might serve any constructive purpose. I disagree. Technology assessment can still play a significant and decisive role by raising questions about who should be involved in making decisions about the future of the HGP; about whether or not to continue funding of the HGP; about which aspects of the Project to continue to support and which to abandon; about how best to regulate the distribution of the information generated by the HGP; about how to guarantee that the fruits of the HGP are fairly and safely distributed to society; and about how to handle the information we gain from applications derived from the HGP. Let me venture some modest proposals about the general characteristics of such a policy framework.

1. Critical discussions of HGP policy ought to be governed by an initial presumption: 'Cautious prohibition until proven probably efficacious'. All technological innovation ought to justify itself according to this presumption. Individuals, corporations, and federal agencies ought to be limited in their initiation, pursuit, and financial support of research on a given technology and its applications until it has passed an initial technological assessment.

Several sorts of arguments support this conservative presumption. The most compelling in our present ethos is the argument from possible consequences — a sort of negative Pascalian Wager. In light of what we know about human tendencies and proclivities in the face of mesmerizing technology, our actions ought to be governed by a 'heuristic of fear' that treats the doubtful but possible as if it were certain.[45] In the present situation, where technologies develop so quickly; where they cost so much (with funding for initial research and development almost always at taxpayers' expense); where the environmental, social, cultural, and psychological effects and consequences of technological wagers remain so unclear for long periods of time; and where new technologies possess the power to transform so completely the lives of so many; social policy agendas must have the power to trump the hypothetical and/or hopeful claims of the 'prophets of bliss'. As a first consideration, then, we must rise 'to the level of moral seriousness . . . [where] . . . we are prepared at least to contemplate saying No. That we are prepared to say it does not mean we must, but it means we may'.[46]

A corollary of this governing principle is that the assessment of a given technology or application must be continual and on-going. Known facts; perceived and understood risks, costs, and benefits; and social needs and desires change. Such new information must be factored into ongoing critical reflections. In particular, the evaluation of public financial support should be a continuous process. Such assessment follows from our moral commitment to the moral principles outlined earlier, including the principle of utility and the fiscal efficiency that it implies. Hundreds of millions of dollars have already been spent on the HGP. But the justification of future funding should rest on complex and sophisticated risk/benefit assessment and critical moral reflection, not on our past record of support or the degree of financial exposure. Indeed, one good test of an authentic programme of technology assessment is the willingness of its assessors to terminate support for a project when it no longer appears able to deliver on its promises.

Additionally, we need more seriously to consider matching funding (and therefore the pace of the final stages of mapping and increasingly sequencing) with the larger task of technology assessment. Reducing funding will allow for more adequate assessment at this crucial juncture in the technology's development (that is, as we move from mapping and sequencing to applying the fruits of that work to functional needs and challenges).

This conservative precondition should not be interpreted as an anti-technological bias. Exactly the opposite is the case. It is because of a fundamental faith that some technological advance is good for human beings and compatible with sustainable existence in our ecosystem; and because of the belief that technological naysayers are wrong in their basic orientation toward and interpretation of the technological undertaking, that we must hold to this conservative presumption. Only technological line-drawing based on this principle can assure the long-term survival of a technological future.

2.   The decision-making process that animates all technology assessment must be open to individuals whose analysis, insights, recommendations, and political support represent the complexity of the society at large. Such decision-making authority should not be limited to (though it ought to include the perspectives of) technocrats, professionally trained policy analysts, or scientists. A number of reasons for supporting this procedure exist. First, good decision making requires numerous perspectives for the simple reason that professionals do not possess privileged knowledge concerning the social propriety of specific policy choices. There is no necessary or essential connection between technical

knowledge of a discipline or profession and the ability to assess that technology as that process has been defined in this chapter (to define risks and benefits; to know the extent of the 'facts' which should be included in appropriate to technology assessment; and to appreciate the ethos and complex moral values affirmed by the society and their relevance to assessments of technology). It is true that this complexity can turn from an asset into a liability (as discussion and debate become carnival and cacophony). But such a risk may be justified in the face of the obligation to protect society against a technocratic reductionism in critical reasoning.

A second reason to aim for diversity in discussions and decision making is that it supports the democratic values — respect for persons, tolerance, and certain substantive and procedural principles of justice — to which our society aspires. Part of what it means to be a liberal and democratic society is to support the establishment of intellectual and social space in which we can pursue open debate, discussion, dissention, and decision making.

A third reason for demanding diverse representation in policy decision making is that it affirms a commitment to a realist assumption about human nature. In light of what we know about decision making and the uses — and abuses — of power among entrenched and unregulated elites, broad representation in decision making provides a counterweight to and a check against the pretensions of individuals who might subvert the process of technology assessment to their own parochial interests. A multiplicity of voices and perspectives dilutes the power of any one group.

A fourth reason to insist on this arrangement is to affirm the enduring importance of political compromise. Supporting such an open process allows us to more successfully deflect later negative public reaction to some bad decisions that might compromise a larger agenda of sound technology assessment. There are costs to public participation — in lost time, efficiency, money, and a loss of clean and unambiguous consensus on hard choices. But when professional elites have restricted public participation in decision making and bad choices are the result, 'the public's disappointment is reinforced by their lack of involvement'.[47] Not surprisingly, this can hamper the growth and development of many other worthy technologies through increased cynicism or new levels of risk-aversion in society.

3. Society must affirm a commitment to an ongoing programme of public education and heightened public discourse in technological and scientific matters. We need to give greater attention and financial support to public education about emerging technologies. If we are committed to public participation in technological debate we also need to be committed to public preparation for such debate. While the 3% of the HGP budget set aside for education and discussions of ethics is a significant start, much more will have to be done in educating at an earlier age (as part of grade school and high school curricular goals and through better teacher education); in broadly disseminating information and seeking an informed public; and in establishing informed debate about technology assessment as an integral part of our social discourse.

4. Society should strive to decrease government involvement in technological developments, but reaffirm its commitment to regulatory oversight of such developments. Communal resources cannot be found to fund the development of every technological innovation that is seen as possibly efficacious (and indeed, governments in general have shown a disappointing capacity to discriminate between effective and helpful technological projects and 'white elephants').

Several reasons exist for advocating this shift for government away from 'technological innovator' to 'technological policeman'. In a pluralistic society where groups of citizens (who are also taxpayers) may object, on moral grounds, to specific technological development programmes, it is not clear that the government is justified in pursuing such developments (though libertarian principles at the foundation of much of our political theory allow for individual citizens or voluntary associations to pursue their interests as long as such pursuits do not harm others). By decreasing government involvement in technological undertakings, society avoids conflicts of interest and affirms this libertarian principle. By supporting public funding for a regulatory infrastructure, we assure that the general wishes and interests (including obligations of beneficence and non-maleficence and protection from risk) of the people are nonetheless factored into the development of technologies.[48]

Such a regulatory mechanism might be established at several levels (local and state; national and international — perhaps integrated into existing commercial, trade, treaty, and security pacts); and address a number of regulatory concerns, including guidelines governing the financing of technological research and development; the substance of assessment frameworks; guidelines for the testing and introduction of the fruits of a given technology; and laws governing the property and proprietary rights of such technologies. Agencies would be responsible to limit research and development if the procedural and substantive goals of technology assessment were not met. But they would also be able to move technological insights that appear strong and efficacious toward earlier development.

Certainly the above task is made difficult by the competitiveness of some technological developments in the private sector and between nations; and the proprietary knowledge involved in certain technological discoveries and applications. But by displaying a dedication to rigorous regulatory control, supporters of many technologies (including the HGP) could do much to disarm their most vociferous critics. By arguing that there are limits that will not be crossed in developing and exploiting the human genome, such researchers protect turf already hard won.

Substantively, such regulation needs to seriously address the concerns involving HGP applications such as genetic testing and screening; the uses and management of information resulting from widespread use of the technology; and environmental safety. These issues are important for practical reasons. They are the issues that we are most able to address and control, and that have captured the interest and excited the passions of a public. But of course other concerns exist.[49]

5. Society must give significant and increasing weight in its assessments of the HGP to considerations of distributive justice. One practical and political reason for this requirement is that freedom and liberty without justice is, over the long run, unsustainable. It is because we are committed to a just, sustainable, and participatory society that we wish the fruits of individual initiative and creativity to be exercised. Our hope is that such activity will, via mechanisms that we have put in place in our society, lead to a society empowered by the discoveries and inventions of the few. At the same time, the commitment to distributive justice suggests that, when publicly funded and supported projects will not be fairly and justly distributed to the larger society, it is difficult to justify government support for such undertakings.

This interpretation of the facts and formulation of the requirements of justice is relevant for several reasons. Because we have given public support to the Project, the imperative of socially rather than strictly marked-controlled distributions schemes will always be relevant in the field of genetic mapping and engineering. Even if public support is withdrawn at some future date (it shows no sign of this yet), the HGP will always and only exist by dint of past public support. If society's financial support of the HGP is to continue to be ethically justified, then broad access to the fruits of the HGP needs to be guaranteed.

Unfortunately, there is little evidence to date that the fruits of gene mapping (including diagnostic tests, products, and related gene therapy) are being equitably distributed. And present pressure to hold the line on health care costs (and to avoid rational rationing decisions for the resources that we do have) raises questions about the possibility of ever attaining fair access to the fruits of genetic research. The push toward a health care system that emphasizes preventive health care might make such widespread access a possibility, but even preventive programmes do not usually increase genetic screening budgets.

There is little evidence that the concerns of distributive justice are of significant concern to those funding and regulating the HGP. Again, this could change substantially as we move from the crude mapping phase to the development, testing, and introduction of tests and products growing out of HGP. My suggestion here would simply be that serious reflection about equitable access needs to be part of broad policy discussions now.

Promises and Perils of the HGP

Should the HGP continue to receive the support of our society? This paper has not conducted a thorough technology assessment on the HGP. Indeed, all I have done is alert the reader to a consideration of such an assessment; and have indicated the terrain in which such an assessment should be conducted. Until such a thorough assessment is performed, I think the question of continuing support should not be answered. I remain pessimistic about our society's ability to reap the fruits of this technology in a way which strengthens its fabric and the life of its members. But my excitement at the promises of the technology and its many applications engenders a hopefulness that the

Project can live up to its promises. The HGP may allow us to more successfully pursue an approach to the practice of medicine and the delivery of health care that is more oriented toward prevention and early treatment.[50] If it is to fulfill those promises, however, society will have to give greater attention to anticipating concerns and issues; reveal the diverse stakeholders in the debate; more clearly articulate the moral values to which it is committed (and provide a clearer picture of how genetic technology fits into the structure of a good society); and come clean on the difficult policy decisions it faces.[51]

Even technological Cassandras must admit that the progress made on the Project to this point is impressive. And as the fruits of the HGP are applied to practical human needs — as is beginning to happen now — the public's support for the Project will grow. But wishing for something good to happen is not the same as being assured that the good will result. For that to happen, society needs to take much more seriously the challenge and the risks of biotechnology.

Notes

1. Tarnass, 1991, 69–72.
2. Long, 1986, 614.
3. Mitcham notes that 'technology is . . . the making and using of artifacts in the most general sense,' Mitcham, 1980, 282. For many thinkers, the issues of major interest surrounding discussions of technology focus on its perceived dependence on or autonomy from human self-understanding and volition (Ellul, Marcuse, Heidegger); issues surrounding the general valuation of technology or identifiable technologies; its 'goodness' or 'badness' (Rousseau, Tielhard de Chardin, Mumford); and the degree to which human beings either consciously or unconsciously appropriate technology (Ortega y Gasset), see Mitcham, 1980, 286–287.
4. A number of philosophers and theologians appear to echo this general tendency linking technological discovery and development to fundamental human ontology. For example, Dessauer posits a 'technological mysticism' in which such activity is viewed as an extension of divine creation and incarnation. Mounier suggests that such a creative impulse reflects humanity's 'demiurgic function,' see Mitcham, 1980, 290–293. The Jesuit Teilhard de Chardin emphasizes the movement of the human spirit toward a moment of ultimate ontological transformation facilitated by and constituting a creative technological mastery of the world, Barbour, 1993, 7, 269. The Uruguayan Jesuit philosopher and liberation theologian Juan Luis Segundo argues that human creative activity ought to seek to establish humanity's 'dominion over nature' as one manifestation of its drive for human solidarity and supernatural transformation, Segundo, 1976, 150. Other thinkers focus on social effects as a means of justifying an optimistic reading of technology (Buckminster Fuller, Herman Kahn, and Alvin Toffler).
5. Ellul, 1964, 1990 and summarized in Mitcham, 1990, 287, 309–312.
6. Barbour, 1993, 9–10.
7. Jonas, 1976, 1984.
8. This argument is developed from various theological perspectives by George Bernanos, David Brinkman, and Emil Brunner. See also Ramsey, 1970, and contributions in Mitcham and Grote, 1984.

9. Annas, 1990.
10. Childress, 1981, 101.
11. cf. Lakoff and Johnson, 1981.
12. Geertz observes that 'Believing . . . that man is an animal suspended in webs of significance he himself has spun, I take culture to be those webs and the analysis of it to be therefore not an experimental science in search of laws but an interpretive one in search of meaning,' Geertz, 1973, 5–7.
13. Geertz, 1973, 9.
14. Childress, 1986, 557, 558; Watchbroit, 1991a. The philosophical underpinnings of cost and risk/benefit analysis are discussed by Rescher, 1983; Wilson and Crouch, 1982; and Douglas and Wildavsky, 1982. Applications to the assessments of genetic technology are discussed by Wachbroit, 1991a, 1991b; Sharples, 1991; Levin and Strauss, 1991; Fiskel and Covello, 1986; Naimon, 1991; Cohen and Chambers, 1991.
15. Childress, 1986, 558.
16. Swazey, 1988; King, 1992, 96–102; Swazey, 1992; Caplan, 1992a, 285–301.
17. Beauchamp and Childress, 1989; Munson, 1992, 30–38.
18. In the United States, the HGP is sponsored by the Human Genome Program of the U.S. Department of Energy and the National Center for Human Genome Research of the National Institutes of Health. The HGP has established the Joint Working Group on Ethical, Legal, and Social Issues in Human Genome Research (ELSI), which receives 3% of all federal funds supporting the HGP. The Human Genome Organization (HUGO) is an international body assisting in coordination of separate national genome programs. The Johns Hopkins University Genome Database in Maryland, USA is a repository for much of the mapping and sequencing information resulting from the HGP. For an introduction to the molecular biology and research techniques related to the Project, see Caplan 1992a, 118–123; Pickering, 1991, 125–127; Beckwith, 1991; 1–8; Judson, 1992; Karjala, 1992, 124–151; Brenner, 1990; Kevles, 1992; Office of Technology Assessment, 1988, 21–75; Davis, 1990. For discussions of the Project's origin, structure, scope, management, politics and funding, see Durfy and Grotevant, 1991, 347–350; McKusick, 1992; Kevles and Hood, 1992, 300–328; National Research Council, 1988; Cook-Deegan, 1991; United States Department of Health and Human Services and Department of Energy, 1990. Ongoing progress of the HGP is covered in *Human Genome News*.
19. Caplan, 1992a, 118–123; Mackler and Barach, 1991, 153–154; Collins, 1991, 260–265; and a rebuttal to such claims by Beckwith, 1991, 5–7.
20. Caplan, 1992a, 124–127.
21. Swazy, 1992.
22. Fletcher and Wertz, 1990. Bibliographies of legal, ethical, and public policy literature related to the HGP are provided in Center for the Study of Law, Science, and Technology, 1992, 223–311; Durfy and Grotevant, 1991; Walters and Kahn, 1991, 1992, 1993.
23. Karjala, 1992, 192–203; Brahams, 1990; Carey and Crawley, 1990, 133–143; Eisenberg, 1990, 1992.
24. Macklin, 1992; Karjala, 1992, 163–166; Draper, 1992; Greely, 1992; Caplan, 1992b, 128–131.
25. Annas and Elias, 1992, 7.
26. Lewontin, 1992, 38; Draper, 1992, S15-S17; Rothman, 1989; Stanworth, 1987.
27. Robertson, 1992; Bonnicksen, 1992; Karjala, 1992, 157–160; Caplan, 1992a,

126; Cowan, 1992; Office of Technology Assessment, 1988, 83–84; Lippman, 1991.

28. Gostin, 1991; Juengst, 1991.
29. Nelkin and Tancredi, 1991; Karjala, 1992, 166–192; Andrews and Jaeger, 1991; United States Congress, 1990.
30. Nelkin and Tancredi, 1991; Lander, 1992; Sensabaugh and Witowski, 1989; Committee on DNA Technology in Forensic Sciences, 1992; Ballantyne, 1989.
31. Capron, 1986, 174–178; Elias and Annas, 1992; Sharples, 1991; Walters, 1991, 269–273.
32. Karjala, 1992, 155–156; Bazleon, 1986.
33. White and Caskey, 1992; Holtzman, 1989.
34. See the discussion of this issue in relation to Huntington's disease in Terrenoire, 1992; DeGrazia, 1991; MacKay, 1991; and Wexler, 1992.
35. Nelken and Tancredi, 1989; Nelken, 1992; Juengst, 1991, 72; Collins, 1991, 264.
36. Carey and Crawley, 1990.
37. Rechsteiner, 1990, 4.
38. King, 1992, 94–96, 98–99.
39. King, 1992; Lippman, 1991.
40. Nelkin and Tancredi, 1989.
41. Swazy, 1992; Caplan, 1992a; Capron, 1986.
42. 'The importance of the Human Genome Project lies less in what it may, in fact, reveal about biology ... than in its validation and reinforcement of biological determinism as an explanation of all social and individual variation', Lewontin, 1992, 34. See also Jonas, 1976 and 1984; and a counter-argument by Charlesworth, 1990, 180–189. Theological perspectives are introduced by Lammers and Peters, 1990, 869; Meilaender, 1990; Ramsey, 1970; and Mitcham and Grote, 1984.
43. Caplan, 1992b; Keller, 1992; Lewontin, 1992, 34.
44. Office of Technology Assessment, 1988, 84–85; Keller, 1992; Wikler and Palmer, 1992; Nelkin and Tancredi, 1989; Nolan, 1992; Bonnicksen, 1992; Karjala, 1992, 160–161.
45. Jonas, 1976, 87–91.
46. Meilaender, 1990, 872.
47. Bazelon, 1986, 83.
48. Bazelon advocates the establishment of comprehensive regulatory law to address these concerns, rather than depending on common law and judicial innovation to answer the society's need for adjudication of conflicts: 'damages must be addressed through regulation to prevent harm rather than litigation to redress it. Control of such risks cannot be left to the ad hoc value of judges through possibly inconsistent determinations at trial', Bazelon, 1986, 78.
49. Skene, 1991; Juengst, 1991, 72–73.
50. Karjala, 1992, 151.
51. Barbour, 1993, 229–230.

References

L. B. Andrews and A. S. Jaeger, 'Confidentiality of Genetic Information in the Work Place', *American Journal of Law and Medicine* 17(1/2) (1991): 75–108.
G. Annas and S. Elias, 'The Major Social Policy Issues Raised by the Human Genome

Project'. In G. Annas and S. Elias, eds., *Gene Mapping: Using Law and Ethics as Guides* (New York: Oxford University Press, 1992).

G. Annas, 'Mapping the Human Genome and the Meaning of Monster Mythology', *Emory Law Journal* 39(3) (Summer 1990): 629–664.

J. Ballantyne et. al., eds., *DNA Technology and Forensic Science. Banbury Report: No. 32* (Cold Spring Harbor, NY: Cold Spring Harbor Press, 1989).

I. Barbour, 'Ethics in an Age of Technology'. *The Gifford Lectures*, Vol. 2 (New York: HarperCollins Publishers, 1993).

D. Bazelon, 'Governing Technology: Values, Choices and Scientific Progress'. In J. G. Perpich, ed., *Biotechnology in Society: Private Initiatives and Public Oversight* (New York: Pergamon Press, 1986).

T. Beauchamp and J. Childress, *Principles of Biomedical Ethics*, 3rd Ed. (New York: Oxford University Press, 1989).

J. Beckwith, 'The Human Genome Initiative: Genetics' Lightning Rod', *American Journal of Law and Medicine* 17(1/2) (1991): 1–14.

A. Bonnicksen, 'Genetic Diagnosis of Human Embryos'. In 'Genetic Grammar', Special Supplement, *Hastings Center Report* 22(4) (July-August 1992): S5-S11.

D. Brahams, 'Human Genetic Information: The Legal Implications'. In D. Chadwick, G. Bock, and J. Whelan, eds., *Human Genetic Information: Science, Law and Ethics* (Chichester and New York: John Wiley & Sons, 1990).

S. Brenner, 'The Human Genome: The Nature of the Enterprise'. In D. Chadwick, G. Bock, and J. Whelan, eds., *Human Genetic Information: Science, Law and Ethics* (Chichester and New York: John Wiley & Sons, 1990).

A. Caplan, *If I Were a Rich Man Could I Buy a Pancreas? And Other Essays on the Ethics of Health Care* (Bloomington: Indiana University Press, 1992a).

A. Caplan, 'If Gene Therapy is the Cure, What is the Disease?' In G. Annas and S. Elias, eds., *Gene Mapping: Using Law and Ethics as Guides* (New York: Oxford University Press, 1992b).

A. Capron, 'Human Genetic Engineering,' 171–183 in Joseph G. Perpich, ed., *Biotechnology in Society: Private Initiatives and Public Oversight* (New York: Pergamon Press, 1986).

N. H. Carey and P.E. Crawley, 'Commercial Exploitation of the Human Genome: What Are the Problems?' In D. Chadwick, G. Bock, and J. Whelan, eds., *Human Genetic Information: Science, Law and Ethics* (Chichester and New York: John Wiley & Sons, 1990).

Center for the Study of Law, Science, and Technology, Arizona State University, 'The Human Genome Project: Bibliography of Ethical, Social, Legal, and Scientific Aspects', *Jurimetrics Journal* 32(2) (Winter 1992): 223–311.

M. Charlesworth, 'Human Genome Analysis and the Concept of Human Nature'. In D. Chadwick, G. Bock, and J. Whelan, eds., *Human Genetic Information: Science, Law and Ethics* (Chichester and New York: John Wiley & Sons, 1990).

J. F. Childress, *Priorities in Biomedical Ethics* (Philadelphia: Westminster Press, 1981).

J. F. Childress, 'Risk'. In J. F. Childress and J. Macquarrie, eds., *The Westminster Dictionary of Christian Ethics* (Philadelphia: Westminster Press, 1986).

J. I. Cohen and J. A. Chambers, 'Biotechnology and Biosafety: Perspective of an International Donor Agency'. In M. A. Levin and H. S. Strauss, eds., *Risk Assessment in Genetic Engineering: Environmental Release of Organisms.* McGraw-Hill Environmental Biotechnology Series, series editors R. M. Atlas, E. P. Greenberg, A. L. Demain, B. H. Olson, and G. Sayler (New York: McGraw-Hill, 1991).

F. C. Collins, 'Medical and Ethical Consequences of The Human Genome Project', *Journal of Clinical Ethics* 2(4) (Winter 1991): 260–267.

Committee on DNA Technology in Forensic Science, National Research Council Staff, *DNA Technology in Forensic Science* (Washington, D.C.: National Academy Press, 1992).

R. M. Cook-Deegan, 'The Human Genome Project: The Formation of Federal Policies in the United States, 1986–1990'. In K. E. Hanna, ed., *Biomedical Politics* (Washington, D.C.: National Academy Press, 1991).

R. S. Cowan, 'Genetic Technology and Reproductive Choice: An Ethics of Autonomy'. In D. J. Kevles and L. Hood, eds., *The Code of Codes: Scientific and Social Issues in the Human Genome Project* (Cambridge, MA: Harvard University Press, 1992).

J. Davis, *Mapping the Code: The Human Genome Project and the Choices of Modern Science* (New York: John Wiley & Sons, 1990).

D. DeGrazia, 'The Ethical Justification for Minimal Paternalism in the Use of the Predictive Test for Huntington's Disease', *Journal of Clinical Ethics* 2(4) (Winter 1991): 219–228.

M. Douglas and A. Wildavsky, *Risk and Culture: An Essay on the Selection of Technological & Environmental Dangers* (Berkeley, CA.: University of California Press, 1982).

E. Draper, 'Genetic Secrets: Social Issues of Medical Screening in a Genetic Age'. In 'Genetic Grammar,' Special Supplement, *Hastings Center Report* 22(4) (July/August 1992): 515–518.

S. J. Durfy and A. E. Grotevant, 'The Human Genome Project: Bibliography', *Kennedy Institute of Ethics Journal* 1(4) (December 1991): 347–362.

R. S. Eisenberg, 'Patenting the Human Genome,' *Emory Law Journal* 39(3) (Summer 1990): 721–45.

R. S. Eisenberg, 'Patent Rights in the Human Genome Project'. In G. Annas and S. Elias, eds., *Gene Mapping: Using Law and Ethics as Guides* (New York: Oxford University Press, 1992).

S. Elias and G. Annas, 'Somatic and Germ-line Gene Therapy'. In G. Annas and S. Elias, eds., *Gene Mapping: Using Law and Ethics as Guides* (New York: Oxford University Press, 1992).

J. Ellul, *The Technological Society*, translated by J. Wilkerson (New York: Alfred Knopf, 1964).

J. Ellul, *The Technological Imperative*, translated by G. W. Bromiley (Grand Rapids, MI: William B. Eerdmans, 1990).

J. R. Fiskel and V. T. Covello, 'The Suitability and Applicability of Risk Assessment Methods for Environmental Applications in Biotechnology'. In J. R. Fiskel and V. T. Covello, eds., *Biotechnology Risk Assessment: Issues and Methods for Environmental Introductions* (New York: Pergamon Press, 1986).

J. Fletcher and D. Wertz, 'Law, Ethics, and Medical Genetics: After the Human Genome is Mapped', *Emory Law Journal* 39(3) (Summer 1990): 747–809.

C. Geertz, *The Interpretation of Cultures* (New York: Basic Books, 1973).

L. Gostin, 'Genetic Discrimination: The Use of Genetically Based Diagnostic and Prognostic Tests by Employers and Insurers', *American Journal of Law & Medicine* 17(1/2) (1991): 109–144.

H. T. Greely, 'Health Insurance, Employment Discrimination, and the Genetics Revolution'. In D. J. Kevles and L. Hood, *The Code of Codes: Scientific and Social Issues in the Human Genome Project* (Cambridge, MA: Harvard University Press, 1992).

N. A. Holtzman, *Proceed With Caution: Predicting Genetic Risks in the Recombinant DNA Era* (Baltimore: Johns Hopkins Press, 1989).

H. Jonas, 'Responsibility Today: The Ethics of an Endangered Future', *Social Research* 43 (Spring 1976): 77–97.

H. Jonas, *The Imperative of Responsibility: In Search of An Ethics for a Technological Age* (Chicago: University of Chicago Press, 1984).

H. F. Judson, 'A History of the Science and Technology Behind Gene Mapping and Sequencing'. In D. J. Kevles and L. Hood, eds., *The Code of Codes: Scientific and Social Issues in the Human Genome Project* (Cambridge, MA: Harvard University Press, 1992).

E. T. Juengst, 'The Human Genome Project and Bioethics', *Kennedy Institute of Ethics Journal* 1(1) (March 1991): 71–74.

D. S. Karjala, 'A Legal Research Agenda for the Human Genome Initiative', *Jurimetrics Journal* 32(2) (Winter 1992): 121–222.

E. F. Keller, 'Nature, Nurture, and the Human Genome Project'. In D. J. Kevles and L. Hood, eds., *The Code of Codes: Scientific and Social Issues in the Human Genome Project* (Cambridge, MA.: Harvard University Press, 1992).

D. J. Kevles, 'Out of Eugenics: The Historical Politics of the Human Genome'. In D. J. Kevles and L. Hood, eds., *The Code of Codes: Scientific and Social Issues in the Human Genome Project* (Cambridge, MA.: Harvard University Press, 1992).

D. J. Kevles and L. Hood, 'Reflections'. In D. J. Kevles and L. Hood, eds., *The Code of Codes: Scientific and Social Issues in the Human Genome Project* (Cambridge, MA.: Harvard University Press, 1992).

P. A. King, 'The Past As Prologue: Race, Class, and Gene Discrimination'. In G. Annas and S. Elias, eds., *Gene Mapping: Using Law and Ethics as Guides.* (New York: Oxford University Press, 1992).

G. Lakhoff and M. Johnson, *Metaphors We Live By* (Chicago: University of Chicago Press, 1981).

A. Lammers and T. Peters, 'Genethics: Implications of the Human Genome Project', *Christian Century* 107(27) (October 3, 1990): 868–872.

E. Lander, 'DNA Fingerprinting: Science, Law, and the Ultimate Identifier'. In D. J. Kevles and L. Hood, eds., *The Code of Codes: Scientific and Social Issues in the Human Genome Project* (Cambridge, MA.: Harvard University Press, 1992).

M. Levin and H. S. Strauss, 'Introduction: Overview of Risk Assessment and Regulation of Environmental Biotechnology'. In M. A. Levin and H. S. Strauss, eds., *Risk Assessment in Genetic Engineering: Environmental Release of Organisms.* McGraw-Hill Environmental Biotechnology Series, series editors R. M. Atlas, E. P. Greenberg, A. L. Demain, B. H. Olson, and G. Sayler (New York: McGraw-Hill, 1991).

R. C. Lewontin, 'The Dream of the Human Genome', *The New York Review of Books* 49(10) (May 28, 1992): 31–40.

A. Lippman, 'Prenatal Genetic Testing and Screening: Constructing Needs and Reinforcing Inequities', *American Journal of Law and Medicine* 17(1 & 2) (1991): 15–50.

E. L. Long, Jr., 'Technology'. In J. F. Childress and J. Macquarrie, eds., *The Westminster Dictionary of Christian Ethics* (Philadelphia: Westminster Press, 1986).

V. A. McKusick, 'The Human Genome Project: Plans, Status, and Applications in Biology and Medicine'. In G. Annas and S. Elias, eds., *Gene Mapping: Using Law and Ethics As Guides* (New York: Oxford University Press, 1992).

C. MacKay, 'The Physician as Fortune Teller: A Commentary on 'The Ethical

Justification for Minimal Paternalism", *Journal of Clinical Ethics* 2(4) (Winter 1991): 228–238.

B. F. Mackler and M. Barach, 'The Human Genome Project in the United States: A Perspective on the Commercial, Ethical, Legislative and Health Care Issues', *International Journal of Bioethics* 2(3) (July-September 1991): 149–157.

R. Macklin, 'Privacy and Control of Genetic Information'. In G. Annas and S. Elias, eds., *Gene Mapping: Using Law and Ethics As Guides* (New York: Oxford University Press, 1992).

G. Meilaender, 'Mastering Our Gen(i)es: When Do We Say No?' *Christian Century* 107(27) (October 3, 1990): 868–872.

C. Mitcham, 'Philosophy of Technology'. In P. T. Durbin, ed., *A Guide to the Culture of Science, Technology, and Medicine* (New York: The Free Press/Macmillan Publishing Co., 1980).

C. Mitcham and J. Grote, eds., *Theology and Technology: Essays in Christian Analysis and Exegesis* (Lanham, MD: University Press of America, 1984).

R. Munson, *Intervention and Reflection: Basic Issues in Medical Ethics*, 4th Ed. (Belmont, CA.: Wadsworth Publishing Company, 1992).

J. S. Naimon, 'Using Expert Panels to Assess Risks of Environmental Biotechnology Applications: A Case Study of the 1986 Frostban Risk Assessments'. In M. A. Levin and H. S. Strauss, eds., *Risk Assessment in Genetic Engineering: Environmental Release of Organisms*. McGraw-Hill Environmental Biotechnology Series, series editors R. M. Atlas, E. P. Greenberg, A. L. Demain, B. H. Olson, and G. Sayler (New York: McGraw-Hill, 1991).

National Research Council, Committee on Mapping and Sequencing the Human Genome, *Mapping and Sequencing the Human Genome* (Washington, DC: National Academy Press, 1988).

D. Nelkin, 'The Social Power of Genetic Information'. In D. J. Kevles and L. Hood, eds., *The Code of Codes: Scientific and Social Issues in the Human Genome Project* (Cambridge, MA.: Harvard University Press, 1992).

D. Nelkin and L. Tancredi, *Dangerous Diagnostics: The Social Power of Biological Information* (New York: Basic Books, 1989).

D. Nelkin and L. Tancredi, 'Classify and Control: Genetic Information in the Schools', *American Journal of Law and Medicine* 17(1/2) (1991): 51–74.

K. Nolan, 'First Fruits: Genetic Screening'. In 'Genetic Grammar,' Special Supplement, *Hastings Center Report* 22(4)(July/August 1992): S2-S4.

Office of Technology Assessment, Congress of the United States, *Mapping Our Genes: Genome Projects: How Big, How Fast?* (Baltimore, MD: Johns Hopkins University Press, 1988).

N. Pickering, 'Ethics and the Human Genome', *Bulletin of Medical Ethics* 72 (October 1991): 25–31.

P. Ramsey, *Fabricated Man* (New Haven, Connecticut: Yale University Press, 1970).

M. Rechsteiner, 'the Folly of the Human Genome Project', *New Scientist* 127(1734) (15 September 1990): 4.

N. Rescher, *Risk: A Philosophical Introduction to the Theory of Risk Evaluation and Management* (Washington, D.C.: University Press of America, 1983).

J. A. Robertson, 'The Potential Impact of the Human Genome Project on Procreative Liberty'. In G. Annas and S. Elias, eds., *Gene Mapping: Using Law and Ethics as Guides* (New York: Oxford University Press, 1992).

B. K. Rothman, *Recreating Motherhood: Ideology and Technology in a Patriarchal Society* (New York: W.W. Norton, 1989).

J. L. Segundo, S.J., *The Liberation of Theology*, translated by J. Drury (Maryknoll, NY: Orbis Books, 1976).

G. Sensabaugh and J. Witowski, eds., *DNA Technology and Forensic Science. Banbury Report: No. 34.* (Cold Spring Harbor, NY: Cold Spring Harbor Press, 1989).

F. E. Sharples, 'Ecological Aspects of Hazard Identification for Environmental Uses of Genetically Engineered Organisms'. In M. A. Levin and H. S. Strauss, eds., *Risk Assessment in Genetic Engineering: Environmental Release of Organisms.* McGraw-Hill Environmental Biotechnology Series, series editors R. M. Atlas, E. P. Greenberg, A. L. Demain, B. H. Olson, and G. Sayler (New York: McGraw-Hill, 1991).

L. Skene, 'Mapping the Human Genome: Some Thoughts for those who Say 'There Should be a Law on It', *Bioethics* 5(3) (July 1991): 233–249.

M. Stanworth, ed., *Reproductive Technologies: Gender, Motherhood and Medicine* (Minneapolis, MN: University of Minnesota Press, 1987).

J. Swazy, 'The Social Context of Medicine: Lessons from the Artificial Heart Experiment', *Second Opinion* 8 (July 1988): 44–65.

J. Swazy, 'Those Who Forget Their History: Lessons from the Recent Past for the Human Genome Quest'. In G. Annas and S. Elias eds., *Gene Mapping: Using Law and Ethics as Guides* (New York: Oxford University Press, 1992).

R. Tarnass, *The Passion of the Western Mind: Understanding the Ideas That Have Shaped Our World View* (New York: Harmony Books, 1991).

G. Terrenoire, 'Huntington's Disease and the Ethics of Genetic Prediction', *Journal of Medical Ethics* 18(2) (June 1992): 79–85.

United States Congress, *Genetic Screening in the Work Place* (Washington, DC: Government Printing Office, 1990).

United States Department of Health and Human Services and Department of Energy, *Understanding Our Genetic Inheritance: The U.S. Human Genome Project, the First Five Years*, FY 1991–1995 (Washington, DC: U.S. Government Printing Office, 1990).

R. Wachbroit, 'Describing Risk'. In M. A. Levin and H. S. Strauss, eds., *Risk Assessment in Genetic Engineering: Environmental Release of Organisms.* McGraw-Hill Environmental Biotechnology Series, series editors R. M. Atlas, E. P. Greenberg, A. L. Demain, B. H. Olson, and G. Sayler (New York: McGraw-Hill, 1991a).

R. Wachbroit, 'What's in a Risk?' *Report from the Institute for Philosophy and Public Policy* (University of Maryland) 11(1) (Winter 1991b): 6–9.

L. Walters and T. J. Kahn. *Bibliography of Bioethics*, Vols. 17 (1991), 18 (1992) and 19 (1993) (Washington DC: Kennedy Institute of Ethics, Georgetown University).

L. Walters, 'Ethical Issues in Human Gene Therapy', *Journal of Clinical Ethics* 2(4) (Winter 1991): 267–274.

N. Wexler, 'Clairvoyance and Caution: Repercussions from the Human Genome Project'. In D. J. Kevles and L. Hood, eds., *The Code of Codes: Scientific and Social Issues in the Human Genome Project* (Cambridge, MA.: Harvard University Press, 1992).

R. White and T. Caskey, 'Genetic Predisposition and the Human Genome Project: Case Illustrations of Clinical Problems'. In G. Annas and S. Elias, eds., *Gene Mapping: Using Law and Ethics as Guides* (New York: Oxford University Press, 1992).

D. Wikler and E. Palmer, 'Neo-eugenics and Disability Rights in Philosophical Perspective'. In N. Fujiki and D. Macer, eds., *Human Genome Research and Society. Proceedings of the Second International Bioethics Seminar in Fukui.* 20–21 March 1992. (Christchurch, NZ: Eubios Ethics Institute, 1992).

R. Wilson and E. Crouch, *Risk/Benefit Analysis* (Cambridge, MA: Ballinger Publishing
    Company, 1982).
L. Wingerson, *Mapping Our Genes: The Genome Project and the Future of Medicine*
    (New York: Dutton, 1990).

Part I

Ethical Concerns in the Age of Biotechnology

* * * * * * * * * * * * * *

Part IC

Biotechnology and Medicine

8

The Conflict Between the Advancement of Medical Science and Technology and Traditional Chinese Medical Ethics

Da-Pu Shi and Lin Yu

From the time of Hippocrates' liberation of medicine from superstition and magic to modern developments such as Watson and Crick's discovery of the double helix, the progress of medical science has been one characterized by difficulties and struggle. One of the central arenas in which this struggle transpires has been and continues to concern the complex ethical issues which arise both within medical science and the clinical applications of that science. Medical ethics has developed as a specialized sub-field within the broader scope of modern ethics. As a sub-field it has its own areas of autonomy but in the end it can never be separated from questions of general morality, traditional values and the various forms of society and social life. In fact, it seems clear that the basic motivation behind medicine is itself a matter of ethics, working out of and giving expression to some of a culture's most lofty ideals, such as helping the weak, the frail, and the sick among us. Medicine as a general practice has traditionally been viewed as 'doing good for others'. This is no less true in the contemporary situation than it was in the past. Advanced medical technology and practice is a vivid modern expression of the highest ideals of a society. However, as medicine has grown into the mature science and practice that it is today, with increasing frequency it finds itself at odds with traditional values and social practices. We find conflicts between the technical ability to do something and the question of whether we have the right to do it.

The Influence of Advanced Medical Techniques on the Traditional Doctor-Patient Relationship

Among the most complex issues faced by modern medicine is the conflict which arises between advanced medical technique and issues of the doctor-patient relationship. Here it is instructive to look at the differences between traditional medical practice and advanced medical technology. Traditional medical practice can rightly be termed an 'art'. Its concern was curing *the person* who had the disease, but as medical technology developed within a general worldview in which there is progressive distance between the 'objectivity' of scientific inquiry and the subjectivity of the scientist. The ideal of 'objectivity', one of the cornerstones of modern scientific technique, is based upon this distancing of the subject and the object. Modern objective science was conceived as being value-neutral. This ideal which originally developed in physics was deemed no less true for the biological sciences. Thus an ideal developed in medical science which demanded an objective 'distance' between the patient (the object) and the doctor (the subject). Thus, other than the broader ethical purposes of medicine as a whole mentioned above, the practitioner was to detach himself from all considerations of morality and concentrate upon practising science.

In modern medical practice, traditional ways of diagnosis and treatment have taken on great changes and thus a new mode of doctor-patient relationship has developed. The continuing clinical application of high-tech diagnostic methods such as automatic, informationalized and remote-control equipment in hospitals, provides increasingly sophisticated physiological data. However, this high-tech approach has mediated the opportunities for direct communication between the doctor and the patient. As a result, it strengthens the reliance by both doctors and patients on the use of instruments and equipment. While it may be argued that such an approach is more physiologically accurate it fails to account for the psychological dimensions of patient care.

Advanced medical technique has absorbed widely and utilized much of the achievements of other sciences. Iatrogenic diseases occur with increasing frequency due to exposure to physical, chemical, biological and electronic factors in the course of diagnosis and treatment. The abundance of ancillary diagnostic procedures leads to what is often an over-dependence by the doctor on machines and a blind faith on the part of patients in those machines. The results are a loss of opportunity for the doctor to practise and improve their own skills as a doctor and at the same time a weakening of trust on the part of the patients in their doctors. Increasingly we trust the machines and not the doctors. In addition, the reliance on high-tech laboratory diagnostic procedures tends to greatly prolong the duration of treatment.

In addition, with the wide application of modern medical techniques, the criteria for judging whether a doctor or hospital is good or not has changed. In the past, patients judged a hospital good or bad by the staff's working attitude, and the medical competence of doctors. But the current attitude judges a hospital by the amount and accuracy (how up-to-date) of the technology it owns. This creates a climate in which all of the hospitals must compete with each other in the rush to buy and use advanced technologies. The resulting financial burdens means that in the present situation in China, hospitals find it increasingly difficult to keep pace and to find ways of balancing and distributing their budget. In the end hospitals pass the costs on to the patients.

This raises yet another issue. The increased reliance on technology and the scientific modernization of supplementary diagnostic procedure has resulted in a dramatic rise in the costs of medical care for the patient. The result is that while patients are released from their physical sufferings, they face the new mental and financial burdens of having to afford services. This poses complicated issues for traditional medical ethics which has been based upon the principle of achieving the best patient results for the best cost. This conflict between the moral responsibility of patient care and the economic interests of medical institution is one which is likely to become an increasingly difficult problem in China.

Finally, the development of modern medicine has resulted in the role of the contemporary doctor becoming much more complex. The doctor's roles and responsibilities now increasingly include meeting not only medical but also non-medical needs. The doctor assumes responsibility for not only the patient proper; as a central figure in the community the doctor must take on responsibility for the whole community or society. The doctor must take both short-term and long-term interest into consideration, and perform a variety of roles which go beyond the traditional roles such as that of cosmetologist, mediator, judge, psychologist, etc. The contemporary doctor must find ways to balance the various new social and professional roles and interests with those traditional medical responsibilities of patients care.

Thus the contemporary view of the doctor-patient relationship has become more complex because it admits the connection to social contexts and thus has reintroduced a great many serious ethical issues into the picture. In other words the doctor-patient relationship is no longer considered to be one which is merely 'objective' but rather one that is full of complex ethical dilemmas which the practitioner must confront.

Quality of Life Issues in Modern and Traditional Medicine

The idea behind traditional medicine is the belief that life is sacred. It has been said that 'Everyone is entitled to live'. Thus issues of quality of life are raised as central to the practice of traditional medicine. Modern medicine also aims at improving the quality of life in its whole process, from birth, through life, until death. However, advanced medical technique and its newfound ability to maintain life artificially raises disturbing questions of quality of life. We often find that the quality of life decreases in cases where advanced techniques are used to maintain useless and vegetative life. Likewise, the ability of modern medicine to save a child with multiple serious congenital defects, who would otherwise die at the hands of nature, values life itself over the quality of life. Such extreme applications undoubtedly bring about unnecessary suffering and burden to family members and to the whole society. These extraordinary abilities of modern medicine raise a number of serious questions for Chinese society: Should doctors and the medical institutions be dedicated to heal and save life without any preconditions? How does medicine and society balance the good health as well as heavy burden modern medicine brings? How does medicine and society go about the task of deciding who shall live and who shall die? How does medicine and society confront the problem that longer life spans and low-death rates achieved by modern medicine contributes to the increase of world population?

The law of nature has been survival of the fittest, which has served to both limit animal and human populations and to ensure that only the best genetic material is passed on. Modern medical science has radically altered this through such techniques as *in vitro* fertilization, and sexless reproduction. Do such techniques contribute to the production of many low quality lives?

Thus it seems clear that much of what we now face with modern medical technique raises profound questions about the quality of life and of how our attitudes with regard to quality of life have changed from what we find within traditional moral positions.

The Distribution of Medical Resources Within Advanced Medical Technique and Traditional Medical Ethics

One of the most pressing issues now and in the future in China is likely to be the distribution of medical resources. This problem arises because clearly there are natural limits and limits may have to be established with regard to the distribution of certain medial techniques. The issue can be broken down into questions of how micro- and macro-distribution will co-exist. An example of this might be the widening application of techniques such as organ transplantation. The result of the increased demands is that an imbalance develops between supply and demand for organs. In this circumstance, how should the limited number of organs be dispensed? This is an issue which has varied responses and one for which traditional medical ethics seems unprepared.

In developed countries, distribution of medical resources is dealt with according to the principle of fair and effective service to the general public, that is, the limited medical resources are dispensed in accordance with both the medical and social standards. Traditional medical ethics takes into consideration only social fairness, and ignores effectiveness. The application of such standards is not easily put into practice. Advanced medicine allocates medical resources both retrospectively and prospectively. The latter, in particular, includes not only the principle of family values but also the principle of scientific research values.

Perplexities and Problems Presented by Advanced Medical Technique for Traditional Medical Ethics

Perplexities of the Problems in Death and Birth

Human beings can create lives. Can they also create deaths? Everybody enjoys the right to live, but how should he protect this right? Although the advanced medical science makes it easier to live or die, can traditional medical ethics, which considers life to be sacred, deal with the issues of the right to death? Life or death, which used to be a personal choice, have now become complex legal, philosophical, social, and ethical issues. Issues which increasingly involve the medical community. Thus, while we can say that life and death become much easier, at the same time they become more difficult. It raises questions such as: Are the infants born through artificial fertilization the 'fruits of love' between man and woman or more like toys we purchase from a supermarket? Is the donor of sperm to be considered a 'father'? Is it possible that the separation of child-bearing from marriage will destroy the existing family pattern, and further destroy the whole social structure? Should sperm be considered a commercial organ transplantation product or the heritage that can be transmitted by the parents? Will regarding sperm as a merchandise lead to its devaluation because it is regarded solely as a source of profit? Should foetuses and babies be considered as valuable as life or should they be equally treasured as a source of biological tissue for transplantation that can be used freely? Do new born babies with serious congenital genetic diseases have the same right to live?

Is it murder to deprive them of their right to live? Is it correct to emphasize blindly the maintenance of life when this actually wastes limited materials and energy and then to justify this as humanitarian? Is it wise and fair to exhaust valuable life to prolong useless life? Is it merciful or cruel to perform euthanasia on the vegetative life and the dying person? What is the standard definition of death? Should a limit be set to prolonging life-span by technology? What standard should this limitation follow: the possibility of science and technology, or the rationality of social development and the traditional morality?

Faced with the dramatically increased 'freedoms' medical technologies present to us to choose life and death, people are confused and at a loss, instead of feeling relieved.

Perplexities and Cogitation on Transsexualism

Is the transsexual operation a method to help the patient lead a new life, or a tolerance to his abnormal psychology? How should the society treat this separation between physiology and psychology? How should people treat the transsexual, as a new existence? Should people ever have the right to choose their sex? It was said that British pathologists have invented a wonder drug to enable a free choice of sex. Is this news a glad tiding or a disaster? Will this freedom in choosing sex destroy the social proportion between male and female? Is this new technique able to be used to change people's concepts and ideas of sexual discrimination?

Is the appearance of 'male mother' a destruction to natural balance? Should the 'synthesized man' who receives organ transplantation be responsible for his former society, or the 'new soul'?

Is the marriage between human beings and animals with organ transplants merely a new creative research area of life science, or does it raise issues of the contempt for human dignity and ethics?

If most of a person's original organs have been replaced by animal's or artificial ones, will this person's individuality and personality be influenced? And now is this person a human, an animal, or a machine?

While some advanced medical techniques and operations cure diseases, they also restrain people's normal behaviour. Is this a scientific issue or an ethical one?

As for the behavioural abnormality caused by social factors, what should be changed directly: environment, or brain?

If we combine the genetic substances of human beings and animals, and create a kind of 'animal men' who are specialized in doing tedious and dangerous work, including fighting in wars, is it in conformity with social morality? Does medical science go further and further from nature while conquering nature?

Perplexities and Anxiety of Medical World

Doctors can create families and babies with artificial reproductive technique, then are doctors matchmakers or 'doctors'?

The organ transplantation technique makes it obligatory for doctors to face the conflict between the death-time of a donor and the transplantation-time for the recipient. Are doctors being placed in the position of being judges rather than 'doctors'?

The development in plastic surgery drags more and more doctors into non-medical areas of practice. Are doctors becoming cosmetologists or is cosmetic surgery the genuine practice of medicine?

What are doctors' responsibilities? What can they do? What should they not do?

Has advanced medical technique obliterated doctor's sympathy and made them indifferent, such that they no longer treat a patient as a life, but a mass of flesh?

What are the connotations of modern medical ethics exactly?

Is the relatively stable, traditional and conservative ethics and morality able to accommodate the active and wilful advanced medical technique? Could it be said that humankind is willing to be reduced to the status of slaves of science?

Essential Principles for the Development of Advanced Medical Techniques

There is always a difference between the development of the theoretical side of a science and its application. It is true for any branch of science that the closer the combination of development and application, the better. This coordination becomes complex and difficult in the case of medical science. Medical science is both a science and an expression of a moral position concerning the care of society's weak and sick. As we have argued, modern medical science has tended to emphasize the technical end of things and forsaken the moral aspects. There must be an ethical foundation which bridges the exploration of medical science and its clinical application. Although the development in medical technology varies and the development of ethics is uneven, the ethical principles that are recognized and followed by the whole humankind should have a common criterion: nature is supreme, and anything in this world abides by this natural law.

Another principle which we find in traditional medical ethics is that to 'let patients know and obtain their agreement'. To a large degree this has been destroyed by advanced medical technique. For example, the donor's identity is kept as a secret when performing an artificial fertilization. Also with increasing frequency, patients do not know what is going on as they are subjected to various procedures. There are now statutes which allow the patients legal recourse when they are unaware of what is going on in spite of agreement. Will these statutes and law cases inhibit the development of advanced medicine?

The goals of medicine are not only healing the wounded and rescuing the dying, but also improving the quality of life. The maintenance and even abandoning of life must take into consideration both the intrinsic value of life and the needs of the society. However, because with advanced medical science there is often a lack of corresponding ethical restraints during the course of application, some mistakes which go against modern ethics of life have emerged. Thus, practitioners of advanced medical techniques should adhere to the following ethical principles during the course of application:

1. *Principle of overall responsibility for patients.*   The medical community needs to take responsibility for both the physiological and psychological dimensions of patient care. Responsibility for both public security and environmental protection are important in order to protect the interests of the majority. The evaluation and propagation of the high-tech medical applications should be practical and realistic, rest upon scientific evidence, and give consideration to the far-reaching social effects, but not exaggerate them blindly. Application of high-tech medicine should take particular care to avoid causing iatrogenic diseases. The application of high technique should harmonize with the goals of the whole society, and adhere to the principle that the overall interests of society should be put first.

2. *Principle of appropriateness.*   The development of medical science should proceed in a rapid and unimpeded fashion. In addition, the introduction and

diffusion of advanced diagnostic and therapeutic techniques should be a priority. However, this needs to be tempered by a comprehensive understanding of China's actual situation. Care must be taken that measures are suited to the country's needs and that there are adequate numbers of qualified professionals to utilize effectively the instruments and techniques.

3. *Consistent principle between two benefits.* We should adhere to the principle that we buy the essential instruments and equipment first, then gradually achieve quality, superiority, and sophistication. We should satisfy the needs of the majority first, then those of special-needs groups. Also, in purchasing the instruments and equipment, we should uphold the following principle: diagnosis first, treatment next, and auxiliary uses last. Further, we should employ the principle of: citizens first, foreigners next; and specialized uses first, comprehensive next. All of this is to ensure that we will be able to receive the most benefits with the least costs.

4. *Principle of fair allocation.* Fair allocation of limited resources is a basic issue. It is a matter of moral responsibility that we balance the value of the needs of each individual with those of the group. The policy-making departments should take into account the balanced distribution of the techniques instruments and equipment so that the highest goal of medicine can be realized: health for all.

5. *Prospective principle.* We should correctly deal with long-term and short-term goals and benefits. We can encourage neither the over-emphasis on the techniques nor excessive financial consumption. We must not ever be timid or in fear of mentioning these goals. Public opinion and understanding should play an important role in the application of advanced medical techniques and these prospective strategies should be applied rationally.

Modern medicine must take the broadest perspective possible, focusing upon such things as the value of life. Attention must be paid to the quality of life at birth, quality in the conduct of life, and quality of the conclusion of life. It should have its eye not only on the people today but also on the quality of life of the people in the future.

Conclusion

We have moved from the ignorance of traditional medical ethics to the wisdom of a modern ethics of life. We have also moved from the muddle of ancient medicine to the precision of modern medicine. Human beings have proven that they have the confidence and ability to face themselves, control themselves, to be the masters of themselves. As long as humankind can create advanced medical techniques, they should make good use of them. Although our hopes are often overshadowed with confusion, and the difficult problems about life stand like a forest, we must have confidence that the train of human civilization will successfully move forward along the harmonious and parallel tracks of advanced medical science and traditional ethics.

9

In Vitro Fertilization and Embryo Transfer: Technological Achievements and Ethical Concerns

Kazumasa Hoshino

In 1978 Steptoe and Edwards in England succeeded with the clinical application of a newly introduced reproductive biotechnology called *in vitro* fertilization and embryo transfer (IVF-ET), allowing an infertile woman to give normal birth to a baby girl, Louise Brown. Since then a series of new medical interventions have been applied to human reproduction. It has become possible for adult couples to bear children without having sexual intercourse.

Artificial Insemination

Until IVF-ET was introduced as an advanced reproductive intervention technique, only artificial insemination was available for infertile couples who wished to have their own children. In artificial insemination, semen of either a male partner or a donor can be used to inseminate a woman, but an ovum has to be naturally ovulated by a female partner. When a woman has obvious troubles with her ovaries, uterine tubes or uterus, she cannot benefit from artificial insemination. When a man is suffering from aspermia or severe oligospermia, his semen is not usable and a donor's semen has to be used for artificial insemination of a female partner. In this case, the genetic father of the child is not the male partner.

Bioethical issues with regard to artificial insemination are important, but beyond the scope of this article.

In Vitro Fertilization and Embryo Transfer (IVF-ET)

For IVF, semen which is ejaculated manually is observed under a microscope and only morphologically normal and healthily mobile sperm are selected and transferred to a Petri dish containing a proper culture medium. Prior to IVF, as many mature preovulatory ova as possible are mechanically retrieved from the woman. The woman is first pretreated with gonadotrophin for artificial induction of excess ovulation. Then, with negative pressure and the aid of ultrasonography, ova are mechanically obtained from the hyperovulating ovaries of the pretreated woman. A number of mature ova thus obtained are observed under a microscope in order to select normal looking mature ova. They are then transferred to a Petri dish for cell culture. Later, some selected sperms are added to the culture media with the ova for *in vitro* fertilization.

When *in vitro* fertilization takes place, the fertilized egg is produced and undergoes a series of cleavages. Embryologically the fertilized egg is designated as the zygote. Cleavage is the process of a series of mitotic divisions of a zygote. The cleavage produces two blastomeres which then produce four blastomeres and so on, in exponentially increasing numbers. It does so without changing the total volume of either the nucleus or the cytoplasm within the original zona pellucida (Fig. 1). During cleavage, the volumes of the nucleus and the cytoplasm of each blastomere thus become reduced to two halves at each division. During cleavage, the zygote is then often called clinically 'the early embryo'. An early embryo containing two blastomeres, for instance, is designated as the early embryo at the 2-cell stage, although both of them are

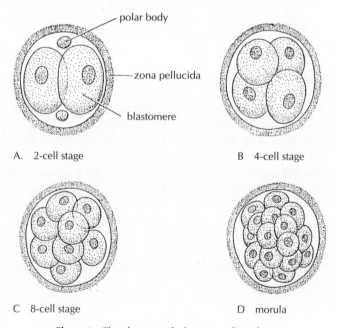

A.   2-cell stage   B   4-cell stage

C   8-cell stage   D   morula

Figure 1   The cleavage of a human early embryo.

located in the same zona pellucida the size of which is identical to that of the zygote immediately after the fertilized egg was produceda. Each time an early embryo consists of 2, 4 or 8 cells, the external appearance of each of them looks just like one cell surrounded by the zona pellucida of the same size at each stage.

Usually when an early embryo reaches the 4-cell stage or a little later, it is transferred from the Petri dish to the uterine cavity for natural implantation to take place into the endometrium. The endometrium has to be pretreated with various hormones to complete its progestational changes, in order to accommodate implantation of the early embryo. Commonly 2 to 4 early embryos are used for each ET in order to increase the success rate of implantation and to lessen the chance of causing multiple pregnancy.

According to the report made at the Eighth World Congress of In Vitro Fertilization in September 1993 in Kyoto, Japan, during the year of 1991, 138,000 cases of IVF-ET were performed in 760 medical centres in 46 countries, and 26,000 patients became pregnant. Among them 19,000 patients gave birth to normal babies: 4900 cases in the United States, 3800 cases in France and 1300 cases in Japan. In Japan, IVF-ET has been and is acceptable socially only between legally married couples. In the United States, however, the donation of either semen or ova and surrogate mothers are acceptable. The combinations of IVF-ET using either male partner's semen or donor's semen with either female partner's ovum or donor's ovum in either female partner's uterus or surrogate mother's uterus make the identity of an offspring so difficult that such procedures have been and are subject to legal, social and bioethical concerns and debate.

Variations of IVF-ET Procedures

There have been several modified methods of the IVF-ET procedures. One of them is gamete intra-fallopian tube transfer (GIFT). In GIFT, instead of using a zygote formed in culture media, both sperms and ova are aspirated together from a culture media into the syringe and transferred directly into the ampulla of the uterine tube with aid of laparoscopy. Sperm and ovum are both designated as a gamete and the uterine tube is clinically called fallopian tube. Thus, this procedure is called gamete intra-fallopian tube transfer (GIFT). The ampulla of the uterine tube is the natural site of fertilization and therefore GIFT is more natural than IVT although there are still considerable amounts of biotechnological interventions in the reproductive process.

Micro Insemination and ET

A more recent procedure is microinsemination and ET. Similar to IVF, sperms and ova are retrieved and placed separately in culture media. Sperms are examined under a microscope. Sperms that are morphologically normal and healthily moving-around are selected and separated in a Petri dish with culture media. Ova are also examined under a microscope and normal looking mature ova are separated. One selected mature ovum is immobilized under a microscope and a very small hole formed in the microscopic stage by gentle suction. The single sperm is then injected by a very narrow injection needle into the selected and immobilized mature ovum.

The ovum is surrounded immediately outside of the plasma membrane by the perivitelline space which is surrounded by the zona pellucida (Fig. 2). Therefore, there are three different spaces where the sperm is injected:
1. into the cytoplasm of the ovum,
2. into the perivitelline space,
3. into a small narrow canal created by either a chemical or a needle in the zona pellucida.

By method 1, the gametes are forcibly fertilized by biotechnological intervention, whereas in methods 2 and 3 the gametes are only helped to fertilize each other more easily. Once the zygote is formed by one of these approaches, ET is performed as same as IVF-ET.

Microinsemination is good news for infertile male patients.

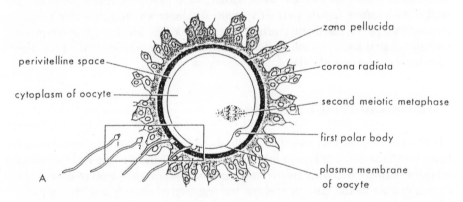

Figure 2   Bisected surface of a matured oocyte (ovum).

The Most Recent Modification of IVF-ET With or Without Preimplantation Genetic Diagnosis

In this procedure, all steps of IVF are identical to the ordinary IVF. Preimplantation genetic diagnosis is performed on one or more blastomere at the 4-cell stage of the early embryo. Thereafter, the embryo transfer procedure is different from the ordinary ET.

At the 4-cell stage of the early embryo, there are four blastomeres, each of which is genetically identical. Despite the fact that the volume of the genetic materials contained in one blastomeres at the 4-cell stage is exactly one quarter of genetic materials of the zygote before the cleavage (Fig. 1), each blastomere maintains the total potentiality to be capable of developing into a normal individual person. Any one of four blastomeres may be sucked out by a negative pressure without damaging any of the other blastomeres and can become subject to genetic diagnosis. This genetic diagnosis is performed in a blastomere before implantation of an early embryo into the uterine endometrium, thus it is called preimplantation genetic diagnosis.

If genetic disorders are diagnosed in the tested blastomere, all of the remaining blastomeres are likewise disordered and must not be used for embryo transfer. When the tested blastomere is found genetically normal, the remaining blastomere must also be normal and can be used for embryo transfer. In order to transfer one or more blastomeres by embryo transfer, another zygote is used and its nucleus is enucleated to make space, into which one or more blastomeres are replaced. This procedure is important, because the cytoplasm and the surrounding zona pellucida are necessary for cleavage to be carried out in order to form the blastocyst prior to implantation into the uterine endometrium.

The newly formed early embryo containing genetically normal blastomere is transferred into the uterine cavity like the usual ET procedure. When ET procedure succeeds to cause implantation and the resulting pregnancy goes normally, a single genetically normal offspring will be expected to be born, regardless of the number of blastomeres contained in the transferred early embryo.

This procedure may be performed also for fertile couples who have the risk of having genetically affected children. For example, in cases where in a previous pregnancy the foetus was found by prenatal diagnosis to have inherited a disease such as cystic fibrosis which is a severe autosomal recessive disease. At the next pregnancy, those couples face the risk of having again a foetus affected with the same genetic disease and have to make the most difficult decision of whether or not to continue a risky pregnancy until the prenatal diagnosis confirms that the new foetus is genetically normal. If and when the foetus is diagnosed as genetically affected, some may choose artificial abortion. Couples who choose abortion may have risks of repeated artificial abortions until they have a normal foetus.

Using preimplantation genetic diagnosis, it would be possible for couples at risk of having affected children to make their decision before implantation of their conceptus in the uterine endometrium, thus avoiding artificial abortion. Thus, this method is certainly advantageous to a couple at risk of having a genetically affected foetus.

There will be some more possibilities that special attempts such as the following may be made: several single blastomeres are isolated from the blastomere which remained after preimplantation genetic diagnosis; thereafter each of these blastomeres is put into a single empty nuclear space prepared by enucleation of blastomeres from other early embryos produced by IVF; and finally each of the newly formed early embryos is transferred into each of the uterine cavities of surrogate mothers. By these procedures it is theoretically possible to expect the same number of genetically identical normal offspring to be born from the same number of surrogate mothers.

When an early embryo at the 8-cell stage, for example, is used for this procedure without preimplantation genetic diagnosis, it is possible to expect to produce eight genetically identical offspring by eight surrogate mothers. This is really genetically identical human cloning as long as mutation does not occur unexpectedly in any of these embryos. Human cloning is definitely not permissible from eugenic, bioethical, social and political points of view, because it is extremely dangerous to humankind. Therefore, IVF-ET using blastomeres must be bioethically evaluated thoroughly and any attempts to extend this particular procedure to human cloning must be legally prohibited. I emphasized this point with my serious concerns at the satellite meeting on medical ethics of the Sino-Japan Medical Conference 1992 held in Beijing, China in November 1992. After the submission of the abstract of my paper to the programme committee in Beijing, my fear of the possibility of human cloning became at least technically proven — Handyside and his associates reported in the 24 September 1992 issue of *New England Journal of Medicine* the first case of the birth of a normal baby girl after *in vitro* fertilization, preimplantation diagnostic testing for cystic fibrosis and embryo transfer. Although Handyside and his associates did not intend to perform human cloning, their procedures succeeded in producing a normal individual person. Thus, human cloning is technically possible with these procedures.

On 24 October 1993, the *New York Times* reported on a meeting of the American Fertility Society in Montreal where Jerry Hall and his supervisor Robert Stilman of George Washington University in Washington, D.C. discussed their attempt to produce human clones using their own techniques in order to increase the number of genetically identical zygotes. In their 8 November 1993 issue, *Time* magazine reported in detail about this happening. According to their report these two scientists said they just wanted to take the first step toward determining if cloning is as feasible in humans as it is in cattle. They used abnormal zygotes, which had been formed by dispermy, which means fertilization by two sperms at once, and thus were destined for an early death whether or not they were implanted. Hall and Stilman saw nothing unethical about experimenting with them, and they got permission to do so from the university.

Their experimental procedures were different from those used by Handyside and his associates. Hall developed a gel from seaweed that could serve as a substitute for the zona pellucida. When two blastomeres were formed, he removed the zygote from the zona pellucida and separated two blastomeres. He then wrapped each of these blastomeres with the artificial coating (the substitute for the zona pellucida). These two blastomeres began once again to grow and divide. Hall repeated this procedure and produced 48 human clones in all. But they did not grow for more than 6 days and died.

This recent report concerning attempts at human cloning are shocking because of the slippery slope which follows from it. Once such experiments are sanctioned where will we stop? Fortunately they did not attempt to develop their procedures into clinical application.

The Japanese Association of Obstetrics and Gynecology declared in 1983 that cloning of human beings should not be attempted. Although this declaration was made ten years ago, it will be important to continue in the future to proceed with caution and vigilance as long as the possibilities of cloning exist.

References

A. H. Handyside, J. C. Lesko, J. J. Tarin, R. M. L. Winston, and M. R. Hughes, M.R. 'Birth of a Normal Girl After in Vitro Fertilization and Preimplantation Diagnostic Testing for Cystic Fibrosis', *New England Journal of Medicine* 327 (1992): 905–909.

K. Hoshino, 'Bioethical Considerations on Preimplantation Genetic Diagnosis and Reproductive Procedures'. In *Medical Ethics: China-Japan Medical Conference*, Vol. V (1992): 921.

P. Elmer-DeWitt, 'Cloning: Where Do We Draw the Line?', *Time* (8 November 1993): 37–42.

10

Moral Risk Assessment in Biotechnology

Hans-Martin Sass

The Jacob Story

About 2500 years ago — during the century of Lao Tzu, Kung Fu Tze and Buddha — Jacob, the father of the House of Israel, served as a herdsman to Laban, his father in law, for many years without pay. Laban was an avaricious and mean person and did not pay Jacob during his years of service. One day Jacob made what Laban thought was a modest request: to get title to all crossbreeds of Laban's herds. After the new contract was in place, Jacob started to increase the number of cross breeds by canny and prudent means of encouraging crossbreeding among previously strictly separated flocks. Incentives included watering and even feeding previously separated herds together to provide for extra breeding time across previously established and protected breeding lines. When the time came to count the flocks, Laban got very angry and Jacob got very rich as his flocks increased exceedingly, or in the word's of the German version of Dr Martin Luther '*daher ward der Mann über alle Massen reich*' (1. Mose, 31:13).

We have two sets of problems in this story, both of which are related to risks in biotechnology. One set represents *four purely technical risk parameters* in indirect biotechnological manipulation by breeding methods and in direct biotechnological manipulation by moleculargenetic methods: *stability* of genetic expression and *survival, multiplication, and migration* in environment.[1] These four risk parameters have been widely described in contemporary DNA hazard management and are mandatorily used in corporate and government risk assessment schemes in agriculture, drug research and gene therapy.[2] Jacob's story plays well before the background of a history of well established means and goals in genetic selection, purification and improvement of wild animals and wild plants into domesticated animals and cultivated plants. Genetic improvement of wild forms of life into domesticated and cultivated forms of life is an essential part of human culture since her prehistoric days. The goal of genetic cultivation was the improvement of human living conditions, better survival risk management and lower risk rates for good, civilized and cultivated forms of life. The technical challenge in conditioning and manipulating hardware instruments and machines as well as living entities such as herbs and plant, dogs, horses, cats and chickens was and is to identify goals and to shape the instruments appropriately so that the job can be done with a minimum of unwarranted side-effects. The Jacob story does not confront us with the beginnings of human cultivation of raw nature, rather it presupposes an already long history of genetic cultivation of nature and describes some technical parameters of furthering the ongoing process of cultivation of already manipulated genetic material, this time by re-merging previously separated genetic lines for a well designed purpose.

The strategically designed goal of Jacob's biotechnological manipulation was not technical improvement of already cultivated stock, rather a business purpose with related moral aspects. And here we face the second set of risks in this story: *moral risk*. Mating and breeding in Jacob's story is not considered to be a moral risk, but his business attitude. He played the cards of his herdsmanship in an unexpected and unusual, canny and prudent way for his own benefit and at Laban's loss. It is the old moral problem of contracting with parties who are unaware of loopholes of contracts and those who exploit the loopholes; we face business ethics issues such as this one in many areas of wheeling and dealing, not just among breeders, horsetraders but researchers and businessmen in modern biotechnology as well. Jewish and Christian ethics, of course, was and is concerned with business ethics; writes the Stuttgart annotated German bible edition: 'Jacob used the trick, calculating the mistakes of the breeding animals. God did not tell Jacob to do so. He let it happen in order to punish Laban for being mean', i.e. the animals were to blame for making mating 'mistakes', and God was not to be blamed for anything as He did not support actively what seems to be a moral, not a legal breech of contract, rather He passively watched and let it happen. Without going into a detailed analysis of the commentator's moral reasoning concerning Jacob's biotechnological deeds, let me finish the story by noting that the bible reports increasing tensions between Laban's house and the house of Jacob and that 'the Lord said unto Jacob, return into the land of thy fathers and thy kindred and I will be with you' (Genesis 31:13).

It is a long way from Jacob's parameters of technical and moral risk to those in modern biotechnology, from breeding sheep and cultivating grain to transgenic forms of life, cross-species hybridization, genetic manipulation in somatic and germ-line cells, organ transplantation and artificial organs, micro-organisms producing human insulin or eating away pollutants. While the technical challenges and moral risks are similar, the stakes in miscalculation and misappropriation of technology assessment and moral assessment and societal assessment have risen. We might take to heart what Lao Tzu's says in this regard: 'the sharper the weapons the people possess, the greater confusion reigns in the realm; the more clever and crafty the men, the oftener strange things happen; the more articulate the laws and ordinances, the more robbers and thieves arise'.[3] The review of the Jacob story leads to my first thesis: *Biotechnology is not new, nor are the technical and moral risks associated with it. But, as the dimensions of knowledge and manipulation have widened, so have associated ethical dimensions which need careful assessment in the light of traditional moral and cultural principles.*

Such re-confirmation of moral and cultural traditions and values and risks associated with their implementation has to include a re-evaluation of

1. concepts of *nature and culture,*
2. knowledge in human *self-understanding,*
3. goals, risks, and limits of *genetic manipulation,* and
4. the ultimate challenge to an *ethics of responsibility.*

Raw Nature and the Cultures of Manipulation

The word and the concept of culture comes from the Latin *cultivare* which means cultivating and plowing the raw ground into productive garden lands and field. It includes the weeding out of unwanted weeds, the protection, nursing, and improvement of herbs, vegetables, fruits for nutrition, medicine, and enjoyment. The *hortus*, the garden, is protected by a fence, a hedge, or a ditch from the surrounding wilderness, its beasts and weeds. Wild nature traditionally had been the enemy threatening and endangering human survival and cultivated and civilized life. Houses, hedges, walls, gardens and fields, domesticated animals protected against cruelty, uncertainty and unpredictability of nature. Cultural and civilizatory evolution can be understood as the prolongation of natural evolution through tools and technologies.[4] Only when the walls of culture have been built strong and high enough do we begin to romanticize wilderness and find in nature a part of our own nature which we feel we have lost in the processes of rationalization, instrumentalization, and cultivation.[5]

The way humans see nature tells us as much about ourselves as it does about nature, we mirror ourselves in the way we cultivate, nurse or dominate nature. This can be shown best by comparing different attitudes towards nature as displayed in different architectural *concepts and designs of parks and ornamental gardens.* The hortological differences between the French and the English park are well known, but such differences also clearly displays anthropological differences in human self-understanding. In the *French park* we find domination, uniformization, rationalization of natural vegetation into geometrically shaped hedges, borders and beds by means of cutting, clipping, and trimming, everything under strictly controlled design, oriented towards the house as the centre of control, manipulation and domination in a timeless fashion. There is a distrust in the genuine powers of nature and a call for high maintenance and permanent control, punishment, and rectification of unwarranted natural powers. The *English park* is famous for protecting, nursing, and appreciating the personality of the individual and solitary tree or of groups of shrubs and trees through the use of low but determined and strategically applied forms of control and maintenance. The borders between lawns and ways are 'naturally' designed, not geometrically designed. The park is open towards the surrounding landscape, not walled in, thus, the house not necessary as the centre. The inclusion of artificial ruins engages a time horizon of the 'memento mori', as a reminder of the limited span of human lives, products, and efforts. The English park looks more 'natural', but is no less a carefully designed product of human hortological biotechnological manipulation.

The same is true for Chinese hortological culture. The *Chinese garden* is not a park, rather a place of well controlled growths and interaction between the cultural and natural side of the owner, who may also be the gardener and who, if climate allows, cares for interrelating house and garden as cultivated living spaces for cultivated and cultivating humans. Greatness and smallness, natural and even bizarre forms of growth, bridges, lakes, fish, houses, boats and humans together form a cultivated landscape which resembles 'naturalness' but is actually as artificial, as strategically designed, as micro-controlled as the European parks. Goldfish are products of severe and intense biotechnological manipulation, so are certain bonsai trees. While the French park stands for representation of power and dominance and the English park for controlled fairness and a culture of low control, the Chinese garden is a symbol as well as an instrument for human interaction with nature by clipping branches, cultivating roses, and feeding fish for the purpose of revering and cultivating nature, for meditation and self-recognition, and a culture of integrating labour and leisure. Where are the *garden of our times*? They are inside the lobbies of luxury hotels and shopping malls; reminders only of nature inside the house, not surrounding the house, truly domesticated biotechnologically controlled and designed nature inside the centres of commerce and civilization, as the spaces outside the buildings have become parking places and driving places towards other buildings.

It was Francis Bacon who in his *Novum Organon* (1670) underlined that the history of nature is never a history of free and uncontrolled nature, but a history of bound and dominated nature, of nature pushed, pressed, and formed by human ingenuity and activity. The point is that the cultural and moral risks of using concepts of 'nature' and 'culture' uncritically effects the assessment of goals, limits, and risks in technological development and application. Such concepts are indicators of our sense of the limits of self-understanding and self-determination. Our review of the epistemological, biotechnological and anthropological aspects of ornamental gardens and parks can be summarized in a second thesis: *The manipulation of nature mirrors human self-understandings, values, and morals; the key to avoiding risk in technology is to strengthen individual and cultural competence in moral risk assessment and personal responsibility.*

Ethics and Risks in Genetic Knowledge

While moral risk associated with genetic manipulation dominates public debates on moral risk in biotechnology, it is the benefits and risks of genetic knowledge which constitute the actual and more concrete challenges which are in need of urgent attention. Knowledge provides for power; power increases opportunities for freedom and self-determination, also for exploitation and domination. Changes in the balance of power also result in shifts of rights and responsibilities among players as moral subjects. The availability of reliable instruments for contraception is a classic example for how biotechnological progress in personal human fertility has changed millennium old scenarios of family planning and sexual culture. The availability of oral contraceptives has done more for the liberation and emancipation of women than thousands of pages of writings and legislation, as it allows for differentiating between procreational and recreational forms of sex. The contraceptive ethos makes women and men more equal, but changes the equations in making moral choices, e.g. not using available technology is a choice deliberately made and may not be excused by deliberate regression into pre-technological innocence: use or nonuse of available technology is always a moral choice, related to responsibility not to technology.

The truly revolutionary explosion of knowledge and the challenges it presents to moral risk competence can best be demonstrated by developing moral and medical scenarios of predictive medicine based on genetic prediction and medical prevention.[6] The medical and moral challenge in predictive medicine is to translate the certainties of hereditary and diagnostic facts within the uncertainties of the parameters of quality of life, health literacy and self-determination of the citizen/patient, and the design of prevention and therapy. The classical nosological difference between health and disease does not hold any more in carrier-status prediction and prevention. Risk factor medicine has started to revolutionize existing forms of medical treatment away from acute crisis style intervention, with the physician being the prime moral agent and the patient's ethics reduced to compliance towards non-acute long-term prediction and prevention, with the pre-symptomatic citizen as the prospective patient being the prime moral agent in making and implementing preventive decisions, and the physician being the expert partner for prediction, information, and education.[7] Solidarity-based health care financing systems will have to include the principles of responsibility and subsidarity into the foundations of workable, affordable and fair systems of health care financing. Individual life-style decisions in leisure activities and carrier planning will have to be based on information of individual health risk.[8] Traditional principles in medical ethics such as truth-telling and confidentiality will have to be reformulated for the scenarios of prediction. As there is a right to self-determination and to protecting one's own health, there has to be a societal and medical duty to inform and to educate the individual on his or her health risk parameters in order to allow for the implementation of rights to health and self-determination. The increased availability of more and more sensitive information means that the protection of data becomes a prime technical and moral issue: research in epidemiology and individual risk management need collection, storage, and differentiated and controlled access of data, while principles of privacy and respect for persons call for strict data protection. A third principle, *the right to know*, carries a new weight and for the first time in modern medicine becomes a leading principle in bioethics, in particular where knowledge relates to severe individual health risk or the most severe forms of genetic disorder in possible offspring.

As far as I see it, there is not only a right, but a *duty to know* about one's own health risks such as diabetes, hypertension, hyperkalemia, and the risks of excessive life-styles including smoking and heavy drinking. I also see positive rights to know, but not a duty to know, where prediction and risk knowledge cannot yet be translated into preventive scenarios, such as information on the carrier status of Alzheimer's disease. I see a definite duty to know about one's carrier status before making reproductive choices, ranging in obligatory weight from some of the severest forms of genetic disorders to those which are less severe. Severe disorders such as the Lesch-Nyhan disease, autosomal dominant polycystic kidney disease, and genetic predisposition for hyperchloremia or Alzheimer need to be dealt with differently. For example in the case of autosomal dominant polycystic disease, the onset can be later in life or can be postponed by prudent risk management and dealt with by means of renal dialysis or organ transplantation. This must be accorded a different status in the rights and duties to know than Alzheimer's which is only a genetic predisposition.[9] The moral challenge and risk is in differentiating scenarios of genetic prediction precisely enough according to technical and moral parameters and allowing for individualized and patient-oriented, better carrier-based, decision making. Knowing that one in 25 British are carriers of cystic fibrosis challenges the moral and medical assessment of new epidemiological and individual aspects of moral scenarios of screening for the medical profession, for the health care system, and not least for the carrier[10]. Again, as I already mentioned, the new scenarios of *duty to know versus right not to know* call for careful differentiated ethical assessment and not for moral generalizations. Such generalizations carry the hazard of indoctrination and the risk of medically and ethically harming carriers in terms of their quality of life and reproductive choices.[11]

Summarizing these reflections on the ethics and risks of new genetic information in a third thesis: *There is a duty to know about individual health risk factors for the promotion of self-determination in life-style and reproduction.* The truly Copernican turn in modern medicine and new knowledge in molecular genetics calls for a shift of emphasis on physician's ethics to emphasis on lay ethics in future medical ethics; this can be highlighted by the following interactive set of maxims in lay ethics and expert ethics for health care which are structured after Dr Gong Tingxian's famous two sets of ten rules each, for the physician and the patient:

Eight Health Care Rules for the Lay Person

1. Find truly educated and trustworthy health experts.
2. Develop competence and responsibility in health risk management.
3. Make extended use of predictive and preventive medicine.
4. Expect healing or relief from acute medicine, but be aware of the limits and risks of any medical intervention.
5. Expect information and advice from medical experts and be a fair partner with them.
6. Define and implement your sense of qualities of life, from childhood to old age, in sickness and in health.
7. Prepare advance directives and name proxy decision makers for circumstances of incompetence.
8. Act responsibly in the use of communal health care funds.

Eight Health Care Rules for the Health Expert

1. Treat your patient as a person, not just his or her symptoms.
2. Assist your patient in developing health risk competence.
3. Integrate the 'clinical status' and the 'value status' of your patient into differential ethics, diagnosis and prognosis.
4. Be aware of the benefits, limits and risks of acute intervention and discuss those with your patient.
5. Be an expert partner with your patient and respect her or his wishes and values.
6. Continuously educate yourself and provide the best possible clinical and personal service.
7. Assist your patient in preparing advance directives and in working with proxies for the benefit of your patient.
8. Act responsibly in the use of communal health care funds.

Ethics and Risks in Manipulation

It was a long way from Jacob's biotechnological manipulation by means of breeding and cultivating to the strategically targeted molecular-genetic design of drugs and multiple forms of life. Stakes have become higher and there are calls for improvements in the ethos and ethics of manipulation. There is a special responsibility in human stewardship towards those forms of life which have been modified by humans — whether by indirect or by direct means — and to those forms of life which may become extinct as a result of human activity. Dachshunds have been designed as assistants in hunting rabbits, dachs and fox, with good technical and moral breeding results. But dachshunds carry a construction blunder as they develop painful spinal cord deterioration in their later years. An improved ethos of manipulation and the ethics of biotechnology would call for terminating the breeding of dachshunds or at least not making them run staircases or be pets for kids. The protection of endangered species of life rests on two strong but different moral arguments. The first concerns the respect for the diversity of life as an end in itself. The second concerns the preservation of as many diverse forms of life as material for future cultivation and manipulation. It would be moral malpractice to call for the ban of certain forms of technology just because they may be misused by 'bad' people. Historically we know that black powder was used in China for cultivating the fine art of fireworks, while in Europe it was used in guns for killing fellow humans. In the stone age the axe could be used either for cultivating the wilderness or for killing foes or friends — three different ethical scenarios with different balances of right and wrong. As in the story of Jacob, different scenarios demand careful technical and ethical analysis and assessment, not moral generalizations and prohibitions.[12] Of particular concern has been the manipulation of human cells and tissue. I do not see that the moral risk in using biotechnologically altered human somatic cells and tissue for healing or relieving suffering would be different than the risk parameters of other forms of medical intervention. Initial experiences in the ethical review of somatic cell therapy[13] have concluded that except for the additional special risks associated with the control of genetic stability, all other problems are either related to technical risks in prediction, professionalism, and support; or to ethical risks in patient selection and informed consent. Before somatic cell therapy was technically possible, a moral risk assessment board, an ethics committee, convened at the US National Institute of Health and developed checklists for ethical risks assessment which then were used when first somatic cell protocols were submitted. Submission of somatic cell therapy protocols have already become routine. They are not sensational or morally curious but do call for differentiated moral judgement rather than moral generalizations.

Worst-case scenarios in human germ-line manipulation have been used to morally condemn biotechnology in general or at least in human medicine. Such scenarios as thousands of identically cloned soldiers or slaves or genetically designed labourers immune to pollution, the so-called eugenic improvement of the human race or of some of the human races are the utensils in Dr Mabuse's cabinet. But this is not a realistic picture of the future of germ-line modification in humans. Traditional forms of manipulating fellow humans by means of indoctrination, exploitation, and the withholding of instruments and means for individual self-determination are still and will, for the foreseeable future, be the most effective methods of reducing fellow humans to means rather than respecting them as persons and ends-in-themselves. It is a fiction that genetic manipulation can do the same job as effectively as disinformation and indoctrination do.

Years ago, the European Community rightly included the right not to have one's identity genetically manipulated into the list of citizen rights. This position should be universally supported by all nations and cultures. Certainly if and when reliable methods become available to 'heal' any of the severest forms of human genetic disorders by means of modification of germ-line cells or genetic therapies, the benefits and risks, medical and moral, will have to be compared to the benefits and risks of indirect 'prevention' such as pre-implantation diagnosis or abortion, or even allowing one to knowingly give birth to severely handicapped offspring without further moral considerations. The decision of whether germ-line intervention is a moral good or bad will be an issue for responsible parenthood.

I consider it a malpractice in moral argumentation to resort to generalizations when particulars of moral assessment are requested; philosophical and theological generalizations are a moral and technical hazard and present great risk for those in need of medical information and intervention. Thomas Aquinas already mentioned that generalizations lose their authority the more one moves to the details of moral scenarios, '*quanto ad particularia descenditur*'. It is the particularities which count in what I call differential ethics. These arguments lead to my fourth thesis: *Progress in methods of manipulation calls for progress in the development and support of an ethos and ethics of manipulation; a ban on manipulation would be moral and cultural malpractice.*

Biotechnology and the Cultures of Responsibility

It is not just in biotechnology that new knowledge and new forms of manipulation challenge the human race and human culture with wider dimensions of responsibility and risk competence. They demand the development of an ethos and ethics of responsibility, i.e. for improved forms of moral risk management in using tools, defining ends, and respecting limits. I take issue with those ethicists who in using worst-case scenarios request a ban or severe forms of governmental tutelage of the development and use of a new technology. Writers such as Hans Jonas single out in addition to biotechnology, nuclear and information technologies.[14] Their thesis is that technological progress has outdistanced human moral capacities and therefore call for a retardation in developing and applying modern technologies. I hold the contrary view based on the study of the history of moral and cultural risk management and on own experience. Regulating technology does not result in a morally and culturally less risky environment, on the contrary heteronomous regulation carries moral hazards and risks of its own as it reduces the individual's options to choose and to follow his or her own conscience. The ethically beneficial response to increased technical capabilities is to increase education of and support for individual risk competence and increased training in moral responsibility.

Moral and cultural traditions play an important role in shaping individual and societal competence to deal with new challenges. But tradition may not be used in an uncritical way, as traditions do not just contain truly moral values but also antiquated customs which have to be cut off like the old queues once fashionable.[15] There are at least three different forms which introduce moral traditions into modern discourse concerning moral assessment and to instruct the individual:

1. the *authoritative and regulative* way which is favoured by the patrons of
    hierarchical value assessment such as recently expressed by the Vatican
    Encyclical *Veritatis Splendor*,[16]
2. the *educative and exhortative way* in which the individual conscience
    seeks guidance from the wisdom of the past, often in seeking guidance
    from God by interpreting classical texts,[17] and
3. the *discursive and adjuvantive way* of making the best use of traditional
    forms of moral risk management.

The risks of the authoritative model include the suppression of the
individual conscience and the promotion of double standards as well as the
risk that the authorities might change the course of fatherly instruction. The
discursive model fits best into the scenarios of moral assessment by educated
and risk competent individuals; it is the model of the future but it needs to
more carefully make good use of the treasures hidden in the moral history of
many cultures.[18]

Since cultural traditions are different, so will be the moral solutions
which they will or will not support. Western definitions of brain-oriented
models for death which are based on concepts of a difference between the
immortal soul and the mortal body or on concepts of understanding and self-
understanding face many obstacles in Asian cultures treasuring the non-divisible
nature of the human person.[19] The more moral issues are related to the basics
of life, death, pain, liberty and justice, the more we will find cross-cultural
consensus for *prima facie human rights and obligations*, the more the issues
are culturally rather than biologically defined the more widespread will be
cultural diversity.[20] The protection of the basics of human and civil rights is
an issue of solidarity within pluralistic societies and among the plurality of
cultures. The recognition of those basic rights, which can be called pre-
cultural rights and obligations as they have to be respected in all cultures of
human dignity. The principle of *subsidarity*, first developed in Christian moral
theology for social ethics,[21] is very well designed to handle bioethical issues as
well. It favours the support of moral risk management by those who are
directly involved rather than by heteronomous rules and requirements designed
by those who introduce general norms from the outside for those who are the
prime and personally challenged moral agents. The principle of subsidarity
relieves governmental and societal institutions from consensus formation and
implementation where consensus cannot be achieved because individual
consciences calculate the moral options differently based on their individual
moral priorities. It also strengthens the individual conscience by requiring
final moral responsibility rather than the formal obedience to regulations and
laws given by others.[22]

As long as the rights of other members of the moral community are not
infringed, the principle of subsidarity should allow for individuals to make
moral choices regardless of whether theologians, ethicists, lawyers and
politicians disagree in such crucial questions as to when unborn life should be
protected or when a human life is over, whether to give or receive organs,

whether or not to differentiate between procreative and recreative forms of sex, whether to have or not to have children and how many. The cultures of responsibility are not threatened by giving individual conscience and risk management too much room for responsibility, rather by giving them too little. As Spinoza observed 1670 in his *Tractatus Theologico-Politicus*, the freedom of individual responsibility from indoctrination threatens neither truth nor society, but the destruction of the individual conscience will finally result in the destruction of those powers of destructive dominance.

Of course, there have to be some *rules and regulations* as to how to handle machines, technologies, biotechnologies, and the technicalities of regulation and enforcement. The moral hazard of over-regulating, however, is a special risk in those areas of technology assessment and moral assessment where technologies are new. Anticipating high technical risks is not unprofessional for good technical risk management; it is even mandated when chartering into new and unknown territory such as expected risks of importing dangerous microbes from the moon or striving for the highest possible safety standards in early DNA recombination. But it also is a part of prudent technical risk management to reduce safety measures as soon as experience tells us that they are far too high. In order to avoid abuse, moral and technical limits to the regulation of technology should be recognized.[23] Rules and regulations are often a moral hazard themselves such as the German Embryo Protection Law, which makes pre-implantation diagnosis for certain severe genetic disorders a crime while allowing early and even late abortion for those cases as medically indicated.[24]

Fletcher has described how new ethical issues evolve in four stages: threshold, open conflict, extended debate, and adaptation. Wivel and Walters have demonstrated that in somatic cell therapy, these four steps have been followed, accepting that new issues such as germ-line therapy will unfold in similar sequences.[25] Many countries have already implemented national or multinational review boards and developed moral assessment strategies for one or the other challenges of biotechnology in agriculture and medicine.[26] Reading the protocols and following the deliberations of these moral risk review bodies, the absence of generalized statements and arguments is remarkable, as is the capacity of ethicists to micro-allocate well-established and supported traditional principles and maxims into new scenarios of knowledge and manipulation. There is great risk involved in biotechnology as in all technologies: technical risk, moral risk, and risk in the calculation of risk. But there are methods to improve and sharpen technical devices and models of deliberation, consensus formation, and accepting ambiguities and diversities in moral choice. There are many prudent ways for government to ease moral conflict and to reduce technical risk; there are many ways to research and to teach moral and technical risk competence and individual responsibility. What finally counts are not these various devices but the wisdom, knowledge and the ethos. In the words of Lao Tzu 'we make doors and windows for a room, but it is these empty spaces that make the room livable'.[27]

Finally, let me summarize my observations of the working of differential ethics in the assessment of technical and moral risk in well defined new scenarios of biotechnology in a fifth thesis: *To master the benefits and risks of modern technology we must further strengthen the ethos and ethics of responsibility in the support of individual self-determination, cultural diversity and political stability.*

Notes

1. Sass, 1987a.
2. Council of Europe, 1990; U.S. Office of Technology Assessment, 1991; U. S. National Institute of Health, 1985; Wivel and Walters, 1993.
3. Lao Tzu, 1989, 117.
4. Kapp, 1877.
5. Jünger, 1960; Kapp, 1978; Sass, 1981.
6. Vogel, 1990; Wertz, Fletcher and Mulvihill, 1990; Sass, 1993.
7. Sass, 1992a; Sass, 1992b.
8. Sass, 1993.
9. Kielstein and Sass, 1992.
10. Asch et al., 1993; Handyside et al., 1992; Kielstein and Sass, 1992.
11. Altimore, 1982; Sass, 1987a.
12. Altimore, 1982; Sass, 1987a; Sass, 1987b; Sass, 1992b.
13. U. S. National Institute of Health, 1985.
14. Jonas, 1979.
15. Sass, 1986.
16. Johannes Paul II, 1993.
17. Fuchs, 1984.
18. Sass, 1987b; Sass, 1991.
19. Sass, 1992a; Sass, 1992b.
20. Sass, 1986.
21. Pius XII, 1931.
22. Sass, 1992b.
23. Altimore, 1982; Sass, 1987a; Sass, 1992b.
24. Bundesrepublik Deutschland, 1990.
25. Wivel and Walters, 1993.
26. Council of Europe, 1990; Lenoir, 1991; U. S. National Institute of Health, 1985; U. S. Office of Technology Assessment, 1991.
27. Lao Tzu, 1989; U. S. National Institute of Health, 1985.

References

M. Altimore, 'The Social Construction of a Scientific Controversy', *Science, Technology and Human Values* 7 (1982): 24–31.
D. A. Asch et al., 'Reporting the Results of Cystic Fibrosis Carrier Screening', *American Journal of Obstetrics and Gynecology* 168 (1993): 1–6.
Bundesrepublik Deutschland, 'Embryonenschutzgesetz', *Bundesgesetzblatt* 13 (Dezember 1993).

EC, Council of Europe, 'Council Directives on the Contained Use and on the Deliberate Release into Environment of Genetically Modified Organisms', *Official Journal of the European Communities* 17 (1990): 1–27.

J. Fuchs, 'Das Gottesbild und die Moral innerweltlichen Handelns', *Stimmen der Zeit* 6 (1984): 363–382.

A. H. Handyside et al., 'Birth of a Normal Girl after In-Vitro-Fertilisation and Pre-Implantation Diagnostic Testing for Cystic Fibrosis', *New England Journal of Medicine* 327(13) (1992): 905–909.

H. Jonas, *Das Prinzip Verantwortung* (Frankfurt: Insel, 1979).

F. G. Jünger, *Gärten im Abend- und Morgenland* (München: Bechtle, 1960).

E. Kapp, *Grundlinien einer Philosophie der Technik* (1877), hg. H. M. Sass (Düsseldorf: Stern, 1978).

R. Kielstein and H.M. Sass, 'Right Not to Know or Duty to Know? Prenatal Screening for Polycystic Renal Disease, *Journal of Medicine and Philosophy* 17 (1992): 395–405.

Lao Tzu, *Tao Teh Ching* (Boston: Shambala, 1989).

N. Lenoir, *Aux Frotiers de la Vie: Une Ethique Biomedicale a la Française* (Paris: La Documentation Française, 1991).

Pius XII, *Encyclica Quadrogesimo Anno* (Rome, 1931).

Johannes Paul II, *Encyclica Veritatis Splendor* (Vatican: Libreria Editrice Vaticana, 1993).

H. M. Sass, 'Mensch und Landschaft'. In G. Höhl hg., *Landschaft und Mensch* (Mannheim: Verlag Humboldt Gesellschaft, 1981), 293–322.

H. M. Sass, 'The Moral a priori and the Diversity of Cultures', *Analecta Husserliana* 20 (1986): 407–422.

H. M. Sass, 'Philosophical and Moral Aspects of Manipulation and Risk', *Swiss Biotechnology* 5(2a) (1987a): 50–56.

H. M. Sass, 'Methoden ethischer Güterabwägung in der Biotechnologie'. In *Fragen der Gentechnologie und Reproduktionsmedizin* (München: Schweitzer, 1987b).

H. M. Sass, hg., *Genomanalyse und Gentherapie* (Heidelberg: Springer, 1991).

H. M. Sass, 'Risiko aus der Sicht der Medizinethik'. In K. Giel and R. Breuninger, hg., *Risiko* (Ulm: Humboldt-Studienzentrum, 1992a).

H. M. Sass, 'Generalisierender Moralismus und Differentialethik'. In *Politik und Kultur nach der Aufklärung. Festschrift für Hermann Lübbe* (Basel: Schwabe, 1992b), 186–205.

H. M. Sass, 'Ethik in der Epidemiologie', *Das Gesundheitswesen*, 55 (1993): 119–126.

U. S. National Institute of Health, 'Points to Consider in the Design and Submission of Human Somatic Cell Therapy Protocols', *Federal Register* 50/160 (1985): 33463–33467.

U. S. Office of Technology Assessment, *Biotechnology in a Global Economy* (Washington DC: Government Printing Office, 1991). [OTA-BA-494]

F. Vogel, *Humangenetik und Konzepte der Krankheit* (Berlin: Springer, 1990).

D. C. Wertz, J. C. Fletcher, and J. M. Mulvihill, 'Medical Geneticists Confront Ethical Dilemmas: Cross-Cultural Comparisons among 18 Nations', *American Journal of Human Genetics* 46(6) (1990): 1200–1213.

N. A. Wivel and L. Walters, 'Germ-Line Gene Modification and Disease Prevention: Some Medical and Ethical Perspectives', *Science* (Oct. 22, 1993).

Appendix to Chapter 10

Ten Steps in Moral Risk Management

1. analyse single technical and cultural risk components
2. assess and group single risk components
3. develop risk reduction and risk avoidance strategies
4. define and assess options for action
5. select one or two options
6. assess arguments against selected option
7. modify and confirm your decision
8. manage moral risk
9. re-assess scenario or case continuously
10. re-assess scenario or case ad hoc

Models of Moral Risk Management

1. REVIEW
    1. Peer Review Boards
    2. Ethics Committees including 'lay persons'
    3. Ethics Expert Review
2. CONSULTATION
    1. Ad hoc Consulting on Request
    2. Contract Consultation, periodically or thematically
    3. Coordinated Consultation between parties
3. INTEGRATION
    1. Ethics Expert in the Team on the Service Side
    2. Ethics Expert in the Team on the Client Side
    3. Ethics Modules or Metalanguages in Expert Systems

Thesis One. Biotechnology is not new, nor are the technical and moral risks associated with it. But, as the dimensions of knowledge and manipulation have widened, so have associated ethical dimensions which need careful assessment in the light of traditional moral and cultural principles.

Thesis Two. The manipulation of nature mirrors human self-understandings, values, and morals; the clue to avoid risk in technology is to strengthen individual and cultural competence in moral risk assessment and personal responsibility.

Scenario Development Procedure

1. IDENTIFY THE PROBLEM
   a. collect technical data
   b. collect significant human data
   c. identify value elements
   d. discuss relations between technical and human values
2. ANALYSE ALTERNATIVE SCENARIOS
   a. establish reasonable possibilities for each scenario
   b. identify ethical principles in each scenario
   c. determine ethical costs and risks in each scenario
   d. discuss ethical and technical cost-benefit assessments
3. EVALUATE ALTERNATIVE SCENARIOS
   a. discuss uncertainty in each scenario prognosis
   b. discuss technical and moral costs and benefits
   c. identify moral agents
   d. discuss benefit-cost-risk balances
4. JUSTIFY YOUR SELECTION
   a. specify your reasons for the selected course of action
   b. clearly present the ethical basis for your action
   c. understand ethical shortcomings of your justification
   d. anticipate and discuss objections to your selection

Thesis Three. There is a duty to know about health risk factors for the promotion of self-determination in lifestyle and reproduction.

Eight Health Care Rules for the Lay Person

1. Find truly educated and trustworthy health experts.
2. Develop competence and responsibility in health risk management.
3. Make extended use of predictive and preventive medicine.
4. Expect healing or relief from acute medicine, but be aware of the limits and risks of any medical intervention.
5. Expect information and advice from medical experts and be a fair partner with them.
6. Define and implement your sense of qualities of life, from childhood to old age, in sickness and in health.
7. Prepare advance directives and name proxy decision makers for circumstances of incompetence.
8. Act responsibly in the use of communal health care funds.

Eight Health Care Rules for the Health Expert

1. Treat your patient as a person, not just his or her symptoms.

2. Assist your patient in developing health risk competence.
3. Integrate the 'clinical status' and the 'value status' of your patient into differential ethics, diagnosis and prognosis.
4. Be aware of the benefits, limits and risks of acute intervention and discuss those with your patient.
5. Be an expert partner with your patient and respect her or his wishes and values.
6. Continuously educate yourself and provide the best possible clinical and personal service.
7. Assist your patient in preparing advance directives and in working with proxies for the benefit of your patient.
8. Act responsibly in the use of communal health care funds.

Moral Risk in Manipulation

1. MANIPULATING NATURE
    1. building houses, preserving fire
    2. manipulating and producing materials
    3. breeding and cultivating animals and plants
    4. transforming nature into culture
2. MANIPULATING HUMANS
    1. indoctrination, terrorising
    2. skill training
    3. responsibility and risk education
    4. withholding education
3. MANIPULATION IN BIOMEDICINE
    1. information and diagnosis
    2. herbal medicine
    3. antibiotics against infectious diseases
    4. geriatrics against aging
    5. psychopharmaca against lover's grief

Moral Risk Management in Clinical Research

1. Medical diagnosis of patient.
2. Value diagnosis of patient.
3. Integrate axioscopic results and medical facts.
4. Share medical and moral risk assessment with patient.
5. Consent of research subjects.
6. Select research subjects.
7. Establish trust based communication and cooperation.
8. Monitor moral design within research design.
9. Protect rights and opportunities to withdraw.

Thesis Four.   Progress in methods of manipulation calls for progress in the development and support of an ethos and ethics of manipulation; a ban on manipulation would be moral and cultural malpractice.

Instrument for Ethics Transfer in Technology

1. ETHICS EXPERT
    integrated in team
    consulting
    reviewing
2. ETHICS COMMITTEE
    anticipatory scenario analysis
    single case consultation
    single case management
    development of moral policy options
    setting of moral identity standards
3. CHECKLISTS
4. GUIDELINES AND RECOMMENDATIONS
5. SELF-REGULATION
6. GOVERNMENT REGULATION
7. LEGISLATION
8. MORATORIUM
9. DAMNATION AND PENALIZATION

Basic Foundations of Ethical Reasoning

1. WORLDVIEW BASED
    Moral rules are based on interpretation of basic metaphysical or metascientific conceptions.
2. PRINCIPLES BASED
    Moral rules are based on selected basic and mid-level principles.
3. VIRTUES BASED
    Role model and character formation are preconditional for acting morally.
4. SCENARIO BASED
    Scenario analysis and assessment determine optimal case management.
5. CASE BASED
    Case history of moral risk analysis and micro- and mix-allocation of mid-level principles justify intervention.

Goals in Real Life Application of Ethics

1. MORAL ENARMEMENT
    1. Introduction of uniform metascience or metaphysics

    2.   Restauration of mandatory values in a closed society
    3.   Power as domination by indoctrination
2. DIFFERENTIAL ETHICS
    1.   Differential analysis of basic values, mid-level principles, and moral micro- and mix-allocation
    2.   Moral cost-benefit and risk-reward analysis
    3.   Scenario analysis and case management
3. QUALITY CONTROL
    1.   Ethical review by boards or experts
    2.   Integration of ethical expertise into management
    3.   Long-term compatibility of agenda with societal setup

Thesis Five.　　To master the benefits and risks of modern technology we must further strengthen the ethos and ethics of responsibility in the support of individual self-determination, cultural diversity and political stability.

Part II

Towards an Ethics for
the Biotechnological Age

11

Anthropology as the Basis of Bioethics

Reinhard Löw (†)

Bioethics, under this name a rather young philosophical discipline, is concerned with the ethical problems of biology and medicine including ecological questions. Its current, sometimes explosive, importance is drawn from the immensely enlarged possibilities of analysis and manipulation in modern biology (above all in molecular biology) as well as in reproductive and intensive care medicine. These fields raise questions, which engage symposia, academies and civic colleges everywhere: whether we may do everything we can do, whether we need a new ethic adapted to the new situation, whether all such achievements are in fact diabolic, and the like. In some sectors, as in the debate on genetics, the opposite points of view take on an ideological character when it comes to questions of the manipulation of human bodies, from the fertilization of egg cells to the artificial maintenance of a corpse for the sole purpose of supplying organs. Here it seems as if several articles of constitutional law and/or medical maxims all stand in stalemate against each other: the dignity of a single human being and its right to life, e.g. against the freedom of research or the protection of the family, or the patient's will against his well-being, and his own well-being against that of others in the future. The constellations are as numerous in their sheer possibilities, as they are in their actual occurrence in the present-day practice of biologists and medical people.

For the following considerations the wide field of bioethics will be limited to the core of its fundamental meaning for human bioethics. The competing conceptions of what it means to be human are nevertheless just as fundamental for the broader sector dealing with animals[1] in exploitation and experiment as they are for the whole field of nature in general.[2] The human sector is exceptional among them in as much as human beings are both subjects and objects of the problem. This means that the anthropological foundations can never apply to one side only, although this characterizes, at least latently, the major part of the current Anglo-Saxon bioethical debate. The first part of this paper refers to the conception of human being predominant in this discussion, the second to a critique of this view, and the third to its confrontation with a substantialist, Christian conception.

The Evolutionistic Conception of Humankind and Its Bioethical Consequences

Before I talk about an evolutionistic conception of humankind, I want to make clear that evolutionism is not quite the same as evolutionary theory. 'Evolution theory' is a well-founded, in parts, even an ingenious theory about the development and mutation of animals and their species over long periods of time. It is primarily concerned with their material bases (genotypical and phenotypical, but also with regard to their changing environment). 'Evolutionism' is evolution theory developed into an entire philosophy (or even ideology),[3] and its categorical basis concerning humankind is the idea that the species *Homo sapiens* is entirely natural, explainable physically, chemically and in terms of evolutionary biology. There is no need for recourse to anything 'supernatural' or 'spiritual', no need for any unique socialization of humankind or for its morals, neither for human's cognitive achievements nor for culture and art: obviously, even less for God and religion. Not 'God created humankind', but humankind invented 'God' as an answer to questions it couldn't answer itself: questions about the course of the sun, the nature of thunder and lightning, about being after death. To these questions, says socio-biologist Richard Dawkins, the idea of a god is a calming answer; according to the theory of selection, tribes which believe in a god who rewards the brave warrior are much better off than those who do not and therefore flee too early from battle. Even for individual psychology it seems more advantageous to believe in a god; it feels better. For the behavioural researcher Wolfgang Wickler, this seems the best reason to believe in a god; after all, he does want to feel good.

As the basis we need only assume that humankind can in principle be explained naturally, scientifically and causally in all its biological as well as intellectual and cultural abilities and achievements. The physiological processes are not essentially different from feeling and thinking. In this kind of human phylogenesis and ontogenesis, nothing needs to be explained by recourse to non-physical phenomena. In order not to remain too theoretical, I want to explain this very conception of humankind with the help of Richard Dawkins' well-known work, *The Selfish Gene*.

The only decisive level to explain the whole human and non-human living reality is for Dawkins the level of genetics. The genes have built themselves machines of survival, also called organisms, and their equipment and tools for eating, reproduction and flight serve only for the preservation and spreading of the genes. 'Serve for', of course, should not be interpreted in a teleological sense. It is the metaphorically abbreviated term for a programme. From this basic statement Dawkins can work out his scientific definitions of human phenomena. 'A mother is a machine, programmed to do everything to transmit copies of its own genes.'[4] Children are interpreted accordingly: 'The genes in children's bodies are selected according to their capability to outwit parent bodies. Children should miss no opportunity to lie, cheat, exploit and deceive.'[5] Again, 'should' is not used in the moral sense, as Dawkins himself notes. It means that 'natural selection will be eager to favour children who act that way.' Now at last a mother has the scientifically enlightened choice between a morally educated or a successful child. What progress!

It should be emphasized once again that this conception of humankind is perfectly plausible on condition that all phenomena which appear in reality are in principle explainable with scientific measure. Human beings are one phenomenon in this reality; they are composed of very complex organical chemical substances, but there is no need for any non-natural scientific aid in order to explain their personal or tribal evolution.

This view has some concrete consequences, for example in the question of the beginning of human life. As the cell of a fertilized human egg is viewed exclusively as a problem of organic chemistry, one can freely experiment with it. In fact, this should happen, if one day we want not only to extinguish hereditary defects, but to breed humans with 'superhuman' powers, with higher intelligence, and, most likely, with an enhanced resistance against environmental disasters.[6] During the famous, even notorious, CIBA-Symposium in 1962, an expert group including many Nobel Prize laureates made very concrete eugenic proposals, for example, to breed new animals by crossing traits of humans and apes. The combination of human intelligence with clawed feet and a tail would lead to a race more suited for space expeditions, the 'one-man-torpedo', or for labour under extreme conditions. The experts were refined enough to think about the possible need to extend some measures of animal protection.[7]

Another issue arises in relation to the very beginning of life. To abort embryos handicapped can be viewed as a moral duty. The Australian bioethicist Peter Singer is only consistent when he claims that, given this view, the killing of handicapped children should be permitted after birth as well. They are human beings, but not persons. Grown shepherd dogs, in his words, develop more emotions and intelligence than do newborn children. He hereby refuses to view birth as an essential phenomenon. It is nothing but a change of position from the inside (the mother's body) to the outside; the physiological and chemical processes remain the same, dependence on the mother is nearly as extensive as before birth, allowing for some incidental changes. These types of rigorous eugenics are matched by issues of euthanasia, although one might better refer to it as 'active assistance towards dying'. In 1989 the debate on its inherent arguments drew for the first time large-scale attention in both German and Anglo-Saxon bioethics.[8]

At its core, evolutionistic anthropology in its view on bioethics is matched by an idea of medicine which understands itself as a subsection of biology. Human life has no special dignity, but at best a certain value; in other words, it is a calculable factor, more precisely: it involves various calculations. Unwanted hereditary features can be eliminated under the aspect of 'public health' just as under those of economy or aesthetics. Unwanted individuals with their own ideas about liberty or dignity should disappear according to the value calculated for their social functionality, just as children's education should be geared to avoid the rise of such ideas from the beginning (as B. F. Skinner explains in his famous book, *Beyond Freedom and Dignity*). Regarding the initial argument that this anthropology should be valid for both the subjective and the objective sides, it can be replied that equality is perfectly realized here as the 'equality of evolution', only that there is a difference between those enlightened by this knowledge, which is future and directive knowledge (be it communist or Manchester-liberal) and the unenlightened, who need to be guided. It is for their good (though not necessarily for the good of the individual) that the bearers of this knowledge have the corresponding physical and psychological means at their disposal. The highest law therefore is that of evolution. This is the right of the strongest, and therefore not a right at all, despite the cynical expression.

Towards a Critique of Evolutionistic Anthropology

Two initial remarks must precede the critique of this conception of humankind in order not to suggest mistaken, 'fundamentalistic' notions. First, it is true that many bio-scientists do consider this evolutionist conception of humankind as genuinely scientific theory, but they would not want to see in practice the bioethical, much less the political or sociobiological conclusions drawn from it. As laudable as this stance might be, it is inconsistent, for if nothing 'super-natural' can be admitted, how can we admit such unique claims to liberty, rights or dignity? Skinner is right: they are not compatible with evolutionism and the closed causal system of naturalistic scientism. Although it might well be good for the practical order to be inconsistent,[9] in this case it would be still better to develop an anthropology free of any such dilemma.

The second preliminary remark is that the following critique of evolutionistic anthropology will not focus on the apocalyptic vision of a socio-biology rigorously applied, however consistently that could be done, but rather on the theoretical foundations of this position. Among the numerous arguments,[10] some of which we have already touched upon, three will deserve special mention here:
1. the self-contradictory or self-defeating truth-claims of this anthropology;
2. the genuine point of departure for scientific explanations;
3. the illegitimate self-authorization and self-exemption of those 'in the know'.

First, we will comment upon the self-contradictory or self-defeating claim to truth. Were Richard Dawkins right with the theses of his book that all human insight and action can be explained as a function of the genes, then his own book would of course need to be interpreted as the selection strategy of Richard Dawkins' genes; it would have nothing to do with the truth as such. The genes have brought their survival machine, the organism named Dawkins, to write books in order to make as much money as possible and thus create better conditions for reproduction. There might have been simpler ways to do this, but the genes are not free to decide what they 'want' to produce or how they want to do so. Should this reductionistic, evolutionistic anthropology raise any independent claim to truth, it would deny itself. It is itself only one more product of evolutionary strategy, a single, incredible paradox, the core of which is something like the sentence, 'I am lying'. If it is true, it is a lie; if it is a lie, it is true.

As to the second point, this kind of anthropology and world-view ignores the genuine starting point for an explanation of phenomena. It is not the Big Bang, or matter, or laws of natural change and evolution, which provide an adequate point of departure for any explanation of the existing reality (evolutionist explanations included), but it is that grown reality itself which is to be examined. Before we can start explaining and reconstructing realities such as humankind, we have to come to an understanding about what belongs to this reality and what does not. True, the consistent evolutionist or materialist unmasks morals, religion, love and art as illusions: because he cannot 'construct' them, they cannot find a place of their own right in his view of the world and of humankind. But this is his special problem, not the problem of humankind in general. The reality of humankind includes its self-experience. The experience of liberty, morality, morals, God, love and beauty is incredibly 'more real' than those of simplistic reductionism and the pseudo-scientific explanations which claim to expose these as prejudices and illusions. Humans determine what is authentic, before they begin to reflect scientifically upon it.

This leads directly to the third argument: the illegitimacy of that exemption those who deem themselves to be scientifically enlightened make for themselves in opposition to all the others whom they analyse 'scientifically'. Let us look at some concrete cases. The first is bioethical in character. Anyone who experiments with human genes, with embryos, or with biological or psychological adults, might with some justification regard them as objects in the process of the intellectual investigation involved, but no scientific investigator can eliminate the fact that as a subject he or she is likewise drawn into the process itself with different status than the objects. Although this subjective component will not usually appear explicitly in publications or the formulation of a generalized law of nature, and even scientists will often view themselves as unimportant for the results. Still they will have acted out of their own interests, their own curiosity, and, in the end, their own liberty. They might also have 'abstracted', even unjustifiably so, from the fact that their object did not want to be an 'object' and that something had been done to it, to which it would never have agreed. To work out so-called 'determinations', scientific, sociological, ethnological or of whatever kind disguises the fact that those performing the examinations and experiments neglect their own determinations or choose freely among them.

The second case is currently of high socio-political relevance, involving those disciples and followers of Karl Popper's *The Logic of Scientific Discovery (Logik der Forschung)* who demand as a mark of scientificality integrity, tolerance, and a kind of freedom from preconceived thought, in the sense that convictions should be dispensed with as being ideological, unprovable and therefore an obstacle to the intellectual process.

The positive side of this philosophical starting point is beyond question. Hardly anything has brought as much misfortune to our century as insane ideologies. But first, this concerns primarily bad convictions. When in 1939 Germany's policy of expansion was at last brought to a halt, it was done not out of critical-rationalistic reflections on tolerance, but out of the conviction that no people has the right to dispose of others at will, and later on, that no one clique of party members has the right to dispose of its own people at will. And yet the ideal of a 'multicultural, pluralistic society' often overlooks the fact that tolerance is a non-arbitrary command of natural law, springing from the conviction that all humans are equal (earlier, and more completely: 'equal before God and as God's image'). This, indeed, is a matter of principle and is not confined only to specific cultural situations.

Those who claim to be in the 'scientific know' make a clandestine exception for themselves and their convictions. Nietzsche already saw that the call to the renunciation of all convictions springs itself from a very strong one: that by such renunciation a better state could be reached for the world, for the people, for oneself. This conviction itself, nonetheless, is viewed as exempt from the rule under discussion. Since it is not self-evident, it leads to a privileging of those who know how to master the situation rhetorically, sophistically, maybe cynically for themselves.

To sum up: if the evolutionistic conception of humankind not only has undesirable consequences in practice and self-contradictory implications in theory, but it also corresponds to the massive self-interest of people who strive to make a greater or lesser exception for themselves, how should the human being be more aptly conceived, considering scientific, technological civilization and, in our case, its bio-scientifical potential?

The Substantialist and Christian Conception of Humankind and Its Consequences

To begin with, I would like to explicate what is meant here by a 'substantialist conception of humankind'. In the proper sense of the word, substance means what underlies something else materially, elements and chemical compounds. Accordingly, the human being is not a substance, but it is composed of substances: about 90% water and the rest carbon, phosphorus, calcium, sulphur and so on. This fits well with the view of evolutionistic anthropology: the whole world is basically one big process of becoming, in which certain material states pass into each other and in the details of which we temporarily find those composite structures we call human beings, animals, plants, pieces of art or machines.

The original meaning of the term 'substance', introduced by Aristotle as *hypokeimenon*, has little in common with this view. Substance does not mean what something consists of, but of everything that can be said of it. When a human being is considered a substance, many things can be said of it: size, weight, appearance, intelligence, knowledge of foreign languages, place of birth and the like. All this is based on the fact that it is a human being. To be a human being is not just one predicate among many, because the bearer of this predicate is the condition for any efficient statement on the predicates of this being. The example of death makes this most obvious. When somebody dies, we do not say: 'X is no longer a human being', but instead: 'X is no more'. The bearer of the predicates no longer exists — at least not in this world.

The substantialist view of human beings proposed here has as its starting point this irreducibility of its formal conception as substance. It is irreducible and incapable of further deduction, because we know what constitutes human beings first of all by knowing ourselves. Although others, the 'Thou', first of all, the mother, play an important role in the full disclosure of the 'I' and its identity, on the other hand they, too, are only discovered from the vantage-point of the 'I', from the irreducibility of my own self-being and my own experience of life. With it, the way opens towards filling the substantialist conception of humankind with meaning and content. How do humans perceive themselves? We perceive ourselves as creatures with instincts, creatures which do indeed 'consist of something'; beings who can, for example, burn their fingers or be subjected to the law of gravity should we lean too far out of the window. All this we experience similarly to the evolutionistic conception of humankind. We are begotten, we have parents and thus there is a history of our species. And yet our being does not end with these moments. In a way that exceeds all these moments, humans perceive themselves as creatures of liberty, of intelligence, with a relation to transcendence. These perceptions build the basis for our ability to act against our 'natural determinations', without complete necessity of following our instincts. They are the reason why the human being, that creature of 'eccentric positionality' (H. Plessner), is the only one to have its own history, to act knowingly and with a hope at odds with its own past and future. We also perceive ourselves as creatures who do not owe their existence to themselves, and no more to our parents than they do to their parents, and thus eventually we perceive ourselves as mortal.

Liberty, intelligence, and the relation to transcendence: Immanuel Kant named these three essential and substantial properties when answering the single question, 'What is human being?', by dividing it into three questions: 'What can I know? What may I hope? What should I do?' If we wanted to articulate the question from the standpoint of evolutionistic anthropology, we would have to ask: What do I consist of? How do I function? How am I doing?

The substantialist view of humankind is fully aware that humans are also natural, social, economic creatures, that they are often tax-payers, traffic-participants, risk-factors. It simply denies that these elements explain what a human being is. We can assume in everyday discussions as well as in scientific ones that we can still agree without too much difficulty on the fact that the liberty of action and the ability of intelligence essentially belong to human beings. But what about the 'relation to the transcendent'? Can't we do without a 'god', this 'slap in the face of subtle thinkers' (Nietzsche)? Is it not, if anything, a private affair? Quite the contrary. First of all we do not need to understand the transcendent as amounting to the Judeo-Christian Creator-God, but instead we can understand it simply as the acknowledged dimension of what is not immanent, inner-human, inner-worldly. Relation to transcendence in this most basic conception means nothing more than that the experience of sense, in action, in love, in art, is regarded as an authentic experience. That means that this dimension is not my own creation and does not have to wait for my explicit consent, but that it even exists where others deny it explicitly. The admission of this dimension, though, sets an avalanche in motion, which does not stop short of the godhead, whether this is interpreted as the idea of the good (Plato), the unmoved mover (Aristotle), the central monad (Leibniz), or absolute spirit (Hegel). All these terms, of course, are meant for the 'god of philosophers'. Nor do they fathom even the substantialist conception of human being in all its depth, for Plato himself found the existence of slavery perfectly natural, and his rigid eugenic proposals would hardly find the consent of modern representatives of the substantial conception of humankind. What is missing is a non-self-evident, intermediate step, that of the equality of all human beings and the manifestation of the relation to transcendence in what we call human dignity, which specifies itself in the inalienable rights of human beings.

Considered formally, this dignity is the pendant to substance. The difference between value and dignity lies in the fact that, before all calculations of value, the human being appears as the subject of calculation. Of course there still are evaluations, and of course humans can and should be seen also as the bearers of functions and as useful means. The restriction Kant makes in his categorical imperative is this: that humans should never be seen exclusively as a means, but must always be respected as the ends as well.

The dignity of humankind specifies itself in the inalienable rights of humans. As a political thought, this is rather new. Its precondition is the principal equality of all peoples on earth, and until the second half of the eighteenth century this had been at best a religious idea, for example in the Judeo-Christian belief that every human being is the image of God. This conviction makes the differences between slaves and free persons, between barbarians and the Greeks, even between pagans and Christians anthropologically irrelevant; at least in principle. During the second half of the eighteenth century, the enlightenment adopted this universalistic anthropology in its sanctioning of human rights, although at the same time it took a critical view of their Christian foundation. Human rights should only and could only be accepted through reason and should need no religious or metaphysical arguments. The utopia of the rational world-state contrasted optimistically with the well-marked darkness of particular religious fanatisms.

Still, one thing eluded this enlightened, universalistic human rights thinking: that it used to be itself a particular idea of certain European intellectuals; its general evidence still fed on the wide-spread conviction of the equality of all humans in Judeo-Christian belief. The secularization of its content had to be the touchstone for the stability of the human rights idea. The result was surprising: after the popular critique of religion, historicism and naturalism, two favorite children of the nineteenth century enlightenment, turned against the enlightenment which had brought them forth and thus against the human rights idea, in the end even against themselves. They found their consistent formation in imperialism and social Darwinism, which indeed paraded certain rites of theoretical-ethical legitimization, but in fact cynically emerged from the superiority of gunboats and the means of production. Friedrich Nietzsche, the great diagnostician of his century, has indicated against the optimistic era of nationalism and the so-called *Gruenderzeit* the arrival of 'the most uncanny of all guests': European nihilism. The radical relativism of culture and values takes all its own convictions as random expressions of a particular culture. Even the idea of tolerance and human rights appear here as merely Eurocentric prejudices, born out of naive exuberance, but totally unreasonable.

It was reserved for the twentieth century with its dictatorships and wars to demonstrate the nihilistic consequence of the enlightened disconnection of reason and absolute values. In Germany this impression was so powerful that the constitutional law for its Western part after the lost war sprang from convictions of natural law. Forty years later we are again at the point where everything seems explainable out of the historical situation and from the difficulty in translating the term of human dignity into jurisdictional practice we conclude that it is better not to use it anymore. The daily violation of human rights and human dignity makes the formulation of its inviolability appear as a nostalgic anachronism.

In a remarkable essay, Robert Spaemann has drawn the opposite conclusion.[11] The evacuation and destruction of the idea of human rights, European in origin but universal in its validity, by its disconnection from the idea of the absolute must be seen as the occasion for clearly giving prominence to the rational connection of human rights and the unqualified or absolute as the starting point for relations between peoples of all cultures. With its scientific-technical civilization, Europe has invaded all other cultures and extinguished more than a few. It would be unacceptable 'to now keep for itself what alone can justify or at least partially compensate this destruction: the thought of what is without qualification, the absolute . . . Its universal plausibility today is realized in the idea of human rights. And the postulate for human rights is underlied by the idea of human dignity.'[12] Since this idea of human dignity cannot be conceived without the idea of the absolute, it is time for the rehabilitation of the latter. 'The evidence of human rights (could) lead to a renewal of what are acknowledged as their necessary presuppositions.

The fact that the universal claim of human rights cannot be explained by their historical European genesis does not necessarily lead to their relativization, but it could be a chance to acknowledge that absolute dimension of humankind, which is manifest in the terms of human dignity'.[13]

For the transposition of this 'anthropology of human dignity' into the principles of a Judeo-Christian bioethics, it would be necessary to trace human life from its beginnings in the womb, to its birth, development, and education towards a free and responsible individual, with sexuality and matrimony, with illnesses and sorrows and finally to death. Since we are talking about bio-ethics as a philosophical inquiry, penetration and evaluation of all these passive experiences and fates, but also of active deeds and life-plans, we cannot expect general or pat solutions. Instead we must indeed discuss all relevant aspects of the respective actions and cases — medical, economic, political, and so on — but always with respect to an ethical-philosophical aspect which is not just one among others, but the right ordering and interrelation of the other aspects. It is obvious that, when the discussion about human existence focuses primarily on its biological nature, where it is exposed to illness, suffering and death, a particularly sensitive consideration of those related to and those treating the afflicted is required. Still, the dignity of the 'object' must have absolute priority, be it unborn children or the handicapped, be it ill or dying persons. This also means that the other sciences, most of all biology, should orientate themselves toward the classical self-understanding of medicine as aiming at the 'well-being of the human.' The opposite option, to understand a doctor primarily as a researcher of the 'object human being', leads directly into inhumanity.

(Professor Reinhard Löw died on 25 August 1994 at the age of 45. R.I.P.)

Notes

1. R. Spaemann: 'Tierschutz und Menschenwürde', in: U. Händel, ed., *Tierschutz* (Frankfurt: Fischer Verlag, 1984) 71–81.
2. R. Löw: 'Die philosophische Begründung des Naturschutzes', *Scheidewege* 18(1988/9): 149–167, and R. Löw: 'Warum Naturschutz?' (1988) 156 *Kirche und Gesellschaft* 3–16.
3. R. Spaemann/R. Löw, *Die Frage 'Wozu?'. Geschichte und Wiederentdeckung des teleologischen Denkens* (München: Kösel, 1991) 239-299, and R. Löw: 'Kosmologie und Anthropologie', *Scheidewege* 15(1985): 306–321.
4. R. Dawkins: *Das egoistische Gen* (Berlin: Springer Verlag, 1978) 145; translated from: *The Selfish Gene* (Oxford: Oxford University Press, 1976).
5. Ibid., 161, 163.
6. F. Wagner, ed., *Menschenzüchtung* (München: C.H.Beck Verlag, 1969).
7. The famous CIBA Symposion is extensively discussed in ibid., with criticism in R. Löw, *Gen-Manipulation. Die geklonte Natur* (Rastatt: Moewig Verlag, 1987) 183–191.

8. To present this problem in its entirety, see: T. Bastian, ed., *Denken — Schreiben — Töten. Zur neuen 'Euthanasie'-Diskussion* (Stuttgart: Wiss. Verlagsgesellschaft, 1990) (including an article of the author).

9. R. Spaemann once remarkd: 'The only thing, which gives me some degree of optimism in regard of the future of humankind is that human luck is inconsistent.'

10. Cf. P. Singer, *Praktische Ethik* (Stuttgart: Reclam, 1984), 177ff; translated from: *Practical Ethics* (Cambridge; Cambridge University Press, 1979).

11. Cf. R. Spaemann: 'Universalismus oder Eurozentrismus?' *Merkur* 42(1988): 706–712.

12. Ibid., 711.

13. Ibid., 712.

12

Reflections on Method in Theology and Genetics: From Suspicion to Critical Cooperation

Anthony O. Dyson

Preface

Simplistic and heavily-loaded concepts of secularization in the sociology of religion, now many decades old, succeeded in distorting what should be recognized as the complex and pluriform relationships between scientific and theological theory. Furthermore, many women and men who claim not to profess a religious faith make the mistake of assuming that religious faith and theological theory stand in a one-to-one connection and that because the former is rejected, so the latter should be rejected too. Theology is, however, not a spontaneous utterance of religious faith. It involves instead the weaving together of aesthetic, psychological, philosophical, experiential, historical, scientific, existentialist and other strands of symbolic and narrative material. It employs a wide variety of forms of discourse. Theology is, furthermore, ambitious in striving to catch hold of that experience and meaning which is related to, but somehow tries to surpass, our own experience and meaning. Thus, theology is, at its best, a living and critical discipline whose principal task is to illuminate and strengthen human communities. At worst, theology mimics or evades the culture which it inhabits and petrifies the religion which it inherits. (The term 'theology' is not confined to *Christian* theology, but relates also to the other traditions, e.g. Buddhist, Jewish and Islamic theology. I write, however about the tradition which I know best.)

In the Introduction which follows, I present a case-study about the presence, and then the absence, of theological dimensions in the rise to prominence of bioethics in the United States over three decades. I shall then consider the accusation, made by some commentators, that the moral-philosophical brand of bioethics has got into difficulties. Turning then to theology, I consider with care some of the *types* of framework which theology has to offer. I look in turn at examples of the *use* of theology to make appropriate judgements in relation to the field of bioethics, dealing mainly with genetics.

Introduction

'There appears to be growing disquiet about the achievements and future of medical philosophy or bioethics.'[1] This statement is not untypical of many being made at the present time, not only by outsiders to the discipline but also by some who are heavily involved in bioethics. And this disquiet, Toon adds, comes after a period of rapid and sustained growth. As for the causes of this disquiet, Toon says that 'disenchantment with the results of medical philosophy arises largely because too much has been expected and claimed for bioethics'.[2] As an example, he quotes from Clouser and Gert's criticism that beneficence, autonomy, justice, and non-maleficence cannot solve ethical problems, though these concepts may provide a useful framework for clarifying them.[3] A similar reservation is registered by Courtney Campbell when he says that we need to broaden the scope of bioethics beyond our current fixation with problem solving, for some problems cannot be solved but must still be faced.[4]

The Fate of Theology in United States Bioethics

'Theologians just may bite. Or perhaps worse, they may not. At their worst they are seen as extremely dangerous. At their best, they are harmless, that is, useless'.[5]

I shall focus my remarks about *theology* upon a Special Supplement which appeared in the *Hastings Center Report* under the title 'Theology, Religious Traditions, and Bioethics', consisting of six essays by able scholars.[6] One of its editors, Daniel Callahan, manifests in the Preface certain diffidence about the venture, which is not surprising given the successful results which 'secular' bioethics has achieved in the United States in some thirty years. Yet it can be demonstrated that in the early years of bioethics, the 'social and medical ethos within which bioethics emerged . . . was constituted in part by *religious questions and religious thinkers*.'[7]

However, Callahan comments that 'this identifiably religious influence on bioethics subsequently seemed to decline'.[8] Whether this was the case can be tested around 1985 when the symposium Theology and Bioethics appeared.[9] Despite a long list of distinguished contributors, the project sounded an uncertain note. In a review of Shelp, a critic observed that the contributors recognize the intractibility of the problems and view the prospects of a neatly wrapped solution with skepticism. A distinguished contributor thought that little had been achieved.[10]

Callahans's historical account of the origins and development of United States bioethics twice uses the term 'secularization', namely 'the unfolding secularization of bioethics' and the 'most striking change over the past two decades or so has been the secularization of bioethics'. This is expounded as follows:

> The field has moved from one dominated by religious and medical traditions to one now increasingly shaped by philosophical and legal concepts. The consequence has been a mode of public discourse that emphasizes secular themes: universal rights, individual self-direction, procedural justice, and a systematic denial of either a common good or a transcendent individual good.[11]

How can the period of religious involvement and influence in the later 1960s and the 1970s be characterized? First, a tried and tested traditional casuistical Roman Catholic moral theology was available in the persons of, for example, Edwin Healy, Gerald Kelly, Thomas O'Donnell, Charles McFadden and Francis Connell. However, this moral theology was found to be very conservative in practice, not least in its dependence on a conservative reading of natural law. (There was no comparable confessional Protestant tome of theological ethics at this time. Some people have attributed such an identity to Joseph Fletcher's *Morals and Medicine* (1954); this, if carefully examined, turns out to be a statement and defence of *rights*!). Walters can say, however, that in the period 1970–75 'it was perhaps Protestants who contributed the largest volume of literature in medical ethics'.[12]

Second, there were great religious expectations of a significant shift in Papal contraception policy; the Encyclical *Humanae Vitae* demolished such expectations. It is instructive to see this event through the eyes of the young Dutch liberal, Andre Hellegers, an obstetrician-gynecologist, who was appointed to, and played a major role in, the Papal Commission on Birth Control which ultimately led to *Humanae Vitae*. Later, Hellegers, in the context of an essay on the Encyclical, remarked on the Papal implication that theology need not take into account scientific data, *but shall reach its conclusions regardless of present or future facts*.[13] Third, a fair number of middle-class American Christian intellectuals had been affected by various brands of theological radicalism in, for example, Harvey Cox's *The Secular City*, Teilhard de Chardin, and the 'Death of God' theologians. But these initiatives were not so much sustained as countered in succeeding years by church authorities. Fourth, the second Vatican Council had roused many hopes of which a large portion were not fulfilled. Fifth, Callahan's reminder should be noted, namely that 'the theological seminaries and departments of religion were in the 1970s drawn more to issues of urban policy and race, and to questions of world peace in a nuclear age, than to bioethics',[14] and, registering two circumstantial remarks made by Callahan:

> Once the field [of bioethics] became of public interest, commanding the attention of courts, legislatures, the media, and professional

societies, there was great pressure . . . to frame the issue, and to speak, in a common secular mode. As the field of medicine became itself more engaged in the issues [for legal scholars], it sought a way of framing and discussing them that would bypass religious struggles. Lawyers and philosophers were by no means seen as congenial allies of doctors, but they were preferable to theologians (especially those who spoke out of sectarian traditions).[15]

It is difficult, however, to make generalizations about the scale of the early religious involvement in bioethics. There are further 'secular' strands not so far noted which have their roots further back behind the 1960s. David J. Rothman, for example, in his book on the birth of American bioethics, links up the selection, in the Second World War, of research subjects from vulnerable populations who were unable to give their consent, with the 1966 article by Henry Beecher about the unethical abuse of subjects in medical research. Following this initiative, 'formal government regulations and an emphasis on the need for subjects' consent brought oversight of medical research into the public realm'. This reflects an early preoccupation with autonomy and informed consent which has maintained a high place on the agenda of 'secular' bioethics.[16]

It is necessary, however, also to look at the wider cultural context of the beginnings of bioethics. If that context changes, then we may expect attitudes to bioethics to change. Callahan observes that the 1960s and 1970s, when bioethics grew up, was an 'era of affluence and social utopianism'. It was culture that was experimenting 'with an expansive array of newly found rights and unprecedented opportunities for personal freedom . . . .'[17] This personal freedom issues in bioethics in the category of autonomy.

So bioethics in America emerged in a period of buoyancy and optimism, putting factual and moral confusion into order. It was caught up, literally and metaphorically, in a growth economy. So, for example, in their heyday, the National Commission for the Protection of Human Subjects and the President's Commission called representatives from medicine, law, philosophy and health policy sciences to give evidence, and in their reports ' showed not the least visible trace of religious influence!'[18] An additional consequence is that this bioethical moral philosophy 'has either intimidated religion from speaking in its own voice, or has driven many to think that voice can be expressed with integrity only within the confines of particular religious communities.'[19] So 'most religious ethicists entering the public practice of ethics leave their special insights at the door and talk about "deontological vs consequentialist", "autonomy vs paternalism", "justice vs utility", just like everybody else'.[20]

Bioethical Philosophy in Question

But what has been the outcome of all this? Callahan avers that the unfolding secularization of bioethics has *culminated in speculative and linguistic narrowness.* A form of moral philosophy was encouraged for use in the market place 'that aspires simultaneously to a kind of detached neutrality . . . and a culture-free rationalistic universalism, which is suspicious of the emotions and the particularities of actual human communities.'[21]

Thus, says Callahan, in ousting religion from bioethics, we have inherited a triple threat against us: first, we are left 'too heavily dependent upon *the law* as the working source of morality'; second, we are bereft of the 'accumulated wisdom and knowledge that are the fruit of long-established religious traditions'; third, we are forced to pretend that 'we are not creatures . . . of particular moral communities'. But, on the contrary, Campbell insists that 'the normative principles of bioethics are not . . . self-applying or self-interpreting, but instead require a context of application and a content informed by moral traditions — professional, secular, and religious'.[22]

I quote from Susan Parson's account of an ethos of moral philosophy similar to that being criticized by Callahan:

> This model of moral reasoning can be broadly characterised as liberal, for it both reflects the liberal society of which it is a product and contributes further to that ideology by the picture of free rational behavior which it paints. Insofar as its portrayal of moral agency is concerned, this model requires the increasing abstraction of the individual from the facts of life — namely the personal relationships, social roles and biological experiences that seem also to be an important part of being human. This becomes obvious in the distinction between the public and the private realms, which is a feature of liberal political thinking. The private realm becomes the repository of all the intimacies, feelings, human ties, and natural events which define the person as a unique and special entity amongst all others. While the public realm, on the other hand, demands that all such realities be set aside in favour of general principles which are to be applied regardless of unique characteristics. . . . This is also the context in which the vocabulary of rights is set, and the cluster of ideas surrounding to concept reveals the detachment of the individual concerned from intrinsic relationships, social involvements or biological necessities.[23]

Theological Forays

I now present some deliberately varied examples of theological forays into bioethics, especially in genetics.

(a) Arnold Voth's basic assumptions are: God is the ultimate source of all our decisions on ethics; humanity is created in the image of God and thus all human life is sacred; the family unit is ordained by God and is thus of the highest importance.[24] Principal rules of ethical decision making include: using the broadest possible scriptural principle where there are alternatives and conflict of principles; choosing the decision with the greatest potential for good and the least for evil. Voth therefore begins with 'Biblical-theological' principles and then proceeds swiftly to ethical implications. Regarding genetics, Voth comments on cloning — a 'gross travesty of man, the creature of God, [which] would have to be condemned out of hand' — and on recombinant DNA engineering which is 'a neutral issue that has enormous potential for both good and evil'.

Here the theological content is minimal; what there is is rigid and virtually incapable of correlation. The Bible is used mechanically.

(b)   Showing both similarities and dissimilarities to Voth, McCormick starts with six 'foundations that deserve the name theological'.[25] One of the six semi-credal foundations reads as follows: 'This ultimate fact [of God's self-disclosure in Jesus Christ as self-giving love] reveals a new basis of context for understanding the world. It gives it a new (Christocentric) meaning. As a result of God's concrete act in the incarnation, "human life has available a new relation to God, a new light for seeing, a new fact and center for thinking, a new ground for giving and loving, a new context for acting in this world".' But after this traditional confession, McCormick takes a different direction. 'Theological work in the past decade has rejected the notion that the sources of faith are a thesaurus of answers. Rather they should be viewed above all as narratives, as a story. From a story come perspectives, themes, insights, not always or chiefly direct action guides. The *story* is the source from which the Christian construes the world theologically'.

The Christocentric method in theology encompasses all reality; it does not let the secular be secular. The increasingly popular use of narrative and story still means that we have an authoritative resource from which we construe all reality. We do not construe the world independently.

(c)   A number of theologians have accused those who deal in genetic engineering of 'playing God'. This is a theological accusation which deserves consideration. An interesting treatment occurs in the response of the panel of scholars chosen by the three organizations (Protestant, Jewish and Roman Catholic) to the request by the United States President's Commission to the Secretaries of the three organizations 'to elaborate on any uniquely theological considerations underlying their concern about gene splicing in humans'.[26] In the view of the advisory theologians, 'contemporary developments in molecular biology raise issues of *responsibility* rather than being matters to be prohibited because they usurp powers which human beings should not possess. The Biblical religions teach that human beings are, in some sense, co-creators with the Supreme creator. Endorsement of genetic engineering which is praised for its potential to improve the human estate, is linked with the recognition that the misuse of human freedom creates evil and that human knowledge and power can result in harm'. But this term 'playing God' also, at its heart, represents a reaction to the realization that human beings are on the threshold of understanding how the fundamental machinery of life works. Fully to understand these powers would be so awesome as to be God-like.

These remarks may be compared with Ruth Chadwick's conclusions.[27] First, the playing God objection, 'is a reminder to a decision-maker that she is not infallible, not a superior being with the knowledge required to decide on the quality of another's life'. Second, 'the force of the objection seems to be an expression of a fear of what will happen if human beings go too far, trying to transcend human limits and rival the omnipotence of God'. The objection serves as a counsel. But it does not seem to be enough to rule out particular courses of action; it points out that care should be taken to minimize the risk of disaster. It cannot provide us with any definite boundaries which should not be crossed. (This is a matter for consequentialist assessment.)

The approach via 'playing God', it is clear, provides much material for correlation of theology and bioethics.

(d)   Paul Ramsey was a voluminous and sometimes arbitrary writer. Here I consider briefly the question of some of his theological presuppositions in relation to genetics. He argues that our fundamental decisions will be made at the point where we accept a particular understanding of man[28] (gender-exclusive language in Ramsey). Thus, anyone who remains within hailing distance of the biblical view of the life of this 'flesh' knows that we are our bodies no less than we are our souls, minds or worlds; he knows that to violate this flesh is a violation of man no less than to violate man's will or freedom. 'By contrast, a so-called scientific ethic . . . which tries to base itself on the intentionality of the scientific mind alone, nearly always regards mind, or will or freedom . . . as the only thing that can be violated in man. According to this view, our bodies and our genes do not belong essentially to human nature. . . . They are rather matter to be used for self-elected ends . . . So there is no reason why man should not become his own maker, the maker of all future generations, and the re-maker of the nature of human parenthood.' Ramsey insists that both Sacred Scripture and sound reason do not promise success to man in history. He has 'only scorn for theologians who have embraced messianic positivism and baptised secular technology especially in the area of genetics and reproduction'. Ramsey cannot accept a perspective which sees human, temporal history so positively related to the Kingdom of God.[29] He neither advances nor affirms any theological justification for presuming a moral development in human evolution. It is not surprising that, at all points, Ramsey opts for the category of 'doing' rather than of 'making'. Christian scholars introduce the language of making and manufacturing 'with great detriment to a truly human and Christian ethics'. One consequence of this is that often the 'individual person will be unjustly subordinated to the non-patient, the species'. In his preference for the first, namely the Heavenly City of which Augustine spoke, Ramsey plays down the positive aspect of humankind which, in traditional theology, rests upon the doctrines of tradition and resurrection.

(e)   In his article 'Germ-Line Cells: Our Responsibilities for Future Generations', Emmanuel Agius explores the criterion concerning the extent to which present human activity is seen to affect future generations.[30] It is highly surprising that this question concerning the future has not surfaced in any of the theological authors who have so far been mentioned. It is my impression that many writers avoid expressing theological value-judgements in this sphere because the manipulation of germ-line cells is *at the present time* highly problematic. But, theologically speaking, the question of future generations opens up the topic of eschatology which takes on various forms and is rich in symbolic material. Agius leans heavily on A.N. Whitehead, whose process ethics is 'open to all technological progress because of its potential enhancement of the beauty of human experience'. But we must also take responsibility for the consequences of our activity on others. 'Given that the human species is genetically interrelated and that human activity has far-distant future consequences, our moral responsibility must necessarily extend in space and time to include all the members of the human species. But this argument is so general and all-embracing, as is Agius' notion of an 'international juridical system . . . to regulate on sound principles the common intellectual heritage of mankind '. The force of some versions of eschatology is that they come from the future urgently into the present and for action now.

(f)   I want to refer here to Karl Rahner's theological perspective. 'Self-determination' defines the nature and task of human freedom as understood by Christianity. According to the Christian doctrine of humanity, the *human* being is the being who manipulates herself or himself. As such, human beings who are free in relation to God, are in a most radical way empowered to do what they will with themselves, freely able to align themselves towards their own ultimate goal. Thus, what is new in this respect is not that the human being is her or his own maker. Rather this fundamental nature of human beings is 'manifested historically today in a totally new way'.[31] Rahner observes that the human being no longer creates itself merely as a moral and theoretical being under God, but as an earthly, corporeal and historical being. This self-manipulation is deliberately planned, programmed and controlled. 'Man no longer makes himself merely with reference to eternity but with reference to history itself as such'.[32] This raises profound problems. In another essay from the same volume, Rahner recognizes that not everything which can be done, ought to be done. The possibilities available to humankind in earlier days were very stable and had been tested countless times. But 'nowadays the situation is different . . . New and practical possibilities are set before us in relatively rapid succession, and they have vast and far-reaching effects'.[33]

In these two essays Rahner grounds the radical opportunities open to humanity in the very depths of the nature of humankind and of God. This may sound very utopian; but it is fully conceded by Rahner that human nature possesses great limitations, not least the 'great limiting situation of death'. He also argues that our genetic inheritance should be accepted, not manipulated. Furthermore, Rahner's style and emphasis sometimes have the character of idealist philosophy; so it has been argued that Rahner's methodology at times does not give enough importance to the physical, the societal, and the political aspects of reality.

The fruitful starting-point is that humanity and the transcendent both occupy the same habitat, namely 'history'.

(g)   Ronald Cole-Turner writes that 'if we are to see our work as cooperative or co-creative with divine creativity, then we must have some sense of what

God intends'.[34] Cole-Turner justifies an extended analysis of Genesis by its similarity with our situation. For if Genesis is concerned with 'the transition of a people into agricultural society, and if we today are faced with the transition from agriculture to genetic engineering, then we should expect some guidance in our time from the turmoil and theological ferment of this earlier era'.[35] As far as divine intention is concerned, '. . . God stands over the processes of nature, working through them to achieve a divine intent which should not be confused with any processes, patterns, or events in nature. God's creative intent is evolutionary . . . Its goal transcends any present achievement and its progress is marked by continuous development . . . God is continually at work not merely sustaining the creation but guiding it toward an intended future'.[36] But, following Peacocke, Cole-Turner goes further. 'Through science, nature (as human beings) discovers the natural processes through which God works, and through religious awareness it senses the divine intent which underlies its own emergence'. Through human beings, *evolution becomes self-discerning.* 'With the capacity to discern comes the possibility of cooperation with the processes of nature and with the intention of God for creation'. Cole-Turner follows Peacocke yet one more step: 'our technology, guided by our scientific understanding of the processes of creation, might add something new to the creative powers of God, for we might be an agent within creation through whom God acts in a creaturely way. . . . As creatures capable of discerning the divine intention, we are one part of creation that is capable of turning divine intent into creaturely activity'.[37]

(h)   In many ways the most impressive standpoint that I have examined is that expounded by Lindon Eaves and Lora Gross — impressive because it makes the heaviest demands upon *both* science *and* theology to be self-critical.[38] In particular, 'many traditional images of God and the God-world relation are inadequate to present religious ideas in a world whose self-understanding has been transformed by genetics. The model of Spirit as the God-world relationship, deploying insights from human genetics, enables us to conceive of human action and behavior as *co-participation* with the whole created order.'[39] In this perspective, it may be concluded that the distinction between *life* and *human life* may not be as radical as many theologians have maintained. The general two-fold implication of this scheme is that theologians have to appreciate more fully the biological foundations which account for much of who we are and which connect us intimately with the rest of creation *and* that scientists — so say the authors — whose notorious suspicion of religion often confines their criticism to what is most superficial, may find in theological constructs a phenomenlogical aspect *which can no longer be ignored.*

Conclusion

I have briefly described and even more briefly evaluated several theological-ethical proposals, nearly all of which are related to genetics in some way or another. It is interesting to speculate which of these writers might carry weight in a multi-disciplinary setting today. It is no mean question, given the rapidly accelerating implications of genetics in science, medicine, agriculture and other spheres. The beaches are littered with the remains of previous inter-disciplinary undertakings left by the outgoing tide. Of the proposals which I have considered in this essay, the most intellectually and emotionally stimulating (but which criteria govern choice in an interdisciplinary context?) is that of Eaves-Gross, perhaps because it demands of those who might share in it the highest degree of intellectual repentance, asking of themselves what they should surrender and what they should reconceive in the being and practice of their vocations as geneticists and theologians. But perhaps the stimulation results also from being carried along, giddily, by the flow of abstraction. More specific communication is required. Or perhaps — and not surprisingly — it is the respect and fear which one feels in the presence of knowledge and power: 'to articulate the religious significance of the delicate ecological and evolutionary matrix in which all of life is embedded and over which humans have such astonishing power'.[40]

Notes

1. Peter D. Toon, 'After Bioethics and Towards Virtue', *Journal of Medical Ethics*, 19, 1990: 18.
2. Toon, 18.
3. Toon, 18 referring to K.D. Clouser and B. Gert, 'A Critique of Principlism', *Journal of Medical Philosophy*, 15, 2, 1990: 219–236.
4. Courtney S. Campbell, 'Religion and Moral Meaning in Bioethics', *Hastings Center Report*, July/August 1990: S7.
5. Richard McCormick, 'Theology and Bioethics', *The Hastings Center Report*, March/April, 1989: 5.
6. July/August, 1990: S1-S24.
7. Callahan, S1.
8. Callahan, S1.
9. Earl E. Shelp (ed), Reidel, Dordrecht, 1985.
10. Namely John Cobb.
11. Callahan, S2.
12. LeRoy Walters, 'Religion and the Renaissance of Medical Ethics in the United States: 1965–1975', in Shelp (ed), *Theology and Bioethics*, 12. Names include Branson, Carney, Childress, Dyck, John Fletcher, Gustafson, Hamilton, Lebacqz, J. Robert Nelson, Potter, Ramsey, Shinn, Vaux.
13. Shelp (ed), 10.
14. Callahan, S3.
15. Callahan, S3.
16. David J, Rothman, *Strangers at the Bedside: A History of how Law and Bioethics transformed Medical Decision-Making*, Basic Books, New York, 1991.
17. Callahan, S2.
18. Callahan, S3.
19. Callahan, S4.
20. Leon R. Kass, 'Practicing Ethics: Where's the Action?', *Hastings Center Report*, January/February 1990: 6–7.

21. Callahan, S4.
22. Campbell, S9.
23. Susan F. Parsons, 'The Intersection of Feminism and Theological Ethics: A Philosophical Approach', *Modern Theology*, Vol. 4, April: 253.
24. Arnold Voth, 'Christian Principles in Medical/Ethical Dilemmas', *Conrad Grebel Review*, 6, 1988P: 29–44.
25. Richard A. McCormick, 'Theology and Bioethics', *Hastings Center Report*, March/April 1989: 6.
26. President's Commission for the Study of Ethical Problems in Medicine and Biomedical and Behavioral Research, *Splicing Life: The Social and Ethical Issues of Genetic Engineering with Human Beings*, Washington, 1982: 51ff, 95ff.
27. Ruth F. Chadwick, 'Playing God', *Cogito*, Autumn 1989: 186–193.
28. Paul Ramsey, 'Genetic Therapy: Paul Ramsey (Theologian)' in Michael P. Hamilton (ed), *The New Genetics and the Future of Man*, Eerdman's, Grand Rapids, Michigan, 1972: 171ff.
29. Charles E. Curran, *Politics, Medicine, and Christian Ethics: A Dialogue with Paul Ramsey*, Fortress Press, Philadelphia Pa, 1973, *passim*.
30. Emmanuel Agius, 'Germ-line Cells — Our Responsibilities for Future Generations', *Concilium*, June 1989: 105–115.
31. Karl Rahner, 'The Experiment with Man' in *Theological Investigations*, Vol IX, Darton, Longman and Todd, London, 1972: 205–224, 213.
32. Rahner, 213.
33. Rahner, 'The Problem of Genetic Manipulation, Vol. IX, 249.
34. Ronald S. Cole-Turner, 'Is Genetic Engineering Co-Creation?', *Theology Today*, 44, 1987: 338–349.
35. Cole-Turner, 343.
36. Cole-Turner, 347.
37. Cole-Turner, quoting from A.R. Peacocke, *Creation and the World of Science*, Clarendon Press, Oxford, 1979.
38. Lindon Eaves and Lora Gross, 'Exploring the concept of Spirit as a Model for the God-World Relationship in the Age of Genetics', *Zygon*, 27, 3, 1992: 261–285.
39. Eaves and Gross, 282.
40. Eaves and Gross, 283.

13

Bioethics and Genetics in Asia and the Pacific: Is Universal Bioethics Possible?

Darryl Macer

Bioethics and Biotechnology

This collection focuses on the ethical questions raised by biotechnology. Biotechnology is the use of living organisms to provide goods and services, and has been essential to the development of civilization for millennia. There are several key questions I want to answer in this paper. Firstly, does new biotechnology raise any different or novel issues that the old biotechnology did not? Secondly, how do people think about these issues and over the use of biotechnology, both in medicine and agriculture? What do they think about disease, and about nature and life? We could say bioethics is love of life, so our attitudes to life are an essential part of bioethics. Thirdly, from examining the reasoning that people use in making 'bioethical' decisions, can we develop universal bioethics? The third question is the most controversial, and sensitive, and perhaps it is fitting to be discussed in Hong Kong, a cosmopolitan meeting point between European and Chinese culture.

The basic ideals of bioethical decision making are love (balancing risk of doing harm versus intended benefit); and balancing individual and/or familial autonomy versus social responsibility. The question of universal ethics rests on what we mean by the word 'universal'. Even within a single community one will find divisions on issues of bioethics, such as abortion, euthanasia and risk perceptions — so it is obvious not all people reach the same decisions. What I mean by universal is rather at the level of using the same ideals, but people may balance them differently to arrive at different decisions. Therefore, universal ethics does not mean identical decisions, but it does mean that the range of decisions in any one society is similar to other decisions found across the whole world. It is also not the same as absolute ethics, saying that there is one correct ethical decision for a given set of circumstances.

The study of decision making can and should be scientifically made, and is a question that we can answer from data and observations. Therefore in this paper I do not attempt to define an ethical or good decision. The correct 'decision', if it does exist, is not necessarily the same as the majority decision. If people in different countries share the same thinking, and reasoning, then we could call this universalism, and it makes the possibility of universal ethics real. If they do not, then what we must aim for is cross-cultural understanding, perhaps with some degree of universalism. At the beginning I should make it quite plain that the use of surveys is only one part of the overall approach we can use to look at cultures, and that the data from the International Bioethics Survey I will describe is intended as a contribution to answering this question, it does not claim to have the whole picture. However, this data is, like all observations, a challenge to all of us to incorporate or explain into any description of the real world, and it cannot be ignored.

Biotechnology and Bioethics as Part of Human Heritage

Bioethics especially includes medical and environmental ethics. The word was mainly applied for issues of medical ethics in the 1970s and 1980s, but the 1960s and 1990s saw much more attention on environmental ethics. However, the concepts and issues of bioethics are much older, as we can see in the ethics formulated and debated in literature, art, music and the general cultural and religious traditions of our ancestors.

Life is diverse and complex and so are the issues that the manipulation of life and nature raises. To resolve these issues, and develop principles, we must involve anthropology, sociology, biology, religion, psychology, philosophy, and economics; we must combine the scientific rigour of biological data, with the values of religion and philosophy to develop a realistic worldview. Bioethics is therefore challenged to be a multi-sided and thoughtful approach to decision making so that it may be relevant to all aspects of human life. Without combining both of these spheres of thought, natural science and values, we can never succeed to even approach a comprehensive ethics. However, bioethics is not just an academic endeavour or an applied part of philosophical ethics, it is rooted in the daily life and attitudes of all people, hence the title of my recent book, *Bioethics for the People by the People*.[1]

The term bioethics should mean the study of life ethics, but it has often been viewed only as a part. The concern with medical ethics has meant that while many people, or committees, are called 'bioethics' committees, they only consider medical ethics. Likewise, ecological and environmental ethics must include human-human interactions, as these interactions are one of the dominant ecological interactions in the world. Both extremes are incomplete perspectives. In the conclusion of an earlier book, *Shaping Genes*,[2] I said that we have much to learn from the issues raised by genetic technology, not just the nature of our genes, but the nature of our thinking about what is important in life. New technology can be a catalyst for our thinking about these issues, and we can think of the examples like assisted reproductive technologies, organ transplantation and genetics, which have been stimuli for research into bioethics in the last few decades.

The title of this book is *Changing Nature's Course* — this is something people have done ever since they began agriculture, began to block a river for irrigation, began to develop medicines, began to live in houses and to learn how to use fire. It is very attractive to think that biotechnology is new, but has been presenting ethical challenges for millennia, whether it be euthanasia, or how much land should be left for the animals to feed on. Human encounters with the environment, the 'bios', life, have always raised ethical issues. Even more issues have been raised by human encounters with each other, which is where the boundary between bioethics and ethics disappears.

Society does not need new ethics to cope with the impact of genetic technology. There is no inherent clash between genetics and human values as some books, including one under the title *Genethics*,[3] would like to have us believe. Almost all of the issues raised by application of genetics are not novel.[4] What is needed is a revival and renewed discussion of ethical values by all members of the community as society interacts with technology. Also we need globalization of the sphere of this discussion as the world becomes smaller and as it becomes easier for people to exploit the absence of controls in neighbouring countries. The pace and magnitude of change has become greater; for example, we now discuss global eco-engineering rather than only national agricultural policy. Likewise in medicine, the sequencing of the human genome may not create new or more difficult ethical dilemmas, but the sheer number of disease-related genes identified is making the number of such dilemmas greater. Life will become more complex, even the supposedly simple case of imposing higher insurance fees on smokers will become more cloudy should we find strong genetic determinants for drug addiction, to add to the environmental determinants we already know.

One of the issues people like to raise as new is germ-line or heritable genetic engineering, and they may say 'never touch the germ-line'. Although many may like to say this, perhaps to naively reassure the public that they have nothing to worry about, the issue of human germ-line genetic manipulation is certainly not resolved. There are some who want a ban on germ-line manipulation, but the somatic cell/germ-line division is less important than the therapy/cosmetic border. In the easy cases of severe disease, safe and inexpensive germ-line gene therapy can make sense, the same genetic sense that tells us sisters and brothers should not marry each other. Eugenic ideas were debated long before genetic engineering, in both philosophy (e.g. Plato) and religion (e.g. Jewish marriage laws).[5] We should encourage discussion of these complex issues, extending our discussions from the debates of old, and in the real world, never say never.[6]

International Bioethics Survey and Cross-Cultural Bioethics

In every country, individuals are facing personal choices in the use of biotechnology and countries are debating policy to regulate such choices. International society is also facing many policy choices for the adoption of new technology. There are many questions being raised about the future consequences that the genetic revolution will bring, especially the social attitude changes that result from the choices that people make. Bioethics is the study of decision making in questions of life, as discussed above; balancing the ideals of: 'do good' and 'do no harm'; and respecting both 'autonomy' and 'justice'. Do individual people and families in different countries actually make decisions by balancing these ideas, and do so differently? We need to look at the degree of similarity and differences, to determine what level of universalism is possible.

At present many countries have their own standards, some of which are based on false assumptions of cultural uniqueness.[7] These standards may be challenged by this data. While it is important to adopt standards that are suitable to each society, such standards should be based on the views of individuals in the society and be realistic. If people are the same then the same standards of bioethics may be applied — universal bioethics, while respecting the freedom of informed choice and responsibilities to society.

How can we answer the question of cultural similarities? In addition to using our widely open eyes and ears to observe, we can also gain data from opinion surveys. Mail response opinion surveys about bioethical reasoning of public, high school teachers, and medical students in Australia, Hong Kong, India, Israel, Japan, New Zealand, the Philippines, Russia, Singapore, and Thailand, were conducted with numerous collaborators in 1993.[8] These surveys included open response questions on the images of life and nature, and questions relevant to agricultural, environmental and medical biotechnology issues. Open response questions are preferable to fixed response surveys which 'lead' the respondent to a particular answer, and the results can differ significantly.[9] The native language of the country was used, and the response rates for the questionnaires ranged from 14 to 90% for different samples. Full details of the results, including collaborators, interpretations, and open responses are elsewhere.[10] Public questionnaires were distributed by hand into letter boxes chosen at random in different areas of Japan, New Zealand, and Australia. Mail response using enclosed stamped and addressed envelopes was requested. Mail response has one advantage over interviews in that lengthier comments were written to the free response questions and at other points in the questionnaire. The samples from New Zealand (N=329), Australia (N=201) and Japan (N=352) were representative of the general population, while the samples from India (N=568), Israel (N=50), Russia (N=446) and Thailand (N=550) had higher education than the general population, as they included not only public samples but also academics. Comparisons to surveys from North America and Europe was also made.

Student samples were chosen from selected medical schools (Australia:

N=110; Japan: N=435; New Zealand: N=96; the Philippines: N=164), a medical laboratory course (Hong Kong: N=105) and biology students (India: N=325; Singapore: N=250; and Thailand: N=290). Students were generally similar to the public within each country, with most questions being age independent.[11] The high school teacher surveys were national, using randomly selected biology and social studies teachers, in Japan (N=560 biology; N=383 social), New Zealand (N=206 biology; N=98 social) and Australia (N=245 biology; N=115 social). The funding for these surveys comes from the Eubios Ethics Institute, with some assistance from the ELSI group of the Ministry of Education, Science and Culture Human Genome Project and the University of Tsukuba. The high school samples in Japan are partly funded by the Ministry of Education as part of a longer term project to develop high school materials to teach about bioethical issues in the biology and social studies classes.

Space does not permit the reproduction of the results here; however, some relevant features are useful for this discussion, and are presented here. In all countries there was a positive view of science and technology, it was perceived as increasing the quality of life by majority in all countries, with India being the most negative. However, less than 10% in all countries saw it as doing more harm than good. When asked about specific developments of technology, including *in vitro* fertilization, computers, pesticides, nuclear power, biotechnology and genetic engineering, both benefits and risks were cited by many respondents. People do show the ability to balance benefits and risks of science and technology.[12] People do not have a simplistic view of science and technology, and can often perceive both benefits and risks. This is necessary for bioethics, the balancing of good and harm, and I have called this an indicator of the bioethical maturity of a society.[13]

Consistent with North American surveys, in all the countries in this survey, plant-plant gene transfers were most acceptable, with animal-animal next, and animal-plant or human-animal gene transfers were least acceptable. A variety of reasons were cited, as was the case in questions about the concerns of consuming products made from genetic engineering. When specific details of an application were given, there was generally greater acceptance, suggesting people have some discretion. It also suggests that if details are given the public will show greater acceptance of an application, especially for human gene therapy.

Approval of public medical funding for prenatal genetic testing is high in all countries surveyed. In all countries except the Philippines there was about 80% support for making prenatal genetic screening available under government funded medicine, with 2 to 12% rejection, and about 70% said that they would personally use it. The level of personal rejection of genetic screening in the United States was similarly high in the Philippines, being among the more negative of countries (32% said they would not use, while 53 to 64% would use; compared to 15 to 18% against in Australia and Japan, and 61 to 69% saying they would use). Education does not seem to be an issue, consistent with results finding no difference in Japan between public, students, high school teachers and academics in my survey in 1991.[14]

The major reasons cited in the open responses for and against genetic testing are most revealing and were similar in all countries. One difference was in Japan where there were less economic reasons given like it would 'save the country's health care system money'. People in Japan may not think deeply about the economic costs of health care, and it will be interesting to see whether this attitude changes as a result of the recession and of the growing health costs and aging population. It may be that the economic recession in New Zealand and Australia, and the general hard times in some other countries, has forced people to think in terms of saving money. It is also true that if taxes are high people have had to face the fact that taxes are redistribution of wealth according to the ethical principle of justice.

Other reasons for genetic screening included saving the foetus; parents' convenience and more positive support for a right to choose and decision to abort. Only 1 to 2% in Japan said the foetus had a right to life; 3 to 4% in Australia and 4 to 8% in New Zealand. In Asia there is more blame and shame for the birth of a handicapped child than in Western societies. This will be affected by genetic knowledge, but until education reaches more people it will be more than just bad luck in the minds of many Asian families, rather it will include guilt or shame. However, social acceptance of genetic testing is high in all countries, and the reasons given are rather similar. Not all the reasons are known in these responses to a paper questionnaire, other responses may be the secrets of people's hearts, but the general nature of the comments suggests that it is a reasonable approximate. There is much greater diversity of reasoning within any one country than the differences between any two countries. This survey focused on the public attitude, and also general student attitude. The public is the user of genetic counselling, and if non-directive counselling is practised then their attitude will be more important than the attitudes of genetic counsellors. The results allow us to form a better picture of the real situation, and of the ideas that people may use in genetic counselling.

Whether eugenic views of improved genes and health for individuals — a positive view in itself — can be separated from the negative eugenic social forces of conformity, and discrimination against people with disease, is a question only time will truly answer. At the end of 1993, a proposal in China for a 'eugenics and health protection' law that would ban the marriage of people with undesirable genes,[15] is another argument supporting the view that economic forces are the major factor in determining the social consequences of genetic testing. The results of a survey in China among medical staff[16] suggest that many people will support the concept, though perhaps less would support the compulsory nature of the law. About 10% of the respondents in this survey in Russia, and many in India also, gave eugenic reasons for support of genetic screening, more than in the other countries.[17]

There is clear support for attempting to do good, and no apparent public rejection of therapy altering genes. About three-quarters of all samples supported personal use of gene therapy, with slightly higher support for children's use of gene therapy. The major reasons were to save life and to increase the quality of life. Few people gave a reason like 'improving genes'. About 5 to 7% rejected gene therapy, considering it to be playing God or unnatural. There was very little concern about eugenics (0.5 to 2%), confirming the results of a different open question in 1991.[18]

Another question about gene therapy shows that people do have significant discretion over therapeutic and cosmetic applications of gene therapy. This is encouraging for ethicists, and a similar discretion was shown in a question about the use of genetic engineering to make a sports fish, compared to a disease-resistant crop. There is extremely high support for use of gene therapy to cure disease, both as somatic cell or germ-line, and high support as an AIDS vaccine. There is rejection of enhancement of genetic engineering in all samples, another indicator of bioethical maturity. However, the success of cosmetic surgery suggests that once it is possible the 20 to 30% who accept genetic engineering to improve intelligence, may do so in practice. Whether this is acceptable is a much bigger question and may require stricter control than today's cosmetics as heritable changes affect future generations.

Attitudes to disease are central to how much people will want to 'treat' someone, or return to 'normal'. The results of questions of knowledge of someone with a genetic disease or mental disease, showed some interesting geographical differences in the number of people who said that they knew someone with a genetic or mental disease. If they said yes, they were also asked to openly cite what disease, which was also interesting to see their perceptions of what is genetic or mental disease. Open comments about people suffering from diseases including muscular dystrophy, schizophrenia or AIDS were also included. Most people expressed sadness or compassion, but a number of people rejected those with HIV or said it was their own fault. However, there were more comments suggesting people are the same, no matter what disease they have, in Australia. Only 2% admired people with muscular dystrophy, though for other diseases no one expressed admiration. For mental disease, such as depression, more people considered the diseases their own fault, in all countries. People were more afraid of people with neurosis.

Confidentiality is a consequence of respecting autonomy. Respect for privacy of genetic information was similar between Asians and Australians. People in all countries are similarly positive about sharing information with a spouse, with 85 to 98% saying that a spouse deserved to know if someone was the carrier of a defective gene or had a genetic disease, with 88 to 98% saying the same for HIV. About 90% of the people in Japan, Singapore or the Philippines said that the immediate family deserved to know, more than in Thailand (83%) or Hong Kong (76%), and less in India and Australia (74%), USA (70%) or India (67%). The difference in the family result may represent attitudes to family involvement in disease and how much disease is seen as a family problem. Both genetic disease and HIV had similar results. A family in all countries may support a sick person, but it is interesting to see where the balance between individuals and families is; which is the basic unit of autonomy.

A difference was that 58% of people in the USA said that insurers deserve to know the information about genetic disease, much more than in the other countries (Australia, New Zealand, Russia 37 to 39%). Less people in Japan (18%) and Israel (6%) say the information about genetic disease or HIV should be shared with them. Although there are many bioethicists in the USA, the public apparently does not value privacy as much as in some other countries. Sharing information with employers was rejected most in Australia and Japan (only 20% agreed), but it was still accepted by a third in most other countries.

Another issue of ethics is who should make decisions, and whom do people trust. A question on the level of trust that people had in authorities who were making a statement about the safety of a product of biotechnology, for example a new drug, revealed differences between countries in who was most trusted. There was most trust in the government in Hong Kong and Singapore, and least in Australia, Japan, Russia, USA and Europe. Despite the lower trust shown in the government in Russia, they had a level of trust in medical doctors. The result is most striking when we compare it to Japan, where doctors were not trusted. In fact it appears the Japanese do not trust anyone very much, but the biggest difference with the other countries was that doctors and university professors were mistrusted, especially so by medical students, whereas Russians show great trust in doctors, and a high level of trust in professors and environmental groups. Companies were least trusted everywhere.

We need to build a bioethics which includes the views of all peoples of the world — not only from the United States (we should not say American, as the USA is only one country of the Americas), neither only European. Also Europe itself is extremely diverse. We need to add Asian and African perspectives. Similar concepts, such as love, social harmony, relationships with the environment are found in the thinking of many regions, both today and in the past. Open questions about the image of 'life' or 'nature' were included in the International Bioethics Survey. The responses from people in all countries revealed many similarities, and also that there is similar diversity in all countries. These open comments are published in English in the book, *Bioethics for the People by the People,* and they add further data to the debate.

In bioethics we should use not only the data of our own interpretations, but rather look for any other data that can aid us in understanding the real situation. Academics may often have abstract ideas; we need to come back to earth and look at reality. The data from surveys and observations reveals that there are fundamental similarities in reasoning by individuals in different countries, despite diversity in social systems and even greater diversity in legal approaches to bioethics. I call this the universal bioethics approach. This is different in focus from the approach of regionalization of bioethics, for example into Asian bioethics. However, both universal or regional desire understanding of local cultures, and should want to recognize the contribution of different peoples to bioethics. In fact we cannot really develop a complete bioethics without including this contribution. Even in Europe, there is a lot of debate about the autonomy, or ego. In Europe they add more emphasis to solidarity. Also in the USA, we can see some shift towards recognizing our duties to other people. Let me move onto further background for universal bioethics.

Universal Ethics and Our Common Biotechnological Heritage

Any ethical approach must consider the biological, social and spiritual heritage and origins of humanity.[19] All human beings are found as members of some society; all accommodate some individualism within a social niche. All societies have some biotechnological and agricultural basis to provide food and clothing, which has allowed civilization to occur. The common biological origin and common needs — material, social order, and spiritual — mean that it should not be surprising that a common ethics exists.

All living organisms are biological beings, and share a common and intertwined biological heritage. Humans are members of the species *Homo sapiens,* one of the millions of species alive on the planet Earth. The method of our creation appears to be via a process of evolution, like all lives on this planet. This is most consistent with the data we have. There is no conflict between a belief in the creation of the world by God and the theory of evolution. The suggestion that there was a conflict was generated by scientists who wanted to replace the Church as the respected authority of human society, something that they have achieved to some extent. Scientists used the theory and the opposition to it to create an image of a 'conflict' between science and religion which has been very harmful ever since. As a more scientific worldview has been adopted, many people continue to think there is a conflict.

People have minds which search for knowledge, and we can understand more and more of the world. A primitive picture of God is to use 'God' to explain things we do not know. This could be called 'god of the gaps'. We use 'God' to explain what we do not yet understand. However, whatever we know of the world we should be appreciative of our existence. Whether the world was created by pure chance or was created with a purpose, is a non-scientific question, a question which no one can ever prove or disprove. The conflict between science and religion led to the view that scientific questions (those that can be disproved by experiments) are higher than non-scientific questions (those not open to proof). However, love, relationships, religions, are not open to experiments — but are more important for most people's lives. Most questions of bioethics are similar, but we need to value both types of questions.

The biological data tells us that all human beings have the same basic set of genes, the variation found in any one population covers almost all of the total variation, and that humans share a common African ancestor. All peoples suffer from genetic diseases and variation. The genetic factors of human

beings are being scientifically determined, and we must await the results of
the human genome diversity project, and the identification of the function of
human genes to get more detailed answers. Changes in DNA sequences have
also been used to trace the ways that different organisms evolve (phylogenetic
trees). We can compare the DNA of species alive today, and investigate
trends in the sequence change. We can also look at DNA from past organisms
which is a more direct measure of the change over time. We could conclude
that the most consistent explanation of sequence comparisons is that all
organisms are related, and when combined with behavioural studies, we can
see some behaviour relevant to ethics is found in other social animals.

Human beings are created in the midst of an intricate biodiversity, which
is yet to be comprehended. The process or time scale over which all life was
made is not so remarkable as the species and ecosystems that we have today,
or those that we can see from the fossils. The debate over the method and
time frame of evolution is likely to continue for a long time, and may not ever
be resolved, but whatever view we hold we can marvel at the diversity of life.
There are economic reasons to value biodiversity, but most people value it
more because of more 'religious' or experiential reasons, as shown in open
questions about 'nature', and 'life' in the International Bioethics Survey.[20]
Human beings are organized into societies, and our social groups include our
spouse, children, relatives, neighbours, religious group, community, workplace,
village, city, nation, and international partners. The social origins can be
studied by sociology and history. Most societies we think of today as countries
are modern artificial creations of historical and present political power systems.
Perhaps the best example of the artificiality of the national borders is the
division of Africa, an artefact of colonial power struggles between Britain,
France and Germany. The attempt to stop further wars in Africa by the
regional congress to stop further power struggles as tribal boundaries were
separated is only a partial success, at best.

We could consider that wars are a sign that universalism is already lost.
However, if we really look at the origins of most wars, we will find that they
are caused not by clashes between ideologies and customs of ordinary people.
Most wars are caused by certain charismatic individuals who are seeking
further power. These individuals may draw upon the perceived differences
between cultures, often generated with the help of the media. They utilize the
sense of national identity that is attractive to one part of human beings — we
all have an urge to be identified as a member of some community. Sometimes
religious groupings are used, sometimes racial differences, and these are usually
combined with ethnic differences and the promise of better economic
conditions.

Language is central to social structure, and one of the contributing factors
to conflict and mistrust. Linguistic trends are consistent with migrations of
humans over the planet traced by genetics.[21] Individual communication systems
are found in other social mammals and birds, and they are used to discriminate
between individuals. Some other behavioural systems may also be shared
with other animals, which raises a number of ethical questions about the

origin of love, altruism and selfishness, and our responsibilities in our encounters with animals.[22]

The complete diversity of attitudes and characters of human individuals is represented in any one society, and shown by personal experience, or surveys. A failing of human thought is that people view their society as being different from other societies, with sweeping generalizations. We describe the English as conservative, the Australians as noisy, the Japanese as quiet. Such thinking is often tied to discrimination, for example men are . . . ; and women are . . . ; whites are . . . ; blacks are . . . ; and Asians are . . . . Such thinking, of 'us' and 'them' is a root of much disharmony in the world, and should be actively discarded from thought, not only because it has bad consequences but more importantly because it is inconsistent with the above data.

We need to look at the world and ourselves. In many countries it is apparent when you walk in the street, or read the newspaper, that the country is mixed. Ever more than before, universally applicable ethical principles are necessary. Many immigrants from a range of countries have come to the new countries like Australia or America, and to the centres of the old European empires, especially Britain and France. The practices that immigrants are accustomed to differ from each other. Their religions may also be different, and certainly some social customs. The indigenous people in Australia and America, and parts of Africa and Asia, have been suppressed and although they have been overrun by culture introduced from the immigrants countries, often a new culture has emerged. At first we may be surprised that so many Chinese in Hong Kong are Christians, but we must remember that Christianity has its origin in Asia, and Europeans were converted from their former beliefs, as with other religions and ideals. This continues to be a source of friction in some countries, because the groups may try to form an 'us' and a 'them'.

One of the fundamental assumptions of bioethics is that all human beings have equal rights. There are universal human rights which should be protected, and recognized. We can argue for the foundation of human rights from secular philosophy or religion, and they have become enshrined in international law. Universal cross-cultural ethics should be developed to allow diverse views to be maintained even within a single community, as well as throughout the world in the global community. Even within a so-called homogeneous culture such as Japan, there is a wide variety of individuals and universal ethics would promote choice. The view of life that people have is individual, despite the often assumed homogeneity.

Economic factors are an inseparable part of society, and trading between adjacent regions has been a major source of cultural mixing, today as in past centuries. The world has become smaller with modern trade and communications, and this is certainly one factor in the growing trend for internationalism. This is epitomized in GATT, signed in 1993. International economics helps break down geographical and linguistic barriers, though globally it has resulted in deepening divisions between rich and poor nations, another hurdle to the recognition that much of human heritage and much of ethics is universal. This is not to say that modern economics is bioethical, as it usually devalues the environment and social values central to bioethics.

The spiritual origins of humanity are less mixed than the social ones, and these have been used as transnational boundaries in the past, and also today. The Islamic countries, Catholic countries, and loosely-called Christian countries, are major regions of the world. Asia has more diversity of religion; for example, Buddhism in Sri Lanka is different from that in Japan. Within Asia there are also many Christians and Muslims, and most of the world's religions.

Despite the scientific worldview that is prevalent among academics, most other people find religions to be a much more important source of guidance in life than science. In questions of ethics, this is true of most people. Any theory of bioethics that will be applied to the peoples of the world must be acceptable to the common trends of major religious thought. This comparison is one purpose of the International Bioethics Survey. The countries chosen in the survey were chosen for two reasons, one being as representatives of the world, and the other in terms of convenience of access. Unfortunately there is no African, South American, or Islamic country among the countries chosen. It is hoped that future studies will look at these questions in these and other countries also, as a test of the ideas discussed here. The countries chosen include India, a country of mixed religion and the major so-called 'developing' country, though it has a biotechnological and social history much longer than most countries. Russia represents the former communist world, another possible dominant force in shaping opinion. The Philippines is a Catholic country. Thailand is a Buddhist country and represents South East Asia. New Zealand and Australia, with some comparisons to North America, and to past European surveys, represent Christian and Western countries. Hong Kong and Singapore represent the Chinese influence, and some comparison to mainland Chinese attitudes is also made. A small sample from Israel was also included, as one Middle Eastern country. In compiling the data from these countries, and comparing to other published data, we can form a better global picture of the reasoning used by people, and whether there are religious differences. In many issues there were not.

We must also learn from traditions, these are another type of data we have. There are a variety of different ethical traditions, and it is essential to consider these for the development of universal bioethics. These traditions are also part of our social heritage, though most have a more spiritual base. These different traditions should be respected to make this universal bioethics also cross-cultural ethics, respected to the extent that they do not conflict with fundamental human rights.

Ethical Progress

We can find many common features in surveys like those described here that are useful to develop universal ethics. The full results — recorded in the book *Bioethics for the People by the People* — include chapters from each region describing the background circumstances, examples of open comments and explanation of the categorization. This provides some data that allows us to actually look at the bioethical decision making of ordinary people, and to examine the question of the universality of responses to genetic disease and biotechnology. This data finds the complete range of comments for most questions is seen within the samples from any one country or group. In every society there are people who want to use new genetic techniques such as prenatal genetic screening, and there are some who reject the concept of selective abortion. In all societies we see high support for gene therapy, or making disease-resistant crops, as could be expected.

Attitudes to people suffering from disease may be affected by the use of genetic screening, but further studies over time will be needed to see whether there are significant attitude trends. In most countries the majority of respondents express sympathy. In practice, however, we may not always see such an attitude. This type of study is one approach to address some of these questions. The results are also being used in an attempt to develop a method for assessing the general 'bioethical maturity' of different societies, which includes the ability to balance benefit and risk; discretion between enhancement and therapy; and the balance between autonomy and freedom/restriction.

The most important message of this survey is that people in different countries share very similar images of life and similar diversity of views on most of these issues of bioethics associated with genetics. The main difference may be in the acceptance of selective abortion, but even people saying they were very religious also supported this. Any universal ethics must include some respect for informed choices of people, and the range of choices people desire is transcultural. Policy should reflect the universality of diversity and reasoning.

The social consequences of biotechnology depend on the society that we make. Individuals in different countries share similar attitudes to these questions, but already the social systems in Asia and Oceania are different. Despite the similarity in the views of individuals, the social system in Japan and some other countries is constructed differently, and may not represent the views of the public.[23] However, universal attitudes reviewed in some parts of the International Bioethics Survey, when compared to other international surveys, suggest that we have to reconsider our view that different social systems are the result of differences between peoples; in fact the different social systems may occasionally be used in attempts to establish differences. Universal bioethics already exists at the level of individual decision making, and therefore it is certainly possible to develop social and educational systems to allow universal ethics at the higher level of social systems.

Notes

1. D. Macer, *Bioethics for the People by the People* (Christchurch, N.Z.: Eubios Ethics Institute, 1994).

2. D. Macer, *Shaping Genes: Ethics, Law and Science of Using Genetic Technology in Medicine and Agriculture* (Christchurch, N.Z.: Eubios Ethics Institute, 1990).
3. D. Suzuki, and P. Knudtson, *Genethics: The Clash Between the New Genetics and Human Values* (Boston: Harvard University Press, 1989).
4. D. Macer, 'No to Genethics', *Nature* 365 (1993): 102.
5. See Note 1 above.
6. See Note 4 above.
7. D. Macer, 'The 'Far East' of Biological Ethics', *Nature* 359 (1992): 770.
8. See Note 1 above.
9. See Note 1 above. Also D. Macer, *Attitudes to Genetic Engineering: Japanese and International Comparisons* (Christchurch, N.Z.: Eubios Ethics Institute, 1992).
10. See Note 1 above.
11. Ibid.
12. See Note 1 and Note 9 above. Also D. Macer, 'Bioethics and Biotechnology: What is Ethical Biotechnology?' In D. Braver (ed.), *Modern Biotechnology: Legal, Economic and Social Dimensions*. (Weinheim: VCH, 1995), 115–154.
13. D. Macer, 'Perception of Risks and Benefits of in vitro Fertilization, Genetic Engineering and Biotechnology', *Social Science and Medicine* 38 (1994): 23–33.
14. See Note 9 above.
15. Editorial, 'China's Misconception of Eugenics', *Nature* 367 (1994): 1–3.
16. W. H. Y. Lo, et al., 'A Survey of People with Higher Education to Genetics and Diseases in Beijing'. In N. Fujiki and D. Macer, eds., *Intractable Neurological Disorders, Human Genome Research and Society* (Christchurch, N.Z.: Eubios Ethics Institute, 1994).
17. See Note 1 above.
18. See Note 1 and Note 9 above. Also D. Macer, 'Public Acceptance of Human Gene Therapy and Perceptions of Human Genetic Manipulation', *Human Gene Therapy* 3 (1992): 511–8. D. Macer, 'Universal Bioethics and the Human Germ-line', *Politics & Life Sciences* 14(1994): 27–29. D. Macer, et al., 'International Perceptions and Approval of Gene Therapy', *Human Gene Therapy* 6(1995): 791–803.
19. See Note 1 above.
20. Ibid.
21. L. L. Cavalli-Sforza, 'Genes, Peoples and Languages', *Scientific American* (November 1991): 72–8. Also *Scientific American* (April 1991): 70–9.
22. See Note 1 above.
23. See Note 7 above. Also D. Macer, 'Bioethics May Transform Public Policy in Japan', *Politics & Life Sciences* 13(1994): 89–90.

14

Future-Perfect? Biotechnology and the Ethics of the Unknown: An Afterword

James P. Buchanan

> They do not, like the old, merely exert a gentle guidance over nature's course, they have the power to conquer and subdue her, to shake her to her foundations.
>
> Francis Bacon

As odd as it may sound, the purpose of an afterword is to look forward, to digest what has come before, and rather than make an attempt at summarization, draw upon it to try and see where we go from here. The conclusion which I draw from this collection (if it can be called a conclusion) is that as we enter an age of biotechnology we have been thrown into a face-to-face confrontation with the unknown. While it is always the case that the future presents us with the unknown, my claim is that the unknown has reached such proportions that it now needs to become one of our guiding principles in the formulation of ethical and policy decisions.

The position which I want to pursue here is that we are entering a new age, one which entails not only the wide-scale application of these new technologies but also new modes of understanding and organizing the world as well as new power relationships. As this occurs we are faced with a situation best characterized by the *ethics of the unknown*. I will claim that the ethics of the unknown is not a mandate to abandon all ethics but rather a *call to a new type of ethics* which results from a sensitivity to both the past and the future. I will argue that the uncertainties about the *is* (the present and future facts) does not absolve us from certain *oughts*, but rather that such uncertainty should become one of the principles upon which our *oughts* are based.

It seems clear from this collection of articles and many other writings concerning biotechnology that there is a general recognition that we have entered or are entering an age which is *fundamentally biotechnological*. In his article above, Sass has spoken of the importance of worldviews in decision making. We have reached a paradigmatic turning point in the history of science and technology and thus a paradigmatic turning point in both human and natural history. To claim that we are moving into an age of biotechnology or an information (cybernetic) age is to view this shift at the broadest philosophical and cultural level. It is intended as a heuristic to help us see general patterns of understanding, organization and practice. In order to help crystallize what I mean by this shift in 'ages' we might schematize the characteristics of contrasting ages in the following table:

ORGANISTIC/MECHANISTIC/BIOTECHNICAL/CYBERNETIC

PRE-MODERN	MODERN	POST-MODERN
Vital force/Energy	Matter/Motion	Information
Participation	Representation	Simulation/Programming
Correlative Thinking	Causal Thinking	Systems Thinking
Holistic	Atomistic	Behaviouristic
Monism/Unity Continuity of Being	Dualism Discontinuity of Being	Pluralism Relationality of Being
Whole to Part	Part to Whole	Reflexive within System or Field
Cyclic Time	Linear Time	Virtual Time
Tradition/Repetition	Innovation/Progress	Creation/Neo-Evolutionary
Dependence upon Nature	Domination of Nature	Reinvention of Nature
Communal Self	Individual Self	Virtual Self
Biological Process seen as Spiritual/Metaphysical	Biological Process seen as Physical/ Mechanical	Biological Process seen as Inscribed/ Signified/Informational
Archaic Technology	Pyrotechnology	Biotechnology/Genetic Engineering/Cybernetics

While a detailed comparison of these characteristics is beyond the scope of this afterword they can provide a useful reference point as we describe what we will call the foreground and the background of biotechnology.

The first issue which emerges from this collection concerns how we define 'biotechnology'. In one sense biotechnology is nothing new. We find biological technologies in each of these ages. Even the most 'primitive' (archaic) forms of plant breeding or animal husbandry; most of what we would term 'medical' intervention; and virtually every other attempt to manage the biological processes of nature through the use of techniques or technology can be viewed as forms of biotechnology. The fact that archaic people had no concept of 'biology' in the sense that we use this as a modern discourse does not mean that they did not have understanding of, and the desire to use and intervene in those processes we now term biological. In fact we are just now beginning to understand and appreciate the depth of understanding which many indigenous peoples had and have of natural processes. Such 'indigenous knowledges' as the use of plants, animals and other natural substances for medicinal purposes; traditional plant breeding techniques and accomplishments; and even land use patterns have all become matters of modern research within the new biotechnology. In the simplest and broadest terms possible, biotechnology is the attempts to control, manipulate or improve natural biological processes by means of technological processes. Humankind as *Homo faber*, the tool-maker, has always sought to control nature by means of technology. So it might well be asked whether there is any real difference between traditional plant breeding, modern techniques of grafting and cross-breeding (both of which are somatic), and the current 'breeding' by means of the manipulation of genetic materials (germ-line) to produce new plants. All are forms of biotechnology — all seek to change and improve upon the natural biological processes, and all use technology or technique to accomplish this.

The difference between what we might call 'traditional' biotechnologies and the newer forms of biotechnology which mostly relate to molecular biology and genetic engineering is one of both degree and of kind. The 'degree' to which society is becoming and will become *fundamentally* biotechnological is something which is open for debate. In part, this will depend upon how successful we are in finding a broad range of useful applications of this new techno-science. The modern period has been rightly characterized as an age of physics (chemistry coming of age relatively late in the period) and physical (mechanical/pyrotechnical) technologies. The new age is one of biological and information technologies. The degree to which this becomes a fact will depend upon how successful biotechnology is in providing useful applications. To understand this we might compare it to the claim in the middle of this century that we had entered an 'atomic age' or a 'nuclear age'. While the claim is true at the level of international politics and balance of power, a broad range of nuclear technologies and applications have not been developed to the degree expected by the early forecasts. Einstein's famous statement that 'with the splitting of the atom everything changed except the way we think' may turn out to be more applicable to the new genetic biotechnologies. Except I would want to argue that the key to a new age is that there is also or even fundamentally a shift in the way we think.

This shift in thinking is fundamental to the shift in 'kind'. Biotechnology needs to be understood within the context of a more general shift in worldviews which we might term the 'information age' of 'cybernetic age'. This shift is one in which the world is literally reconceived in terms of 'information' and systems of information exchange. When Norbert Wiener developed his theories of cybernetics he was not simply developing a theory of information systems as they relate to computers; he intended this to be a general theory applicable to the biological world as well. He says that information 'belongs among the great concepts of science such as matter, energy and electric charge'.[1] In a fundamental shift from either the pre-modern or modern periods, cybernetics is not concerned with what a thing *is* but *how it behaves*. Behaviour is defined as the exchange and processing (action/reaction) of information. It is in this sense that we can speak of new 'ages' or 'epistemes',[2] the broad characteristics of which are listed in the table above. While the modern physicist looked and continues to look for the basic 'building blocks' in terms of an atomistic approach which searches for the smallest particle (the newest version of this being the sixth or 'top' quark),[3] cybernetics sees the basic building blocks as information and information processes because it is this which determines behaviour. Thus, techniques such as genetic engineering are not just the application of mechanical engineering to biological materials but represent a profoundly new way of understanding, ordering and interacting with the world which we might term a worldview shift.[4]

As an example of the way in which different worldviews determine different social practices, we might look briefly at the problem of conservation. Conservation is a discourse (and a practice) which can be constituted in any number of ways. Within the three models characterized in the above table, we can see that along with conservation other key concepts such as 'species' or 'nature' itself are redefined. If we begin with the Pre-modern/Organiztic Model, conservation would be taken holistically. This approach defines a species in terms of the ecosystems within which it exists. A species is seen in terms of that complex set of relationships with the other participants within an ecosystem. Thus, the keys to survival and conservation are the preservation of the entire ecosystem. This is not just an archaic approach but also the one which is basic to the Convention on Biological Diversity negotiated by United Nations Conference on Environment and Development (UNCED). Within a Modern/Mechanistic Model a species is viewed atomistically. By this we mean that a particular species is defined materialistically, or in terms of its physiological traits. This physical approach emphasizes structural characteristics and is consistent with the modern concentration upon matter. Conservation has focused upon saving members (even to individual members) of species in zoos, parks (national and theme), preserves or compounds. These may attempt to recreate, save or approximate the natural habitat in varying degrees but the emphasis is not upon preservation of the ecosystem but upon members of those species. In a Cybernetic/Biotechnological Model the preservation of species reinscribes conservation as the preservation of the information stored in the genetic code. The context of conservation and preservation shifts from the ecosystem or zoo to the gene bank. Such gene banks (both public and private) are being established all over the planet. When argued in isolation from the other options it is easy to see the claim that we are saving a species from extinction if we only save its genetic code and to argue that this is 'good'. But what must be recognized is that in so arguing we have redefined 'species' in terms of a new information-based worldview.

Nowhere can we see this change in worldview more dramatically than the human body. The organic body is always a good critical site at which one can see the scientific, cultural and political ramifications of worldviews. The biotechnical/cybernetic view of everything as inscribed in the form of information and processing is nowhere more evident than with the human body. Donna Harraway makes the point that,'(b)odies are not born, they are made'.[5] The 'body' is organized around the science and technologies of a given period. 'From the mid twentieth century, biomedical discourses have been progressively organized around a very different set of technologies and practices, which have destabilised the symbolic privilege of the hierarchical, localised, organic body'.[6] In the biotechnological/cybernetic age the 'body is theorised as a coded text whose secrets yield only the proper reading conventions and . . . the laboratory seems best characterized as a vast assemblage of technological and inscription devices'.[7] There is here a new genetic determinism and a new genetic reductionism in which the body is denaturalized in the pre-modern or modern sense of 'natural'.

While it is clear that all three ages and types of 'biotechnology' present us with complex ethical dilemmas, here I want to focus upon biotechnology in its current form of genetic engineering as it is this which presents us with the most profound ethical challenges of the future. It is at this broad, perhaps overly broad, level that we encounter the first unknown. If it is true that biotechnology is part of a 'shift' in ages or worldviews then we presently stand at the beginning of this age and what we take as 'fact' and 'knowledge' rather than being 'true' in the sense of being an accurate description or representation of the world, are also 'true' in the sense that they will constitute the world, reshape or reinvent it from that perspective. Science is not 'objective' in the sense that it has often claimed during the modern period. As Ruth Hubbard (a scientist herself) reminds us, 'Scientists construct facts by constantly making decisions about what they will consider significant, what experiments they should pursue, and how they will describe their observations. These choices are not merely individual or idiosyncratic but reflect the society in which the scientists live and work'.[8] Science is both subject to and the generator of all manner of social and political practices and pressures. In fact, historically it is science's claim to be objective that has been a major source of its power within society. 'Science' and 'scientific' become legitimating terms equatable with truth. However, while scientific education actively seeks to deny the direct connection between scientific questions and social/ethical questions, the fact is that '(s)cientists, as a group, tend to provide results that support the basic values of their society'.[9] The *is* and the *ought* are not as easily separable as we might like to think. If we have learned anything from our experiences in modernity, it is or ought to be that while we have the power to accomplish wonderful things through our technologies, there are unforeseen consequences which may not be equally wonderful. One can point to the environmental consequences of modernity's development of a technological/industrial society as but one example. To the early developers perhaps these consequences were unknown but we can hardly claim either ignorance or innocence. While in modernity the fact that such consequences were unknown has been used as a rationale to ignore them, we should have reached a point in human history where we know enough not to ignore what we do not know. Rather than an ethos of 'safe until proven otherwise' or 'what we don't know can't hurt us', we need to practice what Cusanus called a 'learned ignorance' — to know enough to know that what we don't know can indeed hurt us and might well be the heart of the matter.

What I am suggesting here is that the 'fact' of the unknown needs to become part of the question we ask about technologies, part of the problem formation itself. It is not just the question of what difference it might have made had we (humanity) posed the question of industrial technologies with the environmental or social consequences in mind, and whether it might have made any difference in the ways in which these technologies were developed but whether or not we can accept our inability to answer these questions as a rationale for changing the ways in which we allow new technologies to develop and proliferate? Can we learn from our past that the way in which we formulate the problems will determine to a large degree the types and limits of the answers we give? If we pose questions concerning the environmental and social consequences of biotechnology and cannot answer them, admit that they are unknowns, should this be taken into account as part of our decision making process with regard to the direction and rapidity of the development of this new technology? What role should the *unknown* play in both our ethical and policy considerations?

In the seventeenth century when Francis Bacon wrote the words with which this article began, he could have no idea how prophetic they would become for the new biotechnological age. He tells us that nature must be 'put into constraint, moulded, and made as it were new . . . '.[10] With exception of the splitting of the atom and the subsequent invention of the atom bomb, at no time in history has the human race had such power to take nature and 'shake her to her foundations'. For Bacon and Descartes it was a matter of both divine right and moral imperative that humanity instate itself as the 'lords and possessors of nature' (Descartes' famous phrase). They sounded the philosophical and moral clarion which rang in the modern age, defining the world mechanistically and seeking to control nature by means of techno-science. Whatever our current assessment of this shift in attitude and worldview, their intentions were among the loftiest ideals of humanism, namely to free humanity from its bondage to ignorance, sickness, and poverty, to liberate humanity from its enslavement to nature so that it could realize the higher goals for which it was divinely destined. Humanity had been cast out of Eden but there was a road back — a road built by human ingenuity, skill, rationality, and technology. Expressed here is an ethos, crystallized in such notions as 'progress' which says that anything we have the power to do we have the right, indeed even the duty to do. The new biotechnological age continues this ethos, but genetic engineering would accomplish this by taking those 'foundations' of nature and quite literally reinventing nature itself by means of recombinant DNA technologies. Biotechnology is a story written in future-perfect tense.

Albert Borgman speaks of the 'promise' of technology along with its 'foreground' and 'background'.[11] What he terms the promise of technology is related to what Zimbelman here calls the 'technological imperative'. They both note that modern Western society has always been attracted, even seduced, by the promise of technology. Consistent with the ethos of Bacon and Descartes, technology (techno-science) is offered as the solution to virtually all of the problems we face — it is our path into the future. As Borgman says, 'The promise of technology was first formulated at the very beginning of the Enlightenment. It was not the centre of attention but rather put forward as the obvious practical corollary of intellectual and cultural liberation'.[12] It is the promise of technology which ultimately legitimates the technological imperative. Borgman ties this promise into the foreground of technology. It is a fact of historical importance that technology has flourished within capitalistic societies. Capitalism was in some senses an economic system made for a technological society with mutual interests in progress, innovation, individualism, and the domination of nature. According to Borgman, technology within a capitalistic system places its emphasis upon foreground and obscures the background. He notes that particularly within a capitalistic system, '(c)ommodoties and their consumption constitute the professed goal of the technological enterprise'.[13] The necessity of foregrounding has spawned the mammoth advertising industry whose function is both to extol the promises of technology and to manage the demand necessary to sustain the technostructure. Foregrounding is about the artifacts of hope — the hope of a better, happier life. The problem which Borgman sees with this is that our almost obsessive attention to the foreground obscures the background of technology. This includes both the science and machinery which produce the commodity and the implications, issues, problems and threats which are obscured by our attention being drawn towards the promises and commodities which they provide. Borgman's concerns about this focus upon the promises and foreground of technology are that we suffer a loss of 'depth' and that we lose touch with ethical questions which need to be addressed.

If we look at biotechnology in light of Borgman's analysis, we find an industry which, to an unprecedented degree, has been built upon promises and foregrounding. The bioindustry[14] has been forced to place undue emphasis upon promises and foregrounding because of the rapidity of privatization of biotechnological science. While publicly funded research can be carried out without undue emphasis upon foregrounding and promises (this is supposed to be the nature of research), the shift in context of the research lab from the educational or research institution to that of commercial firms, along with the disturbing fact that a disproportionate number of scientists involved in genetic research are directly or indirectly affiliated with the bioindustry,[15] means that economic interests play a large role in presenting the case for biotechnology as well as determining the direction of its development. The other side of this is that the companies are dependent upon such foregrounding to attract the private money to support the research and their continued survival.

There are two points I wish to make here. First, there is the background issue concerning the proper role of university research and of university scientists. This involves issues ranging from the possible conflict of interests, to the privatization of knowledge among researchers which was previously circulated freely, to the control of the directions of research by commercial concerns. Second, there is the degree to which the bioindustry has been built upon promise and speculation. Firms such as Genetech, Biogen, Repligen, ImClone, etc. have all 'capitalized' (literally raised capital) not upon actual products but upon the promise of products. They have mostly done this by public offerings on the stock exchange. It is unprecedented in business history for an entire industry to grow up based upon promise rather than upon existing product. From the scientists to the news media there is constant foregrounding of genetic engineering. Walter Gilbert, a Nobel Laureate, refers to the human genome as the 'Holy Grail'; *Genetic Engineering News*, the widest circulation magazine of the industry and spoken of as the bioindustry's 'bible', never prints a negative or critical word about the industry. It is a magazine totally dedicated to foregrounding. Likewise, the industry has shown itself to be very effective in using the news media. Hardly a week goes by that we do not see or read a report of the latest 'breakthrough' in genetic engineering. From the possibility of new cancer cures to genetic markers for everything from breast cancer, to Huntington's disease, to Alzheimer's, to aging itself, to the newest genetically engineered fruits and vegetables, to microbes which will eat oil slicks, we are told that genetic engineering is the technological key to the kingdom.

The point is not to deny the real and potential contributions of genetic engineering but that a disproportionate amount of money is spent on such foregrounding. It has been estimated that the major US biotechnology companies spend up to 25% of their income on marketing and that up to thirty million visits are made by salespeople to doctor's offices per year.[16] Such massive efforts to keep the public's eye on the prize tends to obscure the background issues. Even governments are engaged in such hyperbolic foregrounding. During the Reagan and Bush administrations it was firmly believed that the long-term economic survival of the United States was directly tied to the development of biotechnology. Forecasts have been made that by the mid twenty-first century between 60% and 70% of the gross national product (GNP) of the USA will be directly or indirectly tied to biotechnology. Whether biotechnology can live up to either its technological or economic promises is unknown.

Another background issue related to this is that to a large degree it is the science itself which is marketed as the product. Biotechnology is different from other technologies in this. We already see this in the marketing of speculative (future) products by the biotech firms. What they have is the science. What they promise is an application. If we take as an example the sequencing of the human genome, the identification of a genetic marker is extolled not just as a breakthrough in science but as if it were already a product. The commodity here is health. In his article above, Golub has spoken about the commoditization of health and the way in which such commoditization exerts controls on the directions of research and products actually introduced. Health becomes the principle legitimation for projects such as the Human Genome Project (in both its public and private forms). The background issue is that there is a gap and potentially a huge gap between the identification of such genetic information and the development of genetic therapies. The science is not the application. Foregrounding not only obscures this gap but also a host of other issues which lurk in the background. What is clear is that as biotechnology is increasingly privatised, as it becomes increasingly a bioindustry, there will be less and less attention given to background issues because such diversions can only serve to impede 'progress', the technological imperative and the pressing need to bring products to market in order to secure return on the huge financial investments being made to develop them. The point is that the contributions to health, agriculture, etc. are unknown; this is nothing unusual for research but in this case the benefits are marketed (as promise or speculation) as if they were accomplished fact.

There are other dimensions of the unknown which can be brought to light here. One which we tiptoe around is the issue of eugenics. Eugenics is the systematic attempt to create better or even perfect humans by means of controlling the genetic material which is passed on. The term itself is explosive because of its connections to the Nazi programmes of eugenics in which they sought to create a purified Aryan race. Biotechnology opens up a new era of eugenics, for the good and the bad of it. We can speak in terms of positive and negative eugenics. An example of negative eugenics would be the use of genetic therapies to remove genetically inherited diseases and to eliminate characteristics which are considered bad. Positive eugenics would be the re-engineering of traits not because they are bad but because we (individually or as a group) consider them good. For example we (again individually or as a group) might consider blue eyes more beautiful than other colours so we genetically alter humans toward this end. As a general rule most seem to agree that negative eugenics is acceptable but positive eugenics is more problematic. The question is where do we draw the line between these? For example, do we take something like male-pattern baldness as a 'bad' or even a 'disease' and thus take its elimination as a social good. It must be realized that 'disease' is a language which we can and do apply to a wide range of phenomena determined by changing political, social, philosophical, religious and economic climates. While we might all accept something like Huntington's as a 'disease', things such as alcoholism or substance abuse are more controversial. We speak in terms of social/psychological illness; the range of traits which can be included here are limitless. Should everything on the list be genetically eliminated if possible? Should this be a matter of individual choice?

Eugenics is perhaps the most extreme example of the future-perfect in biotechnology. It is the promise of future perfection. But the background issue is that of competing goods. The liberal critique of notions of the good is that it can never serve us as a guiding principle because there are too many versions of the good society or the list of goods one would include as part of a good society. How shall we determine the good when it comes to the perfection of the human (or anything else for that matter)? Shall we let the good be determined by consensus? Or shall we let the 'invisible hand' of the marketplace determine what is and is not good? The point is that models of the good and of perfection vary widely over time and cultures. The other side of this is the argument that the strength of humanity (and of nature in general) is in its diversity. Genetically imposed models of perfection will tend towards monoculture. And in the end it may be that monoculture and what Vandana Shiva calls 'monoculture of the mind' are greater threats than the diseases and imperfections we eliminate.[17] Two examples will serve to make my point. Bereano points out that currently genetically engineered growth hormone is being administered to children in the United States not because they suffer from dwarfism or any form of dramatic height limitation but because they are shorter than 'normal' for their ages. Is below 'normal' height to be considered a disease? Do we begin to genetically 'normalize' everyone? Who will determine what the limits of toleration for 'normal' are? What are the long-term social implications of this? As we eliminate diseases in our quest for the future-perfect what else will we eliminate? One can point to a figure such as Stephen Hawkings and ask what the relationship is between the terrible physical limitations with which he lives and the seemingly unlimited expansiveness of his mind.[18] He is only one recent example of figures who suffer or have suffered a range of debilitating diseases but have surmounted these to contribute works of genius to human culture. If we eliminate the diseases how does this affect the genius? Is there a relationship? Again it is unknown.

This confusion between negative and positive eugenics becomes a pressing social and political issue in situations such as the People's Republic of China. Recently China has passed a law which establishes a list of genetically inheritable diseases which when discovered by means of genetic screening require that the foetus be aborted. Are such policies for the good of society as a whole (as a negative eugenics)? And where will the list end? As the Genome Project supplies the information for the genetic markers for more and more characteristics which of these will be determined to be 'undesirable' or 'diseases'? Will we eliminate foetuses with the so-called 'gay' gene? the schizophrenia gene? the smokers gene? the rape gene? The competing goods within a society and competing goods between societies render this quest for a future-perfect a slippery slope which rather quickly obscures the line between negative and positive eugenics. Again the limits of the applications are unknown.

Yet another way to conceptualize this issue of the unknown might be to suggest that one might apply chaos theory to biotechnology. This theory stated in its most simple form says that complex systems can be dramatically affected by changes in seemingly minute factors. The weather is usually the example given. As a complex system with a myriad of small influences, it is rendered unpredictable. The by now famous example of this is 'the butterfly effect'. This says (metaphorically or actually) that a butterfly can flap its wings in Beijing and this will be an element, even a significant element, within the overall systemic behaviour which results in a typhoon in the United States. Chaos theory can be interpreted in radically different ways and to different effects. One perspective says that underlying the apparent chaos and unpredictability of complex systems there is an order. The implication is that given time, resources, method, etc. we can find that order. The other perspective is that complex systems are inherently unpredictable and the more complex, the more unpredictable they become because there are more variables, any one of which can have systemic impact. In either interpretation, in the short-term, chaos theory is a declaration of the limitations of our ability to predict complex systems. With biotechnology we are dealing with extremely complex systems and systems within systems. What happens when we begin to manipulate single or multiple genes with specific purposes in mind? Science knows very little about the relationship of particular genes to each other or the potential systemic impact of seemingly minute changes in the structure. This becomes even more complex if one tries to think about the effects over generations to the gene pool itself. Again we are confronted with the unknown.[19]

The same might be said when it comes to the background issue of the release of genetically modified organizms (GMO) into the environment. As was pointed out in Bereano's article above, as well as by many other commentators, the release of a GMO is not like an oil slick. Eventually we, with nature's help, can clean up an oil slick even though full restoration may take generations. To release a GMO into an ecosystem is to begin a new chapter in the natural (or maybe now unnatural) history of that system. When one takes into account the fact that many if not most of our ecosystems are already suffering undue stress in terms of declines in existing biodiversity and carrying capacity, the release of new life forms could only exacerbate this situation. This becomes particularly important in the context of Asia and other developing regions which presently have no laws regulating the release of GMOs. Will they become experimental dumping grounds for the Western bioindustry? Will the development of such new species contribute to an overall decline or increase in biodiversity? Will we end up with 'laboratorally advantaged' life forms which will overwhelm indigenous species? Will the biodiversity of the future be primarily what comes out of the biotech labs? Without effective scientific predictive ecologies all we can say is that the long-term impact is potentially immense but fundamentally unknown.

Yet another background issue which has been touched upon in this volume is the issue of ownership of genetic information. Two cases highlight this issue dramatically. First the case of John Moore. In the mid-1970s Moore entered the UCLA hospital and was diagnosed as having leukaemia which among other things required that his spleen be removed. During the pre- and post-operative procedures the medical team discovered that Moore's spleen was capable of producing a remarkable blood protein. The research team saved part of his spleen and developed a cell line from Moore's T lymphocytes. The University of California Regents filed for and received a patent on this cell line. Their belief was that this cell line could produce commercially valuable antibacterial and cancer-fighting drugs. Based upon this, partnerships were entered into with Genetics, Inc. and various divisions of Sandoz, the Swiss based pharmaceutical giant. Estimates of the cell line's ultimate value have ranged as high as $3 billion. John Moore was told none of this. When he eventually found out he went to court demanding a share of the profit. His case was thrown out in the lower courts as it was determined that Moore had no proprietary rights over discarded tissue or genetic structure and that it had no identifiable economic value when in his 'possession'. On appeal it was determined that he did have rights and was entitled to partial ownership of the patented cell line. The case eventually went to the California Supreme Court which ruled that Moore did not have proprietary rights over his own genetic structure. The implications of this case, when taken together with the Chakrabarty case[20] legitimizes the ownership of tissues, cells and genes by patent holders. The broader implications of this are expressed in Judge Broussard's dissenting opinion of the Moore decision: 'Far from elevating these biological materials above the marketplace, the majority's holding simply bars plaintiff, the source of the cells, from obtaining the benefit of the cells' value, but permits defendants, who allegedly obtained the cells from plaintiff by improper means, to retain and exploit the full economic value of their ill-gotten gains free of . . . liability'.[21] What are the long-term implication of the patenting of life forms and the wholesale use of tissues, cells and genes within the marketplace?

The other case in point is that the Secretary of Commerce of the United States has filed for a patent upon a cell line developed from the genetic structure of the Guayami Indians of Panama (US Patent Application 9108455). The purpose of the patent had to do with the development of potential cures connected with HIV. This must be seen against the backdrop of the Human Genome Diversity Project in which the genetic structure of indigenous peoples all over the planet are being collected. While this broader project does not intend to develop products or to patent the genetic structures and is only dedicated to the identification and preservation of indigenous people's genetic structures it is hard to see how it can avoid contributing to the applications for patents and the development of products. One background issue concerns the models of conservation noted earlier in this article. It also has to be seen against the backdrop of the Human Genome Project as a whole, in which thousands of patents have been filed for by the National Institute of Health. The argument which has been given to justify these patents is that it is better to have them in the public domain than privatized. However, what should not be missed is that the principle legitimizing the ownership of genetic material is being established here and that this will result in a vast number of applications from private concerns.[22] What are the long-term implications of the patenting of genetic materials? What kind of property is this? Should we have any kind of proprietary rights over our own genetic structure? Patents are in principle global monopolies; is this the best mechanism of ownership for genetic materials? How much are we obscuring the very complex ethical, social and even religious questions and allowing the foregrounding (the development of commodities) within the marketplace to determine the parameters of these issues?[23] Again with the opening of the patenting of life forms we enter an area of the unknown.

The issue of the patenting of life forms draws our attention to yet another case which raises disturbing foreground and background issues. The OncoMouse is the world's first patented animal. The patent is jointly held by Dupont and Harvard University. The foreground for this is that it is a mouse which is genetically engineered to develop tumours so that it can be used in cancer research. The patent was granted based upon the potential benefits to humanity. One background issue is that it is now legally possible to own not an individual member of that species or even a group from that species but to have some level of proprietary rights over the entire species genetically (and again what this means is not clear). This raises again my previous question concerning the constitution of future biodiversity but adds to it the confusing problem of the ownership of it. Will future biodiversity be mainly from our genetic laboratories and all owned by corporate patent holders? In addition, there is another ethical issue which has been raised by the article by Wacks above. He suggests there, following the work of Singer and others, that one of the criteria which should guide us in the experimentation on animals is the principle of not causing suffering. With the OncoMouse have we entred a era in which we will produce species *specifically designed to suffer* (genetically engineered to develop tumours)? An era in which such programmed suffering will be deemed justifiable as long as it can be argued that it is for the benefit of humans? Where will we draw the limits on this? Will we begin to grow semi-humans (perhaps with altered brain stems and no consciousness) for body parts or experimentation?[24] What kind of ethical principles should we apply here? Again we stand on the brink of the unknown.

In his book *The Imperative of Responsibility* Hans Jonas has argued the '(m)odern technology has introduced actions of such novel scale, objects, and consequences that the framework of former ethics can no longer contain them'.[25] Technology presents us with increasingly complex problems of which former ethical theories were simply unaware and with which they seem ill-prepared to deal. Due to what Ellul terms the 'systemic' dimension of technologies, the ethical dilemmas with which they confront us are increasingly both global and generational. How do we begin to think about issues of such proportion at an individual level? How can we even begin to predict the global and generational effects? There is question as to whether we have the ability or the personal and public will to attempt to do so. It is a problem of the unknown. The modern relationship to the unknown has been one of conquest. To expand the realm of the known and reduce the realm of the unknown has perhaps always been one of the primal sparks of humanity. In modernity it is raised to a conscious ethos which has set its goal as nothing short of perfect or complete knowledge. The unknown has been our challenge, even our enemy, that which most motivates us as a species. The fact that we do not know has been the justification for charging forward where we might find the answers. As Jonas says, 'Now, *techne* in the form of modern technology has turned into an infinite forward-thrust of the race, its most significant enterprise, in whose permanent, self-transcending advance to ever greater things the vocation of man tends to be seen, and whose success of maximal control over things and himself appears as the consummation of his destiny'.[26] He concludes that 'technology, apart from its objective works, assumes ethical significance by the central place it now occupies in human purpose'.[27] The arguments on behalf of progress have always been in part ethically founded. It is for this reason that when something is justified as representing 'progress', this is given the force of an ethical argument.

Biotechnology represents progress in our understanding (as science) but does it also represent progress in the ethical/moral dimensions of our lives? Virtually all of the accomplishments or promises of future accomplishments of biotechnology are presented in ethical terms. Thus the foregrounding of biotechnology is not just about the commodities it will provide for us but that most of those commodities are presented as 'goods' in the ethical sense. Such things as better health, better food production to feed the hungry, new techniques to clean up the environment, etc., are for the betterment of the world. Thus it cannot be assumed that the ethical arguments about biotechnology must be against it. Cogent ethical arguments can be mounted both for and against biotechnology. For this reason, it is important that the background issues which have been raised throughout this book not be interpreted as arguments against biotechnology. What seems certain is that biotechnology has complicated the ethical dimensions of our lives in new and unprecedented ways. We are faced with entire categories of questions which could never have been imagined in the past, questions to which we have no answers. Thus, I am not arguing *against* anything, rather I am arguing *for the unknown*. I am arguing that we need to respect the unknown as a guiding principle when attempting to make ethical and policy decisions about biotechnology.

Two things emerge clearly from all of our considerations. First, biotechnology represents a major shift in the direction of contemporary society both in modes of understanding and practice. Such major shifts demand of us that we consider again our past to see what we might learn from it for the future and that we rethink those principles which might have been appropriate for prior contexts but which might not be adequate to the current situation. Second, the complex problems presented throughout this collection make clear that when it comes to the implications and long-term effects of biotechnology, *we have entered a realm characterized by the unknown*. Granted, throwing the unknown into the picture will not help us if our desire is to give simple, clear answers or to make quick, expedient decisions about biotechnology, but it is also clear that there is too much at stake to opt for the least complicated path.

Let me try then to state what I have been trying to indicate as an ethical imperative for our post-modern/technological situation. '*Act so that the effects of your actions reflect your acknowledgement of the unknown as a key dimension of the action*'. Or, '*Act so that the effects of your actions reflect the fact that you cannot predict the effects'*. The statement of the imperative verges on the paradoxical. It could be argued that as a principle, rather than clarifying the ethical decision making process, it complicates, obscures, even negates itself as a principle or imperative and renders ethical decision-making impossibly complicated if not impossible. However, I would argue that it does clarify the ethical decision making process itself because it clarifies the actual dimensions of the ethical challenges to which the decision responds. I am not arguing that the imperative of the unknown would meet Kant's criteria: 'Act so that you can will that the maxim of your action be made the principle of universal law', as I would be hesitant to propose anything like a universal law. The imperative of the unknown emerges out of a historical encounter with the world we have created and are reinventing, with the ethical situations with which we are confronted, and with our own historical sense of limit. On the one hand, I want to argue that in confronting the types of issues relating to technology dealt with here, the imperative of the unknown *ought* to be applied to ethical and policy decision making. But it must also be noted that I have claimed that biotechnology is part of a shift in worldviews which would mean that I would be willing to generalise this imperative to most of the dilemmas with which we are confronted in the contemporary situation.

The imperative of the unknown reflects what I take to be the challenge of making ethical choices in a postmodern/technological situation. It acknowledges that ethical decisions are 'wagers'. Wagers which must be made in the absence of firm foundations such as tradition, sense of self, and even philosophical or religious certitude. It is not that these have totally disappeared (as the more extreme post-modern thinkers would have it) but that our relationship to them, our faith in them and our ability to apply them to the range of contemporary issues is in question. How to make an ethical decision, the process itself, has a dimension of the unknown in it, a dimension which has grown as techno-science has become larger, more ubiquitous, and systemic.[28]

The imperative of the unknown also acknowledges that the issues have become almost incomprehensibly complex and that predictability or the lack thereof is a major dimension of that complexity. Thus, I would argue that the unknown presents the problematics (in this case biotechnology) more 'accurately' if one accepts that part of 'accuracy' is what we do not know, what we cannot predict, and what we have no control over. These dimensions mean that the unknown *ought* to become part of the decision making process. Thus in the relation between the 'is' and 'ought' a significant dimension of the 'is' is the unknown. The larger the scale at which we are considering the effect the greater the unknown. This was indicated by the brief reference to chaos theory. Acting so that the effects of one's actions acknowledge the unknown is not just entering into paradox or playfulness, but acknowledging the 'factual' 'is' in the sense that we now must attempt to consider the effects of our actions long-term, large-scale, out of all proportion with what we have confronted in the past. The 'fact' of our situation with regard to new technologies such as biotechnology is that we now face an abyss in which not only are the answers unknown but the very questions we need to be asking are unknown. Elevating the unknown to the status of an imperative would have the effect among other things moderating the 'forward-thrust' of biotechnology and allowing us to better determine not only some of the answers to questions already raised but to better determine what the questions are which need answering.

Notes

1. N. Wiener, *The Human Use of Humans: Cybernetics and Society* (Boston: Houghten Mifflin, 1954), 278.
2. The term epistemes is taken from the early work of Michel Foucault. It refers to the historical (social, political, intellectual) conditions under which certain truths and practices develop.
3. See 'Got It: After 17 years of searching, physicists believe they have found a missing building block of matter', *Newsweek* 143(19) (May 9, 1994): 37–38.
4. See J. Buchanan 'New Lexicons of Power in an Information Age', *Technology in Society* (forthcoming).
5. D. Harraway, *Simians, Cyborgs and Women: The Reinvention of Nature* (New York: Routledge, 1991), 208.
6. Ibid., 211.
7. Ibid., 206.
8. R. Hubbard and E. Wald, *Exploding the Gene Myth: How Genetic Information is Produced and Manipulated by Scientists, Physicians, Employers, Insurance Companies, Educators, and Law Enforcers* (Boston: Beacon Press, 1993), 7.
9. Ibid.
10. F. Bacon, 'De Augmentis'. In J. Spedding, R. Ellis, and D. Heath, eds., *Works*, Vol. 4 (London: Longmans Green, 1870), 320.
11. A. Borgman, *Technology and The Character of Contemporary Life* (Chicago: University of Chicago Press, 1984).
12. Ibid., 35.
13. Ibid., 48.
14. The term 'bioindustry' is the term used collectively by those engaged in the commercialization of genetic engineering. The umbrella organization which they created to present their case is called The Bioindustry Forum.
15. See S. Krimsky, *Biotechnics and Society: The rise of Industrial Genetics* (New York: Praeger, 1991); and M. Kenney, *Biotechnology: The University-Industrial Complex* (New Haven: Yale University Press, 1986).
16. See for example P. Abelson, 'Biotechnology in a Global Economy', *Science* 255 (1992): 381.
17. V. Shiva, *Monocultures of the Mind: Perspectives on Biodiversity and Biotechnology* (Penang, Malaysia: Third World Network, 1993).
18. Hawkings himself has said that given the nature of his work and the kinds of support he has received from friends and family that his physical disabilities have not been a serious handicap. I want to go beyond this and at least pose the possibility that his physical disabilities might have in fact contributed to his intellectual brilliance.
19. For a good discussion of the new eugenics see R. Hubbard and E. Wald, *Exploding the Gene Myth* (Boston: Beacon Press, 1993).

20. For a good description of both cases see, A. Kimbrell, *The Human Body Shop: The Engineering and Marketing of Life* (San Francisco: Harper, 1993). Also see P. Mooney, 'John Moore's Body', *New Internationalist*, 217 (March 1991): 8.

21. Taken from Kimbrell, *The Human Body Shop*, 210.

22. In fact a number of the core group within the NIH Genome Project have now quit that project and formed their own private firm to continue the sequencing and to explore commercial opportunities.

23. See J. Buchanan, 'New Lexicons of Power in an Information Age', *Technology and Society* (forthcoming).

24. For the best overall presentation of this dilemma see the previously cited A. Kimbrell, *The Human Body Shop*.

25. H. Jonas, *The Imperative of Responsibility: In Search of an Ethics for the Technological Age* (Chicago: University of Chicago Press, 1984), 6.

26. Ibid., 9.

27. Ibid.

28. Again see my 'Wagers into the Abyss: Transversal Reflections on the Contemporary Crisis of Values', *Philosophy East and West* (forthcoming).

Index